The Culture of Islam

The Culture of Islam
Changing Aspects of Contemporary Muslim Life

LAWRENCE ROSEN

The University of Chicago Press
Chicago and London

Lawrence Rosen is the William Nelson Cromwell Professor of Anthropology at Princeton University and adjunct professor of law at Columbia University. Named to the first group of MacArthur Award winners, he is the author of six books, including *The Justice of Islam* and *Bargaining for Reality: The Construction of Social Relations in a Muslim Community,* the latter of which is published by the University of Chicago Press.

The University of Chicago Press, Chicago 60637
The University of Chicago Press, Ltd., London
© 2002 by The University of Chicago
All rights reserved. Published 2002
Printed in the United States of America
11 10 09 08 07 06 05 04 03 02   1 2 3 4 5
ISBN: 0-226-72613-4 (cloth)

Library of Congress Cataloging-in-Publication Data

Rosen, Lawrence, 1941–
     The culture of Islam : changing aspects of contemporary Muslim life
  / Lawrence Rosen.
        p.   cm.
     Includes bibliographical references and index.
     ISBN 0-226-72613-4 (cloth)
        1. Morocco—Social life and customs. 2. Civilization, Islamic. 3. East and West.
  4. Ethnology—Morocco. 5. Religion and culture. 6. Religion and politics—Morocco.
  I. Title.
  DT312 R64 2002
  306'.0964   2002005968

♾ The paper used in this publication meets the minimum requirements of the American National Standard for Information Sciences—Permanence of Paper for Printed Library Materials, ANSI Z39.48-1992.

FOR CAROL, DIANE, AND DAVID

Contents

Introduction

THE SCIENCE OF ASPECTS

[T]here is a science of the aspects of things as well as of their nature; and it is as much a fact to be noted in their constitution, that they produce such and such an effect upon the eye or heart . . . as that they are made up of certain atoms or vibrations of matter.[1]

JOHN RUSKIN

Suppose you held a diamond in your hand and someone asked you to tell them what you believe to be true about the gem. You might begin to describe how once, eons ago, it was just a lump of carbon and how, over the course of countless years, subject to intense pressure and heat, it developed into its current form. Or you might begin to turn it in the light, describing the ways in which it captures and returns reflections, each facet calling up some other shade or image, its perfection and flaws, its associations and promise showing as it is moved from one angle to another. Neither approach could be called intrinsically superior to the other, neither could lay claim to exclusive truth. And yet, depending on the context, one or the other might well be given appropriate emphasis—the geological history for a scientist, the aesthetics for a connoisseur. Imagine, then, how an entire culture, for different purposes and at different moments, may also play up one or another aspect of a given trait and, knitting each aspect together with those that inform other domains of its overall existence, create a vision that contrasts to the emphases of other peoples or other times. To take such an approach is to catch the allure of the anthropological subject as well as the anthropological style of understanding.

During the course of more than three decades of work in North Africa, I have watched the people of the region probe the relationships in their lives and

ix

the concepts in their minds as they explore and enact the possibilities they envision. I have watched them draw connections among the different aspects of their social and cultural life to form a coherent, variegated whole, and I have been challenged to comprehend connections suggested by my own comparative discipline. I have, for example, come to see that for the people of this region the chronology of someone's personal history does not reveal what is most true about that person but that, like the gem turned in the light, it is the contexts of relationships with others that reveal what is most true about themselves and those they encounter. I have come to see, too, that the arrangement of the Qur'an from longest to shortest chapter, like the nonchronological arrangement of many stories, has no great bearing on the way the truths of that text are revealed: Truth is not signaled by what happens "in the beginning" and unfolds through to "the end" but by the placement of man and Prophet in a series of encounters and contexts through which persons are defined and a community of believers is forged. For the Arabs and Berbers among whom I have worked there is indeed a science of aspects—with effects that are no less tangible than the ideas and acts that yield such effects—and what is required of the anthropologist is, therefore, an approach that does justice to their capacious view of the world and to our general understanding of the nature of human cultures and societies.

Anthropologists like myself begin with certain assumptions and orientations. Human beings are category-creating creatures. Having all but replaced instinct during the course of our evolutionary history with the capacity to create the categories of our own experience—and indeed having achieved this capacity *before* we achieved our present speciation—we take the undifferentiated experience that pours in upon us and divide it into meaningful components and still more complex combinations. This anthropological concept of culture thus rejoins, on the one hand, the generation and manifestation of categorized experience and, on the other, the ways in which any group of people utilize these conceptualizations to orient their actions towards one another in reasonably predictable ways. As concepts are replicated and transformed across the different domains of a culture—as cosmological concepts reproduce social arrangements, or economic ties reinforce religious conceptualizations—the resultant set of cultural concepts appears to those who entrust their lives to them to be both imminent and natural. Because anthropologists start by assuming that all of the different domains of a society and culture have some bearing on one another, comparison among cultures and historic periods is vital: Only as one sees how the kaleidoscope of cultural configurations is turned round from one context to another, one moment to another, can one see the forces that inform particular patterns and their implications.

This disciplinary orientation has a direct impact, too, on the interpretation of the societies under consideration in this book. It bears, first, on the parameters of the subject itself, and, second, on the particular sociocultural aspects with which we will be concerned. The predominant focus of this book stems from work done in Morocco but it is not, I believe, restricted to an understanding of that country alone. It is useful in this regard to think, rather, in terms of themes and variations. For while there can be no doubt that, seen from within the universe of Muslim societies, the range of cultural and historical experience is considerable, a close reading of ethnographic and historical materials suggests that these differences may also be seen as variations on a set of shared themes. This is as true when one is referring to those whose predominant language is Arabic or Berber, or for those who are primarily urban versus rural residents, as it is for understanding distinctions that follow national boundary lines. Thus many of the topics covered in this book, though often taking Morocco as a starting point, purposely draw on materials from different periods and places within the Muslim world. Readers will, I hope, ask themselves in what ways those aspects of Arab or Muslim or North African life to which I give particular emphasis carry reverberations—not exact identities, but thought-provoking similarities or implications—for their understanding of other parts of this broadly variant set of social and cultural orientations. While I shall, at times, speak of Morocco and at other times about the Arabs, at times about Islam and at others about Muslim culture, I hope that readers will see in both my particular and my generalized terms not an invitation to distinguish the examples with which they are familiar from my own but a call to ask in what ways these specific manifestations of Islamic and Arab culture suggest analogs and variations to which their own experience can be addressed. Indeed, the desire to speak at once to the concerns of Moroccan experience and to themes that may obtain in variant forms elsewhere also informs the particular cultural aspects that I have chosen to explore.

There are four main cultural themes that the present work seeks to explore, themes that crosscut the topical organization of the chapters themselves. The first relates to the centrality in Islamic thought and society of reason and knowledge. Repeatedly the Qur'an reminds the faithful that God created humans with reason that they might pursue the "rights of man" (*ḥuquq al-insan*) even as they submit to the prerogatives of God. Popular conceptions give added emphasis to this point in the constant search for and respect accorded to knowledge in whatever form it may take. To the Tradition of the Prophet that "there is no distinction except in knowledge" Muslims have accorded the social implication of constantly looking for information that will further the needs of themselves and their dependents. As one follows individuals through many of the stories that will form the bases for analysis in this volume, one sees the immense importance attached to grasping the world through reason and rendering this knowledge useful to one's own situation.

At the same time it is a characteristic feature of North African social life that it is one's relationships with others that define the person and that these networks of attachment constitute, as it were, the molecular units from which society itself is built. Moreover, each of these webs of relationship, though forged through a culturally recognized repertoire, is inherently open-ended, subject to the capacity of individuals to create networks that are at once distinctive to their own social emplacement and recognizable—indeed, legitimate—in the eyes of the others they encounter. It is, to borrow an image, as if a framework were set by the culture at large—an acceptable range or vocabulary of possibilities—within which each person fashions that structure of mutual indebtedness by which he or she will be more or less secured in a world fraught with the potential for chaotic dis-integration. The constant focus, then, is on the situations, the contexts, in which persons interact with others and on the particular ways they have played out their possibilities to create their own social situatedness. Whether it is family or tribe, occupation or level of education, the constant emphasis on the *situated* person runs through every domain of social and cultural life.

In a sense, then, what is at work is a "great game," a constant series of moves aimed at securing oneself in an uncertain world. Like chess—itself the game that, in the early years of Islam, became the theologically correct expression of God-given reason made manifest in a true "community of believers"—the possible moves, though limited by the rules, are, at least to devotees, endlessly varied and alluring. And as one plays out the series of informed encounters to build the contexts that yield one's own identity, everything from political practice to memory of the past are marshaled to effect. Thus, historic memory is structured, in no small part, according to whether events continue to have an impact on current networks of relationship or may be stored in some past—regardless of chronological ordering—reserved for those relationships that no longer have social implications. In such a cultural environment one can also see why political ties tend to be focused on the situated person, rather than on impersonal institutions, and thus how events come to be described in terms of those involved more than in terms of forces beyond the control of situated actors.

To those who play chess there is little reason to change the rules—to add new pieces or alter the shape of the board—because of any imagined inadequacy or frustration with what the game is able to accomplish. In the sociocultural life of the people with whom we are concerned change does, of course, occur all the time. Yet in the Arab world it occurs with one foot, as it were, solidly planted in the form that the game has long possessed. When change of fundamental concepts or relationships occurs, it presents the analyst with challenging theoretical problems. How do we distinguish "fundamental" change from simple variation; to which metaphors—whether of agglutination, incorporation, or replacement—do we turn for guidance in comprehending alteration? And when change does seem to come—particularly from the margins (such as through the experience of living as an immigrant in Europe)—how do these purported changes appear to affect deep-seated orientations towards the world that Muslim society and culture have long afforded their adherents?

In order to explore these and related themes the topics in this volume have been chosen and organized with an eye to both continuity and discontinuity in social and cultural life. Each part begins with a story that incorporates some of the themes that run through every chapter in that section. Part one, therefore, approaches a number of the central themes of Arab society and culture from the vantage point of understanding the nature and role of cultural ambivalence. Using as its baseline the story of a group of friends who must create a sense of civility in a world of petty corruption, the deep-seated ambivalence of Arab cultural and political orientations is raised in a very human context. Of course, social scientists have not always afforded ambivalence the importance it deserves. Whether its role is due to the evolutionary propulsion to maintain, especially through language and category formation, the possibility of adapting to changing circumstances, or because ambivalence allows a multitude of personal orientations to find sufficient commonality for each person to be able to orient his or her actions meaningfully towards others, the place of ambivalence in everyday life commends itself for direct attention. Certainly there are those societies that address ambivalence by making every effort to suppress it, while others seem to play it up. Arab societies form an especially good instance for exploring ambivalence because they appear to avail themselves of its possibilities for keeping alive the great game of negotiating relationships such that new players and new maneuvers always seem to be available. Thus the issues related to cultural ambivalence can be taken up in several different domains.

Corruption, at first sight, may not seem a particularly fruitful domain for understanding the role of ambivalence, yet as one watches people cope with it on a daily basis one can see the twofold aspect—the struggle for advantage, the discomfort with exclusivity—that it presents. Chapter one thus follows a group of people who set out to assist one of their number in a marital problem that incorporates attending to the petty corruption associated with certain legal proceedings. More to the point, it becomes a story of how, given ambivalent attitudes towards accomplishing desired goals in such an environment, efforts are made, largely through the narration of their common circumstances, to carve out a zone of solidarity and beneficence in a climate of unpalatable means. The ambivalence that relates to power is addressed more directly in chapter two, where the diverse approaches to religious, political, and interpersonal concerns are seen to be fraught with just that deep-seated ambivalence towards power that is central to the overall social and cultural pattern. Even the very concept of a tribe and how it operates in the North African context (the subject of chapter three) can be seen as a cultural and political form whose amoeboid quality, capable of extensive implication precisely because of its shape-shifting capabilities, has a profound impact on numerous domains of social life. When, in the final chapter in this section, we turn to the ways in which one can understand institutions in a world of personalistic orientations it is to these same considerations—of ambivalence and context, negotiability and framing structures—that our attention will be returned.

Part two begins with an attempt to see how memory itself has been reconstructed over the course of the years that I have been working in North Africa. This section starts with the story of how the people of a Moroccan city came to contest whether their patron saint might actually occupy a Jewish holy site, and how the various versions of what "really happened" became a better indicator of the uses of memory and ideas than might be supplied by concentration on what "really" occurred. From this baseline one can then raise the question of how memory has altered in a number of different domains over the past several decades. The concern here is not, however, with the present uses of the past: Rather, it is with the question whether cultural ideas have so changed in the past generation that the very terms by which the same people capture past events now is different from the way they did so when I first encountered them several decades ago. Indeed, as chapter seven suggests, when one encounters what appear to be such fundamental conceptual shifts as the introduction of a concept of probability or a shift in notions of causality and responsibility, the hard question is posed for the analyst as to what shall be taken as indicators of real change and what as the verbal exploration of merely plausible cultural worlds.

Increasingly, Muslim encounters with life in Europe have begun to affect the ways in which cultural and political orientations develop back in the home countries. In part three we look first at the stories of several marital situations involving cross-border influences and see how the conflict of laws and transnational encounters that now characterize the lives of many Muslim migrants play out in the context of family law proceedings. Indeed, it can be argued that a kind of European Islam has begun to develop around the experiences of many of these migrants, and with it some of the central features of Muslim practice and belief may be undergoing alteration. The result may be a kind of Euro-Islam in which accommodations and alterations made "at the margin" have begun to influence the shape of Islamic institutions more widely. It is in this context, finally, that one can look back at Salman Rushdie's novel *The Satanic Verses* not primarily for the political and religious conflict it engendered but to see why it may be a far deeper challenge to Islam to consider the role of doubt within religion than it is to focus on questions of blasphemous utterance.

Throughout, then, the unifying elements of these essays remain those very sociocultural conceptualizations whose unity and diversity, whose continuity and discontinuity the people of North Africa and the Middle East are addressing in their everyday lives. Chapters crosscut one another's themes because the themes themselves crosscut domains: Memory and sainthood are both about ambivalence, corruption and tribalism both incorporate aspects of negotiating relationships, Rushdie's challenge and that of European forms of Islam are fraught with contestation over the concept of the self. Through the concrete instances of their encounters, the everyday expression of their possibilities, one can, perhaps, grasp both the power of a cultural pattern of enduring merit and the challenges posed to these cultures by the elaboration of the contexts in which their adherents now find themselves operating. For the social scientist, no less than for the people involved, the challenge to rethink fundamental propositions is unavoidable.

This book was completed before the commencement of terrorist attacks on the United States on September 11, 2001. Although it was not intended to address the issues brought on by these events or the specific issues that lie behind them, there is, I believe, a link between the topics with which I am concerned and the overall context of Muslim/non-Muslim understanding. To address the question of why personalistic politics remains so prevalent in the Arab world or why tribal attachments come back to concern the West in Afghanistan, to consider how faith and doubt are challenged by fiction or how decent people cope with everyday corruption is indeed to face some of the underlying conditions of contemporary Muslim life. No single work—or single life's work—can hope to answer all of the questions that perplex those who genuinely want to understand Islamic cultures in the present day. But no work—or life—that has been enmeshed with those who place their faith in the Prophet's message can fail to hope that the efforts of scholarship may, in whatever way possible, contribute to the mutual understanding and forgiveness that alone will make true peace possible.

∾∾∾∾∾

The essays in this book have benefited from the support and criticism of numerous individuals and institutions over the years, and I am most grateful to each. Support was, at various times, received from the John D. and Catherine T. MacArthur Fellows Program, Princeton University, the Fulbright Program (for work in Morocco, Tunisia, and Malaysia), and the National Science Foundation. Portions of the manuscript were prepared during my tenure as a Visiting Fellow of Corpus Christi College, Cambridge University, and the Rockefeller Foundation Study Center at Bellagio, Italy, and I am immensely appreciative of the splendid working environment afforded me by each of them. Several of the essays were tried out on audiences I addressed as a Phi Beta Kappa Visiting Lecturer, in seminars and conferences at the University of Leiden, Boğaziçi University, the University of Chicago, and Cambridge University, and during my stay as a visiting professor at the Ben Gurion University of the Negev.

I am also grateful for the assistance of the many people, private and governmental, who facilitated my fieldwork in Morocco, Tunisia, and Malaysia, especially those at the Ministry of Justice and local officials throughout Morocco—particularly in the city and region of Sefrou—who have always respected the curiosity and independence of the visitor among them.

My debt to individual scholars is extensive beyond indulgence, but for those who recognize in these essays either arguments to which they directed me or arguments from which they tried to steer me clear my gratitude should in no way imply any other culpability than my own. In particular I am enormously grateful to Akbar Ahmed, Katherine N. Bennison, Clifford Geertz, Abdellah Hammoudi, and Leonard V. Kaplan for the insights and patience with which they have helped me think through these issues. Much of the work on this book was completed during summers in Castine, Maine, and I am grateful to the administrators of the Maine Maritime Academy and Witherle Memorial Libraries for their hospitality, as well as to my fellow sailors—Terry MacTaggart,

Peter Vielbig, and John Zoller—who were often captive to my conversation and still managed not to toss me overboard. Of the essays in this book only chapter seven appeared in an earlier form, in the volume I edited entitled *Other Intentions* (1995), and is reprinted here by agreement with the original publishers.

On the day this manuscript was completed I learned of the tragic death of a young Moroccan friend, Saʿad Moumen. Saʿad was perpetually intrigued by his culture, and that enthusiasm contributed greatly to my own understanding of the world in which he lived. I am ever-mindful of the grace with which his family invited me into their lives and I will always cherish the joy of having known Saʿad as a kind of younger brother.

Arabic spellings throughout this work generally follow the system used in Hans Wehr's *A Dictionary of Modern Written Arabic*, with allowance made for some Moroccan colloquial distinctions. Wehr's transliteration has, however, received several modifications: š becomes *sh*, ḳ becomes *kh*, g becomes *gh*, ṯ becomes *th*, and ḍ becomes *dh*. Each term is transcribed with full diacritics only the first time it appears in the text. Terms that have gained currency in English—such as *Qurʾan, qadi,* or *shariʿa*—will be presented in recognizable spellings rather than with precise Arabic orthography. The index will also serve as a glossary inasmuch as a brief translation of each term is indicated while the number in bold type will direct the reader's attention to the place in the text where the term receives its fullest definition.

PART ONE

Ambivalent Culture

The Circle of Beneficence
Narrating Coherence in a World of Corruption

Every man is bound to leave a story better than he found it.
MARY AUGUSTA WARD[1]

෨෨

I want to tell you a story. Or, maybe, it is really a story about the telling of stories. It centers on a trip I took while I was in Morocco. The Arabs have a saying: "Men show themselves in journeys." Ours was not the dangerous trip of a lengthy pilgrimage nor the arduous hazard of a trading expedition, ventures in which the honesty and courage, to say nothing of the humor and generosity, of traveling companions may affect survival, to say nothing of comfort. But the trip called for no less in the way of thoughtful support for the friend on whose behalf it was organized. For what was really at issue was the way that the story of these travelers' mutual concern could be related and enacted as they all set forth into a world of petty corruption.

In the West children (and sometimes adults) play a game in which a chain story is created: Each person takes a turn moving the story along and each new person who takes over must maintain some consistency in the narrative while being free to take the story in other directions. Scholars of the common law have also used the image of the chain story to great effect in describing the way one court's views are carried along by the next, an image that is all the more fitting in the present context since, as I have argued elsewhere, Islamic law may be seen as a variant of common law.[2] And the image of the chain story is also appropriate here because each person who came into contact with the core group, as well as each of the main participants, had to pick up on the theme of cohesion in a world of corruption and carry it into new though always connected domains. It is for these reasons that we may treat the situation described here as a story of story-making, the formation of a narrative, the making of a world of compassion and understanding for those who find in its making a way of attending to their world and to one another's needs.༄༅༄༅༄༅༄༅༄༅༄༅༄

And the tale floats on the rivers,
And you, my friends, are generous givers.
MOROCCAN FOLKTALE FORMULA[3]

It began the way all those outings seem to begin: Someone needed to see someone about something, and a few friends had come along for company and support. It is never clear who else will be visited or might join in during the course of the travels or where exactly a bed will be found for the night. But over the years there is one thing I have come to expect with great regularity: The outing will always develop some unstated theme, some unspoken and un-abstracted thread to which all the stories to be told, all the examples to be cited, will be marshaled. Whatever their personal reasons for embarking on the trip a common motif will develop, one that binds the voyagers' separate orientations to a shared, if inexplicit, direction. The trip itself is uncertain: It is the travelers who give it shape and import.

On this occasion our point of departure was clear. Our friend Muhammad was involved in an extremely complex and lengthy dispute with his wife and her kinfolk, and we were on our way to see a judge from a distant city whose advice about how to proceed might be useful for the next phase of Muhammad's case. We were all aware that Muhammad had been caught up in a situation in which his opponents had used both favoritism and bribes to gain certain advantages in the case, and that Muhammad himself had had to learn how to fight fire with fire. Our trip was therefore taking place against this context of unwanted and embarrassing corruption.

In all there were five of us traveling together. Muhammad's contact to the judge was one of the two lawyers handling his case, a man who was also a close personal friend. Omar had served his apprenticeship with Muhammad's senior lawyer but had now set himself up in business and was coming to be much sought after for his precision, his clarity, and his overall savvy. Still in his thirties, sensible to the ways of the world and knowledgeable in the law, Omar was eager to exercise his talents but perfectly prepared to do whatever the system required to get his clients a favorable outcome.

Accompanying us were two other friends. Ali was in his fifties, a trained agronomist who, owing to a variety of personal circumstances, was at that moment without any regular employment in his field. He and Muhammad shared a common background, both having been raised in the same large city and both having extensive experience with Western languages and cultures. In this they were also matched by the fifth of our number, Tahar, who came from a small city in central Morocco but whose work required extensive travel all over the country and abroad. At that moment, however, his position in the government ministry where he worked—and indeed his personal freedom—was in jeopardy as the result of the machinations of some of his enemies.

Individually and collectively, these backgrounds, connections, and the moment at which each of us found himself in life, coupled with our initial purpose in accompanying Muhammad in his search for "justice," contributed to the theme that began to emerge over the course of our long weekend's voyage.

We left Rabat in Muhammad's Mercedes in the late morning and drove north to pick up Tahar. We had stopped along the way to place a "for sale" sign on a piece of property owned by Omar, the lawyer. As we walked over the land, with Ali explaining various features of the property's potential to us, there was reference to the need to get certain licenses if someone wanted to add a building or extend a well. No one said anything about how these licenses might have to be obtained. On the road there was also a touch of nervousness as we passed one group of gendarmes after another: They were part of a recent crackdown on speeding, but everyone knew they also had the right to halt cars for any reason, and while Morocco is certainly not a country in which one feels an omnipresent police presence, the stories of inappropriate blockades began to be related. Someone mentioned that the police had stopped a relative who had a young woman in the car with him to inquire as to their relationship, and a discussion, full of similar instances, ensued over whether the real aim of the police was to protect women from illicit relations. No one said anything about other aims the policeman may have had in mind. At each stopping point we were waved through, but the stories flowed without interruption.

By late afternoon, with everyone on board, we stopped to look at another piece of land with which the lawyer was involved. Because the dirt road was very rocky and the heavily laden car may have scraped bottom, Muhammad and the lawyer went ahead while I and the others remained along the deserted road for a while chatting. Ali began by saying that, like the place where we had stopped earlier, in a few years this area would also be totally built up. There is no sense of planning here, he said, no regularity. Then, in what might have seemed like an unrelated shift of emphasis, he added: "The Muslims are no good at business, not like the Jews. If a Muslim goes to another town and buys a glass for one dirham he will come back and try to sell it for two. He will say he had to travel to get it, that he had to do this and this and this, and so he won't sell it for less. The Jew goes out of town and buys the same glass for one dirham and comes back and sells it for one and a half. He sells a thousand of them. And the Muslim sells two. The Jews," he concluded, "sell their houses and buy businesses; the Muslims sell their businesses and buy houses." As always, the reference to the Jews was not said with rancor or hostility. To the contrary it was said with genuine regret at their absence.[4] For some time we strolled up and down the country road—all together, in pairs, alone—the conversation turning from the land to the government to the Jews, until Muhammad returned and we all tumbled into the car to continue on.

By dusk we had made our way to the home of Omar's sister, a farmstead where the sister, her husband, and their children greeted us and served us tea in the guestroom of the adobe house set in the middle of their field. Earlier, at lunch, in one of those burgeoning strip towns along the road, Ali had gone into the café and asked for a mat that he could use while saying his afternoon prayers, and now Tahar used the small bathroom to wash himself and then set about saying his own prayers. Several people wandered in and out of the room, and as the conversation moved along from one example to another—of land use and licenses, people who did business with each other and the relationships each had had with people they encountered in their travels—the newcomer would listen for some time, then add a story of his own, and a moment later be gone. It was not until the evening was well along that we set off to meet the judge.

Had anyone told me—a week before, much less thirty years before—that I would ever spend an evening with a *qadi* watching him get thoroughly drunk, I would have thought the person more than a little mad. But that is exactly what happened. It began when we picked up the judge at his house and were heading to a kind of resort located some distance outside one of the large cities. The others remembered having come to the place to swim in the sweltering summers, and they talked about how it was now a large complex incorporating several hotels, shops, restaurants, and pools. On this occasion, however, we headed towards one of the bars that was set off below and to the side of the other facilities.

Had I known him to be a man of impeccable reputation I might have found the chubby person with the wide-eyed gaze and boisterous mien now seated beside Muhammad to be a charming if boyish fellow in his early thirties, someone who possessed none of the stuffiness one might associate with a law court judge bearing an ancient religious title. If I had heard nothing but praise for his character I might have been touched by the way, when we picked him up, he gleefully kissed everyone, myself included, on both cheeks, an act of unselfconscious Moroccan bonhomie. And almost certainly I would have found his quick, though involuted, legal mind an admirable, if unseasoned, concentration of personal enthusiasm and well-earned responsibility. But since, in fact, I knew from Muhammad that this judge drank himself drunk almost every night and heard him openly boast to Muhammad as we drove to the bar about a bribe he had recently taken, I could only regard the man who now joined us as a smarmy little toad whose giggly speech and smutty leers were at one with the corruption that ran through his entire being.

The bar was an appropriate place for our meeting. At one end of the long, narrow room a band of musicians from the Rif Mountains played amplified native instruments so loudly one had to shout to be heard. A female singer of large dimensions—blessedly clothed in a long gown, her belt low across her hips—sang and shimmied, every portion of her wriggling flesh the subject of intense concentration by the several men and couples who were scattered about the room. The singer was not, however, the focus of attention of the single women who drifted in to sit at the bar near the door. One of these young women dealt a serious blow to my image of the hardened working girl by actually drinking her beer through a straw. Nearby, at an empty table, stood an empty bottle of the same "Speciale" beer, a candy-striped straw peeking out of the green neck at a rakish angle, whether as mute testimony to a success earlier in the evening or evidence of a new style of beer drinking I shall forever be deprived of knowing. As Muhammad and his lawyer tried to shout inquiries into the judge's ear and the others nursed their beers in relative quiescence, I reflected on the instances of corruption that I had been encountering in the couple of weeks since I had returned to Morocco.

In the late 1960s and through much of the 1970s it was not uncommon to hear of situations of bribery involving public officials. But the extent of such corruption was largely described to me as rather limited: the court clerk who, for a sum, would register a lower than truthful land sale price in order to help avoid taxes; the notary who could be paid to record dishonest testimony that might later help one make a case against an opponent; the market official who, for a price, would siphon off some food aid for his friends. Such matters were not trivial, but few people spoke of these actions as being particularly extensive or as upsetting the means by which people formed and maintained their obligations along relatively predictable lines. But by the 1980s the tone had changed, and by the late 1990s the stories I was hearing were of such rampant corruption that it seemed to enter into the smallest matters of daily life.

Only a few days before a friend had told me how he was helping his domestic employee to purchase a site for a house. The plot was technically part of

a collective property regime and could not be sold, but such clandestine building has its own regularities, and since the government would almost certainly
help illegal residents to relocate at a later date, the investment was a worthwhile
gamble. The day after the employer agreed to pay for the new site the employee
came to work clearly upset: The local administrator was demanding a sum of
money equal to the value of the site itself just to register it as the employee's
official address, a necessary act if one was to be eligible for any later government recognition of a housing claim. Because the employee could never afford
such a sum, my friend was going to have to ante up the bribe to accompany the
gift. When I asked what would happen if they reported the administrator's demand, I was told that the employee would probably be accused of criminal li-
bel and would risk a large fine and imprisonment. In another instance a bribe
was solicited from a friend who needed immunizations to go on the pilgrimage to Mecca. I learned, too, that Moroccans working abroad who previously
sent money home to build houses were increasingly refusing to repatriate their
earnings because of the bribes necessary to get building permits. On a recent
television program a Moroccan working abroad had openly said that he had
expended eighty percent of the capital he intended to reinvest in Morocco on
bribes alone, and that it was still not enough to get his business started. So numerous and diverse are the creative forms of soliciting and subdividing bribery
that, as one man put it to me, "We Moroccans have become veritable techni-
cians of bribery." Although we had not come to be in the bar with a judge to
engage in any bribery, my traveling companions were mindful of how much
money and favors now play a role in everyday contacts with officialdom, and
how much the judge we had come to consult represented this extremely dis-
tasteful if unavoidable kind of encounter.

We stayed at the bar for several hours. Muhammad and his lawyer huddled
with the judge, screaming into each other's ears, trying—as the judge put away
one drink after another—to get a few suggestions about how to pursue their
case. Tahar went off to say his prayers, then returned to order two beers which
he nursed through the evening; Ali, too, did not go beyond the two beers he or-
dered in succession. At times the others would wander outside to be able to
hear what was being said, at another moment an acquaintance who also had a
legal case dropped in to get the judge's advice. It was only after we got back to
the farmstead of the lawyer's sister that both the drinking and the storytelling
were able to commence in earnest.

In short order the lawyer presented the judge with a gift he said came from
Muhammad—a new bottle of Ballantine's scotch ("By appointment to the late
Queen Victoria and the Late King Edward VII"). The normally goggle-eyed

judge set to: About three inches of scotch and a bit of Coca-Cola went into each of three glasses, that of the judge, the lawyer, and Tahar. Ali and Muhammad abstained, while I, who under other circumstances might have participated just so I could later say I once drank with a qadi, also demurred, the better to keep my anthropological wits about me. The judge was also taking snuff from a little squeeze bottle and something else went up his nose from a little black pouch over which he and Omar giggled secretively. Except for Tahar's one drink the entire bottle of scotch was consumed by the legal profession within a rather short space of time. Dinner was served around midnight. Someone then drove the judge home and the lawyer, who was barely able to stay upright, was put to bed in another room. In the quiet of their departure and still unsure where we were bedding down for the night, the best part of the evening's entertainment now commenced.

Having shaken off the effects of two beers and a scotch, Tahar now came alive—and with him the whole unspoken theme of our voyage began to find its fuller narrative voice. For it was in the stories that Tahar began to relate, and in the connected stories that each of the others developed, that the common concerns and orientations of the group began to emerge. Tahar's extraordinary raconteurial skills were now on full display as he would often jump up, take various speakers' roles, and portray each of the actors who figured in one of his stories with wonderful élan. Even Ali, who was stunned by the performance, turned to me at one point and described Tahar with open admiration as "un vrai homme de salon." One tale at a time, the stories began to build on the whole point of our weekend together.

The stories were initially elicited by, and perhaps must be understood in terms of, the context of discussion that led up to them. Ali had returned to a point that kept arising during the day, namely that when people deal with one another face-to-face they always manage to find a way to get along. The motif of Muslim-Jewish relations and Jewish business practices, so characteristically embedded in the earlier comments made along the roadside, now returned. So, too, did the references to interpersonal dealings that cut across political lines. One unstated aspect of those late-night tales emerged without explicit statement: No one is reducible to a single feature of his social identity, and if governments stay out of their way individuals can traduce boundaries with little difficulty. It was an aspect of the developing theme that was wholly consistent with the experience of each of the men in the room.

Tahar had been in the military for a number of years, including a long period of training abroad. In 1963 he found himself at the front in the Moroccan-Algerian border war. He told a long story about how they had taken an Algerian prisoner and how one of their own commanders wanted to torture the man to get information out of him. But others convinced the officer that they could get what information they needed without torture, by being gentle with the soldier, and Tahar told how they were careful to get enough to be helpful to their side without making the prisoner betray his comrades. As in each of the tales related to this theme the moral was neither explicitly stated nor self-serving: They were stories of honorable men, not stories about some abstract concept of honor.

From the story of the captured Algerian Tahar turned to the story of his own capture by the Algerians. ("The thief becomes the victim of thievery," said Ali, as we warmed to the tale.) Tahar had been taken prisoner, along with a small group of others, who were then interviewed by an Algerian officer. The man seemed to take a liking to Tahar—he saw he was educated, well-traveled, and an intriguing conversationalist—and they talked at length over several days. The officer never pushed Tahar for information—he had none to give, said Tahar, and the officer, a man of the Kabyles, a strong and independent people, could readily see that for himself. In time, the Algerian officer returned Tahar and his men to the front, gave them sufficient water to make it back to their own lines, and set them free.

It was not until twenty years later that Tahar and the Algerian were to meet again. Tahar was now working for a government ministry and was preparing to visit several factories in Algeria when he happened to recognize the name of one company director as that of the man who had captured him all those years earlier. When he arrived at the man's office he sent word in, just giving the man his name and asking to see him. The director immediately came out, having instantly recognized Tahar's name. The Algerian not only put Tahar up in Algeria at his own expense but later put him in touch with his own brother in France who hosted him and "gave him money for his pocket." As Tahar finished the story Ali breathed a single word: *'Ajub,* he said—extraordinary, wondrous, miraculous! *Tatshuf,* replied Tahar: You see!

A still more striking story followed, one involving Tahar's own nephew, who was serving with the Moroccan forces that had been sent to the Golan Heights during the 1967 Israeli-Arab war. The nephew was placed in charge of a reconnaissance mission sent out from Quneitra, but in short order they were captured by the Israelis. In line with their instructions, each of the Moroccan soldiers stripped off his insignia of rank before surrendering. When the Israeli commander began to question them, however, he said to Tahar's nephew: You're an officer, I can tell—the way you speak and carry yourself. Tell me, he said, where do you come from in Morocco? Tahar's nephew replied, I come from such-and-such a town. Really? said the Israeli: Tell me, what are the names of some of the important families in that town? The nephew mentioned a series of names. I see you're telling me the truth, said the Israeli captain, because I too am from the same town! Now listen to me, he continued: I promise that you and your men will come to no harm, just answer one question for me—are you an officer? Tahar's nephew replied, Yes. Good, said the Israeli, now I want you and your men to come with me. And he gave them a car and a driver and sent them to Tel Aviv. He gave them a guide and the freedom of the city, and "he gave them money for their pocket." After a few days they were returned to their own lines, unquestioned, unharmed. *'Ajub*, said Ali. *Tatshuf*, said Tahar.

Story prompted story, the connections unstated, the theme swirling through and beneath the current of the instant. Ali remarked on Moroccan Jews who were investing back in Morocco in ventures with Muslims, which in turn evoked stories of such dealings in the past, which in turn yielded a story of a Moroccan Muslim who went to New York, met a Moroccan Jew who was also from the same city, and the Jew helped the Muslim—gave him food and "gave him money for his pocket"—and helped set the Muslim up in business, and they are now partners and both are prospering in New York.

Tahar's work as a meteorologist even came into play as he detailed the way in which clouds are seeded to produce rainfall. The others reveled in his knowledge and his clarity, probing to understand the personal and technological expertise on which seeding is based. They relished the fact that Tahar combined experience from work in Europe, America, and Africa in his base of knowledge, and only when I asked if this meant that Morocco was capturing clouds that would otherwise have been destined for Algeria did Tahar, as if it were an unwanted side-effect, acknowledge that seeding was a veritable "combat for rainfall."

The same emphasis on persons relating across frontiers also set the tone for a series of stories that followed about the American missionaries who still worked in the town when Tahar was a schoolboy. Tahar began to play an imaginary piano keyboard and sang out the Arabic ditty the missionaries had taught: "Jesus loves us, every one!" I was there for the chocolates they gave out, said Tahar, but he went on to relate how they loved the old missionary lady and how she had raised several brothers from the town when she returned to America, and how Tahar disagreed with the brothers when they came back to Morocco after many years and said they thought Christianity was the superior religion, but how much they got along despite that. And Ali said, *'Ajub*; and Tahar said, *Tatshuf*.

After the wartime capture narratives and the stories of how men can relate to one another better without government involvement, a series of instances was mentioned about how rulers favor themselves in various ways. Tahar told a hilarious story about how an entire airplane was sent to England to bring back a couple of dogs for the King's daughter, long thin dogs (said Tahar, jumping up and posturing to mimic their appearance), dogs that looked like snakes. Others told of visiting dignitaries who, upon seeing a cow they admired, had it shipped to them on a special airplane, or how passengers were bumped from other aircraft to accommodate a royal shopping expedition, or how an entire plane was diverted from its scheduled stop so a royal relative could buy a trinket in a store. No direct mention of corruption was made, no overt antiroyalist sentiment uttered.

There was a lull in the stories now. The hour was late, but still nothing had been said about where we would be sleeping, or when. But it was clear that we were all enjoying ourselves, that each had caught the drift of events and that little had to be made explicit for the theme that bound us together to be self-evident. It was at this point, however, that Ali made a gesture and remark that captured the tone of the entire trip. Looking at each of us seated around the low, round table, he leaned forward and with genuine emotion described in the air with both of his hands a rough circle, and looking at each of us with obvious pleasure, said, in Arabic, *hadi l-khayyir:* This is the goodness, the beneficence, the right and proper thing for people to do. That his gesture was inclusive yet imprecise, that he did not run his hands along the edge of the table but embraced our circumstance in a motion of indeterminate exactness, was entirely fitting. And that he should choose the word *khayyir,* with its rich overtones of blessedness, the good aspects of life, the gift of divine bounty, the good things men do for and with one another—all these associations captured quite dramatically his and our sense of what we had been sharing together over this out-of-the-ordinary evening, why what had been created here was, indeed, a circle of beneficence.

Corruption had never been mentioned. What had been stressed—exemplified, articulated, demonstrated—was that people could deal across boundary lines best when government kept out of the way. The constant emphasis, as in Moroccan cultural perceptions generally, was on the socially constructed and situated person, that concatenation of associations and attributes that each focuses on in forming ties with another. Reduction to a single feature is contrary to such a view of persons, contrary to these men's ways of dealing with others. Hence the category Algerian or Jew or missionary or professional are elements of a person's overall identity, not an essential feature to which, alone among all traits, a relationship is reducible. But corruption interferes with this way of perceiving and dealing with others; it *does* render the multifarious singular, it *does* make official position and money the only viable aspects of a relationship. And in this regard it both defines what is so corrupting about corruption and renders it so clearly unpalatable to the men who were gathered around that table.

I had, of course, wondered on many occasions over the years what it was that qualified as corruption for the Moroccans I knew, and my mind was now cast back to another encounter I had had a few years earlier that served to clarify things for me. I was in the Middle Atlas Mountains at the home of a Berber friend of many years' duration where the men of the settlement were gathered for the main meal after prayers on a Friday afternoon. At one point my host, Hussein, turned to me and asked quite straightforwardly: Is there corruption in America? I said, of course. Give us an example, Hussein asked. So I mentioned Watergate. Ah, no, he said, that is just *siyasa*, politics. So I gave him an example of a kickback arrangement. Oh, no, he repeated, that is just *biya ou shra'*, buying and selling. So I dug still deeper and came up with an example of nepotism. No, no, no, he chided, that is just *a'ila*, family solidarity. And as I paused, trying to come up with an example that would save the honor of my country for being every bit as corrupt as any other, Hussein turned to the assembled men and said with open admiration: You see why America is such a strong country? They have no corruption!

Naturally, I was curious to know what Hussein and his compatriots regarded as corruption. The answer I received was one that I have heard right round the Middle East, namely that corruption is the failure to share with those with whom one has forged ties of dependence any largesse that comes one's way. Corruption is, in the Arabic idiom, "to eat" the good things that should be shared with others. In this sense corruption can be seen as interfering with the "the game," as getting in the way of the formation of negotiated ties of interdependency by which society is held together and by which individuals form the associations in terms of which they are themselves known. Perhaps that is why, too, common sayings reflect the greater harm of social chaos (*fitna*) than corruption: "tyranny is preferable to chaos," "an unjust government is better even than corruption," "to make a person live in chaos is worse than killing him." It is significant that the stories of corruption in Morocco have, in my experience, altered somewhat over the years, from stories that were mostly about ministers of the government who "ate" the benefits themselves to a far wider range of persons whose greed and selfishness are part of a larger social estrangement. Several examples came immediately to mind.

A fundamentalist leader by the name of Fqih al-Zamzami wrote a pamphlet in the late 1970s called "The Position of Islam vis-à-vis the Rich and the Poor." In it Zamzami condemns the corruption of public officials with the following example:

> It is said that a king gave the prime minister a thousand dinars and told him to spend it on the illumination of the capital on a certain night. The prime minister took half the money for himself and gave the rest to the mayor (*muḥafidh*) of the capital. The mayor kept half of this and gave the rest to the head of the *muqaddims* in charge of the city's neighborhoods. The head of the muqaddims kept all of this money for himself and told the inhabitants of the city that the king had ordered them to illuminate the capital on such and such a date. On the designated night, the king observed the city and saw that it was indeed illuminated as he had ordered by means of the money he had given to the "prime thief."[5]

Another example is recounted by John Waterbury:

> X, Y and Z are prominent businessmen with connections in the Palace and, more often than not, close relations or friends in the Ministry of Finance. They approach a thriving French textile plant and propose that they be allowed to acquire a certain proportion of the company's stock, let us say 15 per cent of all outstanding shares. It is understood that they will pay nothing for the shares but that dividends will accrue in their names until they are the equivalent to the value of the shares on the day of "purchase." The company can use those dividends as they accumulate, and, depending on the bargain, include interest in the purchase price. In the meantime, X, Y and Z will have been "elected" to the board of directors with salary. Without investing a penny, the three entrepreneurs can each pick up a salary and eventually a share of the company's assets. The more influential they appear to be, the more often they can repeat this gambit. In return for what is essentially protection money, they do favors for the company, such as arranging duty-free importation of machinery or keeping the labor inspector from closing the place down for violation of safety regulations.[6]

The style of giving gifts and favors in Morocco is, of course, integral to the way in which power is distributed within a system of intense personalism. Abdellah Hammoudi captures this sense very clearly when he writes, in his study of Moroccan authoritarianism, that it is imperative that the King, and, by implication, those mimicking his style, dispense gifts to those with whom ties of interdependency have been forged.[7] Failure to do so undermines the expectation of obligation that holds the entire system together. Outright bribery has even been seen by some Arabs as a vehicle of "democracy" inasmuch as the capacity to undercut what a person in power commands by bribing an underling to do something else constitutes a check on the power of the dominant figure. Although corruption among ministers remains a theme in corruption narratives generally, it is, however, much more common now to hear stories that relate to all levels of officialdom, from the royal family itself to a low-level civil servant, and for the thrust of these stories to suggest far more pervasive corruption than was true in the past.[8] If this is so the question could not help but arise, as I listened to the tales told by my traveling companions over the course of our weekend voyage, as to why such occurrences seem to be more extensive than in the past.

Ali had described a circle in the air, a figure within which an imprecise yet not indistinct group of individuals had forged bonds to one another such that they might share in both their common benefits and their sense of mutual indebtedness. That image, of circles within circles and circles intersecting circles, implicit in the image that Ali invoked, may help to account for the actual increase in the corruptibility of public officials over the course of the past decade or so. For if people have come to move around physically a great deal more than in the past, and if the intersecting ties of their various circles of affiliation have decreased, then the multiplicity of bases of interpersonal obligation might no longer account as effectively for the ties and expectations that hold groups together. It is as if the intersecting circles of attachment—what anthropologists have at times referred to as the multiplex ties that crosscut relationships and stitch them together in overlapping and multifarious ways—had begun to retract, the circles no longer overlapping, spaces appearing in the interstices. Into these voids the need still arises to make the connections that hold one's own network together, and money, favors, official contacts begin to replace the running imbalance of interpersonal relationships previously based on multiple, crosscutting ties of obligation.

Such an image was constantly the subject of reference, both explicit and anecdotal, among the people with whom I had been traveling. At one point, for example, I asked the lawyer why it was necessary for Muhammad and both of his attorneys to go hundreds of miles to the courts of two different jurisdictions just to get a copy of a document that one should have been able to obtain by phone or mail. The lawyer replied: "If you have an itch can you really expect someone else to scratch it at the exact spot where you feel it? If you feel the itch, aren't you the only one who knows precisely where it needs to be attended to?" The lawyer was referring, elliptically, to the fact that without seeing the matter through personally—and greasing the way with a few gifts to the appropriate clerks and assistants—Muhammad and his lawyers may have sustained a long delay in obtaining the document, or failed to get a true copy altogether. His way of putting the matter was wonderfully appropriate: It called forth that intense personalism of Moroccan social interactions—the need to attend to matters oneself and the need to focus on *who* it is that one is dealing with—and the need to be sure that it is clear to those with whom one is dealing that it is you, and not someone else, who is both the source of the "favor" and the one expecting its proper recompense. Without some connection of kinship, locality, or history—increasingly unlikely as people move around and relationships are more single-stranded—money becomes the vehicle for attachment. Thus even corruption necessarily partakes of the patterns and assumptions of interaction that run through the entire course of Moroccan person perception and social structure.

The decline in intersecting ranges of obligation is also revealed in a number of other ways. Increasingly one hears statements of causation drawn less in terms of who has caused something to happen than in terms of the impersonal forces at work; increasingly one hears a language of circumstantial evidence in courts rather than characterizations of persons based on their backgrounds; increasingly one hears a language of probability, where the very meaning of the Arabic term itself conveys not the earlier sense of an authoritative opinion but an assessment of likelihood to which any knowledgeable person might be able to apply himself.[9] Gaining the favor of a public official remains a matter of intensely personal contact rather than a structured set of cozy arrangements involving whole classes of persons and, in this sense, fits very closely as well to the way in which the whole story of corruption and cohesion was being narrated during the course of our travels.

Indeed, the lack of explicitness to the theme of the weekend was by no means an isolated phenomenon in the style of narrative characteristic of Morocco and other parts of the Arab world. Each story built on the one before, each partook of an unstated principle that nevertheless suffused the totality of instances. The cultural emphasis is that of the synoptic view, the cumulation of instances, the demonstration of a precept not by abstract articulation but by constant exemplification. At each point another example shows another facet of a variegated whole, the differences of situation revealing the multifarious contexts within which each feature resides. At each juncture, too, a choice is being made, and repetition actually reinforces not similarity but the opportunity—indeed, the necessity—for choice. At different moments, in different contexts, different aspects of a person may be highlighted, while the telling of numerous instances shows how important features vary with context and why intelligent people must gain knowledge of innumerable instances so they can read any situation wisely. These qualities are present in numerous cultural domains of Arab life. One scholar has, for example, spoken of "the Arab frame tradition," in which there is not a structuring principle in terms of which all instances are organized but a general outline to which particular manifestations are attached. Thus in architecture the rooms are added on, each carrying forth and developing a theme but not constituting part of an original governing design. So, too, in music where variations are added on to basic themes, in mathematics, where the invention of the zero operates as a placeholder for particulars generated around it, and in literature, where the accumulation of examples, rather than a series of increasingly abstracted propositions, bespeaks the overarching theme.[10] The same is true in social perception, where each case is seen as distinctive yet each reveals an aspect of a whole—like a gem turned in the light—until the widest possible range of instances gives one the overview necessary to be able to adapt to constantly changing contexts. In the endless quest for understanding others as situated in a continuously varying array of negotiated relationships, this synoptic, exemplified, highly situational sense of events and persons conveys the Arab sense of what is true about people and about the way one grasps an ever-changing set of maneuvers in the world of human contacts. The stories my traveling companions told of cohesion and corruption built on these cultural assumptions and by their very replication reinforced the standards of appropriate interpersonal behavior that could cross bounds of unitary identity even as their inability to be sustained in the face of changing social circumstances seemed to open the way to an alienating range of corrupting forms that undermined my companions' sense of cohesion and wider beneficence.

It was a little after two in the morning when one of the young men of the household brought in blankets and pillows, and it finally became clear where we would be bedding down for the night. Muhammad went off to another room to sleep, but I stayed up to listen to Ali and Tahar who continued telling stories. After some time Ali said that if I was tired I should feel free to go on to sleep, and a few minutes later I made up a bed on one of the banquettes near the end of the room and climbed in to get warm. As I listened to my companions talking I found myself thinking back to other aspects of the conversations I had been hearing throughout the day. I recalled how, at one point while we were driving along, Muhammad had asked his lawyer why he found this particular legal case so interesting. The lawyer said there were three reasons: because it involved so many different domains of the law and thus afforded him a chance to see how each related to the other; because so often cases are settled before going to decision that he now had a chance to see a complex case through to final resolution; and because Muhammad had lived abroad for so many years and was rather naïve about how things really worked in Morocco and he wanted to help his friend see matters as they really are. It was, I thought, a heartfelt statement about how much the lawyer wanted to exercise his professional skills—just as his companions had taken such delight in the details of Tahar's account of cloud-seeding—and demonstrated how crucial to their own self-image and mode of forming relationships is the value set on being a knowledgeable person, a person who has developed his or her reasoning powers, transformed knowledge into worldly consequent effects, and shared the benefits of that knowledge with others in his circle.

I thought back, too, to an incident that had occurred when I traveled with Muhammad and both of his lawyers to the courts of the south the week before. After lunch I was standing beside the road with Muhammad's senior attorney and asked him what future he saw for the development of law in Morocco. He motioned to the traffic on the road—the usual hodgepodge of motorized vehicles, animal-drawn conveyances, and meandering bicycles and foot traffic of every description. "We must," said the lawyer with genuine passion, "have some rules for the way things operate on the roads or Moroccans will go every which way: The law has to supply some boundaries, like these at the edge of the road, some general sense of how to proceed. Moroccans," he continued, "will never be comfortable with strict rules, but look and you will see that as long as there are some bounds people really do develop orderly ways of moving without always bumping into each other or starting fights." I was reminded by his comment of the refrain so common in the text of the Qur'an: "These are the bounds of God, do not overstep them." The lawyer's image was thus a fitting one. Like the narrative theme that had developed over the weekend, the image that came to my mind was not one of sharp boundaries but more like the Gulf Stream that flows along the Atlantic coast of the United States, out to sea, and across the ocean. It is not, as some have characterized it, a river in the ocean, for it has no settled banks, no limitations to which, short of cataclysm, it adheres. Yet it has both distinctive attributes and, at any given moment, a definable shape. Like the Gulf Stream the view of human relationships is one of eddies and blendings that are imprecise, as attachments present themselves and the sheer exuberance of attaching, of watching, of displaying rhetorical and relational skills draws people together in shared experience and values. On the road people push as close as they can, never sure until it becomes manifest whether another will yield. But it is not agonistic: People do not get enraged; if the other yields it establishes where the eddy is at that moment; if they push too close, the hand raised near one's head in a screwing gesture suggests that the other person has not caught the sense of the boundaries and is a bit screwed up. But it is not done with anger—an elaborate dance, a probing, but not without a well-accepted sense of bounds. So, too, the law, like the traffic, is not without its regularizing effects even though Moroccans are more comfortable with the law establishing flexible boundaries than ordering precise actions. Corruption, I heard them saying, disturbs this ability to exercise their knowledge, to display their abilities, to be in the world of negotiated relationships as people ought to be. The unstated premise—that corruption is so deeply alienating—ran, like the current of the stream, through every aspect of their concrete examples and their collective experience.

After some time Tahar and Ali too made up beds on the other banquettes, turned off the lights, and settled in for the night. Then something quite remarkable happened. They began to talk again, only now in those very quiet tones that people use when the lights are out, when the day is ended, but when you still don't quite want to give up the sense of the encounter. Perhaps their hushed tones were meant not to disturb my supposed sleep; perhaps it was just an instance of that familiarity of tone when the intimacy of the night prevails. Though sleepy my anthropologists' ears, like those of any other beast of burden, seemed to swivel around to catch their words, but now it was the snatched phrase, the tone, that I heard. People can always deal with one another, said the one; there are people who are wonderfully knowledgeable, said the other. It was better with the Jews, said the one; it could be better for us all, said the other. *Ajub,* breathed the one; *Tatshuf,* murmured the other. They whispered with feeling, they mused with detachment. They wanted things to be different; they wanted things to be as they had been throughout our journey.

As I listened to the quiet intensity of their nighttime thoughts, I thought how wrong were those who characterized Arab society as a "closed circle."[11] To the contrary, I thought, this circle is extraordinarily open-ended. It may be indeterminate, as are social ties generally, but it is not indistinct; it can expand to include all who relate as persons to other persons. When it does expand it validates the very process which is at its core; when it contracts everyone feels the loss of overlapping ties and the intrusion of officialdom, bureaucratic impersonalism, corruption.

I thought, too, how painful was my friends' sense of this alienating corruption, now so much a part of daily activity. I thought of that famous line attributed to Edmund Burke, that the only thing necessary for the triumph of evil is for good men to do nothing. But these *are* good men, I said to myself, and they have not done nothing. Muhammad works with a human rights commission in Morocco, an effort that is not without its risks in the context of a political system that, for all its efforts to portray itself as benign and responsive, is in fact wholly subject to the will of a single man. I thought of Ali and how, after we had eaten in a roadside café earlier that day, he had gathered up the extra food on our table and made two huge sandwiches which he then gave to a poor family looking on from the edge of the street—and how I had seen him repeatedly engage in such acts of ordinary generosity in the time I had known him. I thought, finally, of Tahar, who had the courage to report to his superiors on a vast scheme of corruption he uncovered in his own government department—only to discover that the superior to whom he reported the matter was himself part of the scheme. Indeed, the man had subsequently tried to cover his tracks by framing Tahar, for which only an appropriate payment to officials was eventually to keep Tahar free from a six-month jail sentence. Far from giving in to evil, these good men had taken their stands even as they found themselves forced into the small corruptions that each encountered on a daily basis and for which they found themselves guiding and supporting a friend who shared both their need to get by and their sense of entrapment.

I trust these men. I believe them to be good men. I do not know what I would do in their place. But I have faith in them, and in the circle of beneficence they had sought all through our shared voyage to re-create. And so, in time I drifted off to sleep, beneath the heavy, earth-colored Berber blankets, nestled on my right side, my knees bent, my face to the rising sun, like a Muslim awaiting the final judgment, unaccountably content.

Ambivalence towards Power
Approaches to Authority in Postcolonial Morocco

∾

"There exists no land of impiety that does not hide some faith; nor act of obedience which does not hide a worse disobedience; nor any devotion plunged in meditation with God that does not hide a lack of respect; nor any claim to love that does not contain a want of decency."[1] So wrote the renowned martyr/ heretic al-Hallāj, and though his fate at the hands of the legalists of his day was extreme his sentiments in this regard are anything but unusual. For it is a common feature of culture itself that the conceptualizations formed reach out in alternative, even contradictory, directions, sustaining their ability to encompass new and changing circumstances through the sheer flexibility of their constituent overtones. How a particular culture addresses ambivalence— whether by suppression or elaboration, by fearful avoidance or joyful exploitation—will undoubtedly connect to and serve as an indicator of its overall approach to diversity of thought and relationships.

In Islamic cultures, and in the Arabic language, the inherent ambivalence of innumerable concepts is on full display. Single words often contain a proposition and its direct opposite, just as popular sayings and self-evident actions demonstrate the two-edged nature of many connections and associations. The following essay takes up the challenge of ambivalence to social science—once readily accepted but inappropriately abandoned in more recent decades—by considering the ambivalent attitudes and actions revealed in the daily lives of Moroccans. Whether it is in their approach to questions of gender, political authority, or saintly legitimacy, a common theme of ambivalence towards power runs through many of the cultural forms found in the Arab/Muslim world, and it is through such circumstantial instances as those presented here that we can, perhaps, comprehend the seeming contradictions by which power is brought within the ambit of everyday life.☙☙☙☙☙☙☙☙☙☙☙☙☙☙☙☙☙☙☙☙☙☙☙☙

EXEMPLARY AMBIVALENCE

Fez—July 1967   In the early hours of the morning the wedding procession had left the home of the groom's family and made its way through the darkened streets of Fez Jedid to a gate beyond which no automobiles could pass. Snaking our way through the oldest part of the city to the sound of robust singing and drums banging, past shuttered stalls and the labyrinth of dead-end streets, our party arrived at the house of the bride's family. Once admitted to the enclosed courtyard of the ancient, high-bourgeoisie Fez house, the professional bridal assistants (*ngagaf*) appeared at the upper-story balcony. The men below began to chant: *'aṭina dyalna u n'aṭikum dyalkum, 'atina dyalna u nmshiu fhalna—* "give us what belongs to us and we'll give you what belongs to you, give us what is ours and we will go our way."[2] The bridal assistants began to taunt the men below: "What pathetic little things you are," their leader called, "do you expect us to give you what is yours when you are so weak? Is this your strength? Are you no more than women?" After a good deal of repartee and noisemaking we were finally assured that, if we left, the bride would come out. When she did, dressed in an elaborate gown and surrounded by her attendants, the mood grew uncertain. She was to enter the car that had been brought round, a white Mercedes with the diplomatic pendants of the groom's uncle waving from the fenders—but she refused. At first it seemed part of the reluctance a bride is expected to display when leaving the parents' house on her wedding night. But this was beginning to go on much too long. People began to whisper: Could it be happening, could she *really* be refusing to go, could all the expense, the elaborate negotiations and preparation be for nothing? After some hasty conversations—the women watching from the windows above, the men nervously clustered below—the bride finally entered the car and the wedding party—now including her father—drove off quickly in the direction of the groom's home.

Immouzar du Kandar—July 1969   It was the usual weekly market day in this Middle Atlas mountain village: The temporary stalls of the people who made the market circuit were erected, the fires of the food sellers were glowing, the scents of the nearby animal market wafted past those who were settled on the ground to eat a midday meal. He came wearing a green turban, the sign of a saintly descendant and member of their brotherhood located on the edge of the Sahara, well over the mountains to the south. He also carried the flag of his brotherhood mounted on the end of a long staff. And he bore himself as one to whom much was due. The marketers—most of them Berber-speakers from the surrounding tribes—were approached in their small groups, and his gesture was far less that of one who was requesting a contribution or conferring a blessing for alms received than of the imperious expecting their proper desert. The men hunched their shoulders and, averting his eyes, reached into their leather purses and dropped coins into the outstretched hand, its curled fingers and rigid arm as unyielding of return as his domineering stance and immobile face. As he moved away they grumbled, their looks a mix of uncertain homage and unrepentant reserve, their quiet conversation flowing back into normal tones as he moved beyond their range to the groups reclining further off.

Sefrou, Morocco—July 1969   They had been standing on the stadium field for three hours in the intense heat while the local notables sat in the suffocating stands above growing equally restive. The forty-five men below were awaiting the ceremony at which the government minister would present documents granting each of them a share of the former French farmland in the district. The minister was not from the city, but his brother was the mayor there and he had himself once been the agricultural representative for a nearby area. When eventually he did arrive, the minister spoke to the assembled about the generosity of the government, even though his own figures showed that only one out of four hectares seized was being redistributed. He said it was not government policy to support large landholders and then proceeded to define "large" in a way that pleased neither those below nor those in the stands. When it came to handing out the documents, he yanked his hand away from any of the unkempt rural folk who tried to kiss it, chided one man for not being able to read the grant, and when another man gave his surname as that of a woman, explaining that it was because his father had died and he was raised by his mother, the minister commented that that seemed to him to be a rather silly custom. Recipients and guests were respectful but wary, deferential but forthright, and though they broadly respected the minister for his background and position, they smiled knowingly as they commented later about the ways of those in power.

ANALYZING AMBIVALENCE

There was a time, in the 1950s and 1960s, when a number of American social scientists were intrigued by the role that ambivalence played in social and political life. Prompted in no small part by the postwar concern about how people come to follow mass movements, giving over much of their own critical sense to the supreme leader or the sentiments of the crowd, the sociologists' ideas were situated within the theories of the day—that form of functionalism that stressed deviations from conditions of relative stability, and that type of social structural analysis that was concerned with roles and their attendant behavioral norms. In part, theirs was an attempt to take back an issue of central importance to social organization from the psychologists who had situated ambivalence at the level of "feeling-states" and personality types.

Robert Merton gave particular impetus to these concerns in his appropriately titled 1963 essay "Sociological Ambivalence."[3] Critical of the psychological emphasis of his predecessors, Merton argued that status positions—such as particular professions—expose their holders to ambivalence "not because of [the individuals'] idiosyncratic history or their distinctive personality but because the ambivalence is inherent in the social positions they occupy."[4] Whether it is an apprentice, whose structured position vis-à-vis his master is fraught with the antipathies of admiration and the struggle for independence, or the scientist, who must appear neutral in the pursuit of knowledge yet personally ambitious in its very acquisition, Merton saw roles as the combination of major norms and minor counter-norms whose alternate governance of behavior yields an ineluctable ambivalence.[5] Indeed, he argued, "only through such structures of norms and counter-norms . . . can the various functions of a role be effectively discharged."[6] In what may have been his boldest thesis, Merton went on to assert that relations that are presumptively enduring actually cumulate ambivalence over the course of time, and that the more such ambivalence accumulates the greater the dissatisfaction each party may be able to sustain before feeling that the relationship must be broken. Thus it is not, in Merton's view, simply a matter of personality differences that yield ruptures between individuals but the extent to which the institutionalized relationship itself supports a backlog of ambivalence.[7]

In his own explication of the theories of Merton and others on ambivalence, Edgar W. Mills points out several related arguments. Dissonant norms and values contribute to individual autonomy and actually protect society against extreme behavior: Sociologists (such as Louis and Rose Coser, Alvin Gouldner, and Talcott Parsons) argued that, far from yielding neuroses based on such incompatibilities, "sociological ambivalence allows individuals to create autonomy for themselves by means of legitimated inconsistent behavior."[8] Recalling the original interest of these scholars in authoritarianism, Mills says of those who fail to deal with these "structural and cultural indeterminacies": "People who are unwilling or unable to tolerate such dissonance, or who are caught up in groups which destroy the social supports for multiple reference orientations, are likely to become collaborators in the reduction of their own moral freedom."[9]

Much of the work of Merton and his contemporaries focused specifically on the relation of ambivalence to authority. Merton's professionals were examples of such authority figures, and he noted generally that "however great its legitimacy, authority is known to have a high potential for creating ambivalence among those subject to it. Authority generates a mixture of respect, love and admiration and of fear, hatred, and, sometimes, contempt."[10] Merton was more concerned with professional than with political authority, but others, coming at the issue from alternative theoretical orientations, have addressed the relation of ambivalence to political authority more directly. William E. Connolly, for example, has argued that while there may be "a presumption in favor of the exercise of authority," the constant danger of its abuse suggests to followers an element of the arbitrary, the possibility that benefits and burdens are distributed asymmetrically and hence could be arrayed differently.[11] He refers to those societies in which, through a variety of myths and rituals, both the authority of the existing order and the arbitrary elements it embraces are celebrated, explored, and only occasionally resolved. Similarly, he says, "modern politics, again at its best, is the institutionalization of ambiguity; it keeps alive that which might otherwise be killed by the weight of authority or necessity; it helps that which is subordinate to find its own voice and perhaps, to expand the space in which it can be for itself rather than only for the order."[12] His argument recalls some of the features of Richard Sennett's analysis in *Authority*, where he suggests that, in the United States, the fear of being deceived by authority has led to its being negated in the very context of a market economy which had generated the image of paternalism as a response to the fractionation of the family and community under modern capitalism.[13]

Political philosophers have also been much concerned with issues of power, and their choice of definitions for the concept indicates the extent to which they recognize ambivalence as an inherent aspect of it. Whether it is Weber's somewhat limited view of power as the probability of getting one's way despite resistance,[14] or the more expansive views of later observers (such as Parsons,[15] Lukes,[16] Galbraith,[17] or Foucault[18]) who, in very different ways, see power as incorporating consensus, proportionate response, or diffuse impacts on the image of the self, modern concerns with ambivalence towards power have been largely tangential and allusive. Ambivalence does surface as an issue in some discussions, as for example in the "problem of dirty hands," where even well-intentioned politicians may be forced to engage in immoral conduct.[19] But for the most part the direct concerns of Merton and others have been lost to sight, perhaps, as we shall see later, because of what Donald Levine has called the larger "flight from ambiguity" in social science.[20]

Anthropologists, too, have occasionally noted the problems, both substantive and methodological, associated with the study of ambivalence.[21] Connolly's reference to trickster figures and rituals of ambiguity acknowledges the predominant way in which anthropologists have concerned themselves with the issue of ambivalence towards power.[22] Some, continuing in the vein of psychological anthropology, cite William James's assertion that "nature implants contrary impulses to act on many classes of things" including "sociability." They follow this assertion by adopting the more recent claim that "ambivalence, rather than averaging, seems the optimal compromise" in social relations and conclude that both ambivalence and compromise are essential aspects of human nature itself.[23] Jack Goody takes a related approach when he argues that cognitive contradictions inherent in the human situation show themselves with particular force in systems of representation: Realizing the inherent contradictions of power, even in the deity, there is, he argues, always a "kernel of doubt"—a kind of "ambivalence in the actor's mind"—that shows itself in representational forms.[24]

As useful as many of these accounts of ambivalence may be, at both the theoretical and the comparative level they remain largely inchoate, detached from the details of specific ethnographic situations, divorced from the daily experience of ambivalent relations towards power in the lives of particular individuals and societies. However, the recent study by Abdellah Hammoudi, entitled *Master and Disciple: The Cultural Foundations of Moroccan Authoritarianism*, has the advantage of being both highly circumstantial and directly germane to my own long-term interest in ambivalence towards power in North Africa. I want, therefore, to take a more extended, critical look at Hammoudi's account and then, relying on the various insights that he and the proponents of "sociological ambivalence" have given us, to return to the three case studies set forth at the outset in order to interpret each in the light of a set of broader propositions about the distinctive form that ambivalence towards power takes in postcolonial Morocco.

AUTHORITY AND AUTHORITARIANISM IN MOROCCO

Hammoudi's study of Moroccan authoritarianism approaches the issue of ambivalence towards power very directly: "The same social actors may exhibit diametrically opposite attitudes in different situations, assuming an attitude of humble submission, which often borders on obsequiousness, when in a subordinate position, but expecting strict obedience when in a position of power, an attitude that takes precedence over any legal mediation. . . . [T]he submission relation, which now can be seen as a waiting period and the price to be paid for access to power, is associated with a high degree of ambivalence, as might be expected."[25] Hammoudi sees in the array of Moroccan "cultural schemata" a series of rules "fraught with strong undercurrents of ambivalence" that are, most significantly, "grounded and sanctified by the concepts and procedures involved in the process of mystical initiation."[26] It is this relationship of Sufi disciple to Sufi master, ecstatic follower to venerated saint that is replicated in the relation to a father, a chief, or a monarch. Each incorporates inversions of position and essence which, by their very ambivalence, sustain—indeed reproduce—their particular religious pattern and the structure of Moroccan authoritarianism itself.[27]

The inversion to which Hammoudi refers takes on many forms. It appears most particularly in sexuality—where the disciple is feminized in the course of being subservient to the master, where the religious acolyte's submission to the saint incorporates signs of feminine weakness, and where the politically impotent stands in unmanly posture (often with his hands crossed over his genitals) before his superior. It appears, too, in those rituals of power where the inversion is portrayed in the drama of the event—whether it be that of an ordinary mortal masked as a figure of great power, or that of a student, crowned sultan for a day, who is licensed to issue commands to the real sultan.[28] Even where, particularly in more recent times, the King is portrayed less as a figure of command than as a mediator and arbiter, the attitudes expressed towards such a role—in which the interests of the monarchy and those closest to it are commonly seen to govern the professed neutrality—underscore the dual nature of authority itself.

Hammoudi also employs his view of ambivalence to account for the relationship of authority to rebellion. At the level of the monarchy, the appearance is always given of a close relationship between King and subaltern, a relationship that is reinforced by gift-giving, etiquette, and the refusal to publicly acknowledge those instances when royal trust has been misplaced. Elites accept even humiliation as the price of access, but they do so "with an ambivalence which oscillates between submission and rebellion, reverence and irritation vis-à-vis the system and its operators."[29] Similarly, at the local level, which replicates the style and structure of the center on a smaller scale, "since [power] has no clearly institutionalized limits, antagonism inevitably arises."[30] Not infrequently, says Hammoudi, "ambivalence manifests itself not only in conversation but in coups and assassination attempts. For the master is also the one that others try to elim-inate—in order to take his place—and who, as a consequence, must often chas-tise the disciples and keep them under surveillance."[31] Particularly at moments of transition—the death of a King, the intrusion by foreigners—"given the ab-sence of formalized succession rules and the lack of stable institutions that would allow a civil society to act as a counterweight, one may go from total obe-dience to one's chief to murdering him."[32] Colonialism, Hammoudi concludes, only rendered this pattern static, while the contemporary bureaucratic appara-tus "sees its rules constantly subverted by concrete codes of interaction geared towards building closeness through gift exchange—that is, through the same procedures we found at work in the master-disciple relationship."[33]

Hammoudi's thesis is filled with provocative insight and he undoubtedly goes farther than any of his predecessors towards accounting for the cultural patterns upon which Moroccan authoritarianism is based.[34] Nevertheless cer-tain caveats may be in order. One could see in Hammoudi's account too great an emphasis on distinctively Moroccan attributes of the Sufi/saint complex at the expense of other cultural foundations. The answer to this objection may, of course, be that even though relatively few people belong, or probably ever did belong, to Sufi orders and even though the saint complex is sometimes mingled with that of the Sufis and at other times kept quite distinct, the sym-bolism of master and acolyte still constitutes an important template through which many relationships are rendered both comprehensible and sublime. More tellingly, it may be argued that the pattern of authoritarianism in Mo-rocco is also prevalent throughout most of the Arab world (and much of the Muslim world beyond), even though in many places neither Sufism nor saint complexes form part of the overall cultural milieu. Whether the sacralization of leaders as descendants of the Prophet, commanders of the faithful, or "secular" protectors of the faith is sufficient to support an argument favoring the centrality of the religious over other sources of authoritarianism may ulti-mately be unresolvable. Hammoudi is particularly arguing against those ac-counts of authoritarianism that are based on modes of production. Neverthe-less, it is always risky to portray a given cultural form as particularly central when the whole point about culture is that features are so thoroughly repli-cated in a variety of domains that no single arena appears to summarize, much less be generative to, all others, the sheer prevalence of the pattern everywhere giving it the air of the impersonal, the immanent, and the natural.

At the risk of reifying certain elements of which Hammoudi himself is only too aware I would like to shift the emphasis somewhat in my own assessment of ambivalence. Ambivalence in Morocco (and broadly in its Middle Eastern

form) is, as will be argued in greater detail in the next chapter, very closely related to the combination of tribal forms of political organization and the specific forms of religiosity to which Hammoudi himself refers. Tribes, as we shall
see, have several characteristics—ranging from rituals and joking patterns to
the ease of social movement and proof of qualities through direct action—that
contribute to the frequent leveling of power. Broadly speaking, tribes are structured so that too much power does not cumulate for too long in too few hands.
Moreover, the very "structure" of tribal forms, like that of an amoeba, lies not
in a given shape but in the capacity to be molded to exigent forms. The result is
a type of political organization that, like a wallpaper pattern design, can sustain
severe diminution in size yet not lose the plan from which it can be regenerated.
Until well into the twentieth century, probably no more than 5 to 10 percent of
Moroccans lived in cities, and even there the pattern of neighbors and quarters,
religious scholars (ʿulamā) and teachers (fuqahā) contributed to a convergent
pattern of power dispersal. Authoritarianism was reinforced by the particular
modes through which Islam supported the principles that were consonant with
tribal organization: the proof of merit by action, the legitimization that arises
from achieving control of the reins of power, the image of the admirable man
as one who uses his reason to create webs of dependency that contain both his
own momentary power and the seeds of contrariety. Prior to the arrival of the
French, it could be argued, Morocco was not an example of a state structure at
all but of a kind of paramount chieftainship, with all the contradictions of
power and emphasis on personality that such a political form entails.

Seen from this perspective power itself can be constructed from a wide
range of resources, and the maintenance of the emphasis on ambivalence keeps
all such mechanisms in play. Steven Caton has argued that persuasion, rather
than force, is far more common in the tribal structures of the Middle East than
others have acknowledged.[35] Although he is imprecise about what persuasion
is and fails to give the examples whose absence he decries in the work of others, one can certainly acknowledge that the capacity to capture the terms of discussion—if only for the moment—is one among many resources by which
people can build a base of power. Ambivalence is thus not only deep-seated in
every mechanism by which a network of dependents is constructed but is also
deeply writ into the very conceptualizations, the very instruments of construction, by which Moroccans orient themselves in a world of others.

Take, for example, the place of ambivalence in the structure of many Arabic linguistic constructs. Berque, Charnay, and their colleagues have been particularly instrumental in recapturing the role that ambivalence plays in linguistic and grammatical forms, particularly as exemplified in that body of

literature known as the *ad'add*.[36] In a host of terms that import both the thing and its opposite, that broader principle to which Franz Rosenthal referred—that in "the Muslim view . . . all matters human have a positive as well as a negative side"—comes sharply to the fore.[37] Paired meanings embraced by a single term include "to bring close / turn away," "to have many debts / many debtors," "to gather / separate," "to be sincere / say useless things," "to doubt / be sure," "to be just / unjust."[38] The logic of these coupled antinomies says much about the domains of ambivalence that characterize Arab culture and the limitations that language itself incorporates in the representation of these ambiguities. The same quality has long been visible in those institutions of high Islamic culture, where the indeterminacy of situation and characterization also remain prominent: The acceptability of a judge's or scholar's opinion has depended on the force of their own constructed networks of supporters; the inability of any person to articulate matters with final certainty militated against any system of legal appeals; and the punishments to which a person could be subjected were commonly expected to be proportionate to the range of a man's network and hence the extent to which his act might cause social harm. So, too, the emphasis on making force appear to be an act of persuasion even when it is raw constraint reinforces the importance of controlling language and maintaining multiple avenues for constructing power.

Ambivalence is thus both deeper and more broadly based in the culture of Morocco than may have been appreciated. In Hammoudi's approach, the test for ambivalence comes in rites of passage—precisely the domain anthropologists have, almost by definition, marked off as the place to find ambivalence in any society. By contrast, I prefer to draw on the insights of the scholars of ambivalence referred to earlier and explore the implications of this ambivalence in several domains of Moroccan social and cultural life. Towards that end, I want to return to the three case studies set out at the beginning of this essay and see what the theories of the sociologists of ambivalence, the Moroccanists, and the informants themselves can add to our understanding of the place ambivalence towards power occupies in these and similar events.

AMBIVALENCE REVISITED

"Rituals of Ambivalence": Sex, Gender, and the Power of Weakness
Weddings are one of the preeminent moments in Moroccan culture in which multiple social interests come into direct contact, and often conflict, with one another. As one Moroccan said to me years ago: "In your country it is very easy to get married and very difficult to get divorced; in Morocco it is the other way

around." The rituals surrounding marriage also form an equally entangling and no less contentious realm for various anthropological interpretations. This is not the place to attempt an analysis of the criteria for better and worse interpretations, and though I shall unashamedly engage in what might be called "the hypocrisy of the interpretive turn" (all interpretations have merit, but mine of course is best), I will discuss alternative views of these wedding ceremonies in trying to understand what happened that day in Fez when a wedding seemed to be breaking down.

Traditional weddings in Morocco are indeed fraught with actual, as well as symbolic, demonstrations that power is not always what or where it may seem to be. In what is surely the most comprehensive and (based on my own work in adjacent areas) accurate description of marriage ceremonies, Edward Westermarck noted a series of these features. Perhaps most striking are those acts in which, in much the sense that Hammoudi also notes, there occurs an inversion of sexuality, particularly in the feminization of the groom. Not only are the groom's hands painted with henna,[39] but the groom is often actually dressed up in women's clothes as part of the festivities. Describing weddings in Fez at the turn of the twentieth century, Westermarck writes: "In the evening a feast is given in his [the groom's] father's house, with musicians and invited guests. After supper the so-called *ngagef*—free negresses whose business is to assist women on festive occasions—dress up the young man as a bride with garments which they have brought with them."[40] The bride, too, may be dressed up in a man's clothing, carrying a dagger, her face painted with mock whiskers.[41] Moreover, the hennaed hands of the groom are bound up, thus rendering him both immobile and symbolically incapable of reciprocating the gifts bestowed upon him.[42] Given the absolute centrality to manhood of being able to move to effect in the world and being able to ingratiate oneself to others to construct a network of support, this tying up demonstrates both femininity and, perhaps more important, the contingencies and ambiguities of power associated with any role.

Perhaps the most stunning moment in the wedding night in Fez that I have described occurred when the bride seemed to be balking at going along to the groom's residence. Some hesitancy may be ritually expected: Westermarck notes that commonly the bride was actually carried into her new home as "a ceremonial expression of the reluctance which a virgin pretends to feel against being given away in marriage."[43] And such a transition doubtless frightens many young women to this day. But when reluctance becomes misgiving, when the bride's capacity to bring everything to a screeching halt is manifested, the particular sense of discomfort changes from mild concern to virtual disorientation. The "solution" that night in Fez was as uncharacteristic as it was disquieting: The father of the bride actually went along to the groom's house with his daughter. Westermarck again notes: "At Fez, as we have noticed, the girl avoids her father at the time of the betrothal, and nowhere in Morocco does the father go to his daughter's wedding."[44] Nowadays fathers of the bride do attend the festivities, but they always keep a low profile and never accompany her to the groom's home. Indeed, when the wedding party arrived back at the groom's home the father of the bride sat looking particularly disconsolate, and the other men, though sympathetic, were clearly very embarrassed. This collective unease was not simply due to the threat of a social bond failing to achieve completion; it was, like the taunting of the bridal assistants, a demonstration of how such disruptions make visible the multiple bases of power and the ever elusive need to sort power by relationship and context.

The events revealed by this wedding are usually analyzed by anthropologists in terms of rites of passage and the inversion of gendered roles. But to assume that such events are examples of being "betwixt and between" fails to consider that one may be in a situation not interstitial to any position—and dangerous for being out of place—but, at this moment no less than at any other, existing in multiple contexts simultaneously. Thus it is tempting to say that what we have here is the reverse of the usual anthropological paradigm, in which women are said to represent nature while men represent culture, for when a bride balks the men are made to look the embodiment of nature—driven by their passions to this impasse—and now the men must become as women truly are—creatures of culture—by approaching the bride's actions through the language and tools of relationship. But the alternative exists that this is neither a case of liminality nor of inversion but a demonstration of multiplicity, a representation of the belief that power has many bases and that every moment is a critical juncture in relationship formation inasmuch as man or woman, saint or sinner, patron or client may be able to dig into the repertoire of such resources to form ties with systemic and unpredictable consequences. The rituals of the bride do not simply render the groom "weak and harmless like a woman"[45] or preeminently an example of "the obligatory passage through feminization simultaneous with a radical negation of it":[46] When the acts of anyone—a bride no less than many others—become unpredictable, the ambivalence inherent in all power is simultaneously displayed and deployed, and both possibility and danger are given equal reign.

"A Snake in the *Zāwiya*": Spiritual Ambivalence

Moroccan culture is intensely personalistic. It is the socially constructed person—that concatenation of created obligations and attributes that perdure only as long as the individual in whom they are reposed operates to effect in the world—which is the fundamental unit of society.[47] Not surprisingly, this personalism is evident in the realm of religion as much as any other domain. With it, too, comes that inherent ambivalence about the power that others can exercise over oneself. What occurred that day in the market in the Middle Atlas mountains, when the descendant of a saint was making his rounds (*ziyāra*) collecting alms, was no more or less characteristic of this ambivalence than what occurs in other domains of social life. But as in each such cultural domain, the way in which this ambivalence is inscribed and the implications it possesses always have their own distinctive emphases.

In addition to Hammoudi, many students of Moroccan culture have noted the ambivalence towards living saints. Gellner, in his analysis of tribal structure and interpersonal trust, argues that specialization is anathema to tribesmen, who find in it the very antithesis of that set of obligations set forth in structures of segmentarity that bind society together along the lines described by Ibn Khaldun. Tribesmen not only despise specialists, he says, "but they are also somewhat ambivalent about the religious arbitration specialists who in a sense are above them, and whom they nominally revere, not without irony. There is an Algerian saying [that] there is always a snake in the *zawiya* [brotherhood lodge]. The tribesmen look up to the holy men but they also laugh at them. Specialists *as such*, of any kind are morally suspect."[48] Westermarck, too, had written that "holiness implies not only that there is supernatural energy in the holy individual or object, but also that they are susceptible to all kinds of baleful influences, especially those of a supernatural kind, like evil spirits, magical tricks, and the evil eye."[49] Moroccans refer to the white egrets that follow a plowman as *mrābṭin* (marabouts, saints) because, they say, they appear elegant and untouched by the dirt but are actually benefiting from the hard labor done by others in turning up food for them. The ambivalence felt towards saints may even combine with that felt towards women when it is said of a man taking refuge with a Berber tribeswoman that "a woman is like a saint."[50] And the old saying "beware a woman from in front, a mule from behind, and a saint from all directions" could not better encapsulate the attitude of the men in the market that day at Immouzar.

Perhaps the central importance Moroccans and those who study them give to saints may be coupled less with the specific roles that saints play in the structure of society than with their cultural importance as heightened expressions, archetypal embodiments, of the more generalized features of ambivalence towards power in Moroccan life. For if the power of saints is not all that different from that seen in other domains—fraught with ambiguity, dependent on ratification by other persons, only as lasting as one's recent accomplishments—then saints become a reified version of a broader pattern rather than the archetype, the anchor, or the exception to it. Given such a perspective one can even understand why, from the Moroccans' point of view, the only good saint is a dead saint—because it is only by interacting with power directly that one can both render it dependent on one's own acceptance and undermine its capacity to become firmly rooted.[51] In a society in which competition for valued connections is rampant, it is by treating all forms of power ambivalently that the channels remain open through which power itself may be acquired.

Political Power, Authority, and Legitimacy

In Morocco, as throughout the Middle East, power is ipso facto legitimate. This version of the common proposition that nothing succeeds like success has, in the Moroccan case, several important historical and contemporary implications. As far back as the medieval period, says Bernard Lewis, "there were significant changes in the definition of legitimacy and justice, and consequently in the definitions of usurpation and tyranny. The first requirement, legitimacy in terms of qualifications and manner of accession, was progressively reduced to the point where, in effect, only two conditions remained—power and Islam. As long as the ruler possessed the necessary armed strength to seize and hold power, and as long as he was a Muslim, however minimal and however nominal, that sufficed."[52] Neither Islamic law (the *shari'a*) nor the "oath of allegiance" (*bay'a*) constitute significant political checks on power: The former grants extensive powers without positing any procedures for their limitation, the latter (for all its contract-like acknowledgment) usually confirms an established fact or thrusts forward a pretender to the throne.[53] But the absence of forms of limitation familiar from Western experience, and of the sort that alone usually qualify in Western theory for the honor of being called "institutions," does not exhaust all the ways in which power is regularly adduced, confined, or accommodated in many Muslim cultures.

As in tribes and chieftainships everywhere, there are in Morocco a host of ways in which power is consistently hedged. Techniques include the use of bribes as a way of controverting the commands of the powerful to their subordinates, systematic limitations on the amount of destruction one can honorably do an enemy, the need for any leader to be effectively ratified in his own position through recognition by his foe, and the constant tension placed on the very meaning of words by those contending for their application.[54] All of these mechanisms are themselves grounded in that ambivalence towards power that continually disperses it and forces any who would grasp it for a time to round it up again and try to hold on to it despite all the centrifugal forces operating to the contrary. Success alone legitimizes the acquisition of power. Once this takes place various supplementary propositions also come into play, ranging from the idea that it is better to have an unjust ruler applying just laws than the reverse, to the preference for adverse rule as opposed to the proliferation of chaos (*fitna*). In each instance, what is being asserted is that the game must remain open, the players must all be able to rally alternative resources on which power is based to build their own greater and lesser constellations, and that only if the game itself is rendered unplayable (e.g., through absence of capacity to ingratiate, or the need for large amounts of money to ante up at the outset) will the legitimacy of the entire enterprise come into question.[55]

When, therefore, the government minister came to distribute land to the peasants arrayed before him in the stadium at Sefrou, his attitude—and more importantly the perceptions of his attitude—became the focal point for much of the ambivalence with which people in the stands and on the field regarded him. As a descendant of the Prophet in the line of the reigning dynasty, he cumulated in small many of the attributes of the monarch himself; as a minister, he was a convenient target for asserting failures at the top without criticizing the King directly; and as a clumsy politician he exhibited just those traits of formal power and uncertain personal effectiveness that add to the ambivalence with which Moroccans approach the modern bureaucracy. In the years following his appearance, many incidents were to occur that underscored ambivalence towards the power of King Hassan II himself: On the one hand there were his nearly miraculous escapes from attempted assassination and the attributions of blessedness that accounted for the avoidance of ecological disasters; on the other hand, there were the times when all pictures of the King disappeared from shops in protest against his taxation for construction of an extravagant mosque or his support for the allies in the Gulf War. Such actions could only have taken on their distinctive Moroccan form given the underlying shape that ambivalence towards those in power takes within the culture at large.

AMBIVALENCE RE-ANALYZED

As one might expect, the three domains from which our examples have been drawn overlap. They are expressions of common principles applied to variant situations. They demonstrate features about the nature of power as it is configured in this part of the world and speak to some of the more theoretical formulations of power to which we averted earlier.

A number of observers have remarked on the fact that power is highly dispersed in Morocco. For Ernest Gellner: "In the traditional situation, rural political relationships are often symmetrical and participatory. There is a great deal of diffusion of power."[56] What this meant for Gellner, however, was that there was a *structural* diffusion of power: The organization of a segmentary system, in which groups coalesce at ever higher points on a genealogical charter while lower level conflicts receive saintly mediation, is itself the form through which power is contained by orderly distribution. But power as dispersal may be seen not, as it was for Gellner, as a way of making anarchy sociologically possible but as a description of how power generally escapes being fixed in one person or one place. Foucault thus argues that the way power is distributed is like a network or a chain, a system in which, by virtue of participation, each person takes on attributes that define each of them as individuals and as participants in the system.[57] Seen from this perspective some intriguing aspects of Moroccan political culture suggest themselves.

John Kenneth Galbraith has argued, as a general matter, that the usual response to an unwanted exercise of power is to counter it with a similar form of power. He distinguishes between various kinds of power—those involving coercion, enticement, and conditioning—and argues that "symmetry in the dialectic of power is the broad rule."[58] But Moroccans do not fit neatly into this paradigm. Recognizing that power may derive from a variety of sources to yield identical results, they counter power of one sort with power of another sort: The bride counters male dominance with role reversal and uncertainty; the follower of a saint demonstrates that it is the believer who judges the presence or absence of spiritual power; the political dependent underscores that he can find others to whom he can grant support if the sharing of largesse does not benefit him to the appropriate extent. In each instance the concepts used to describe and conduce attachment are themselves kept open to ambivalent meanings, and, with them, the relationships they inform remain an open array of possibilities through which social options are maintained and dependencies negotiated.[59]

Social positions, in such a system, are, then, less like the statuses described by classical sociology than the momentary end results of ongoing processes. Women, saints, and politicians possess normative attributes allowing us to generalize about them at one level, but their normative qualities are regularly "disproved" when the attributes are drawn from alternative sources. Thus the *educated* woman, the *foolish* saint, and the *awkward* politician are not seen as contradictions but as possibilities inherent in the contrariety of the ways in which a common process may cast up divergent yet acceptable results. Merton says of his professional status holders that they actually intensify the uncertainties of those dependent on their expertise. In much the same way, Moroccan women, saints, and politicians—like fathers, patrons, and monarchs—can heighten the sense of unease precisely because they constitute focal points for inherent cultural ambivalence rather than predictable relationships sorted by role. Unlike some societies—and the way they have been portrayed by analysts who see power as linked to certain positions—for Moroccans the landscape of power is indeed diverse and the cultural means utilized to keep it open to various styles of exploitation jealously guarded.[60]

It is also worth recalling here the argument that ambivalence, rather than averaging, has been demonstrated in various psychological experiments to be the optimal solution to social relationships that could otherwise end in conflict.[61] Such a proposition connects, too, with Merton's suggestion that when one cumulates ambivalence in a relationship one actually increases the likelihood that the parties will not break their tie. Thus, contrary to Gellner's claim that specialization is anathema to Moroccan tribal organization, some degree of specialization, like that of Merton's professionals, may actually enhance the very ambivalence by which power is diffused in Morocco. One could then argue that the Moroccan solution to the distribution of political power entails, in part, the preservation of sufficient ambivalence to hold people in relationships. Indeed, pursuing Merton's other point—that such ambivalence also militates to some degree against extremism—one could also argue that the relative lack of success of fundamentalism in Morocco is itself due in part to this same ambivalence towards power in any form. Just as the "problem of dirty hands" is countered by the greater fear of social disorder (*fitna*), so, too, the use of rituals of ambivalence, a language of ambivalence, and the emphasis on the situated person using multiple sources to construct a base of dependents all support a system which generally eschews extremism in favor of orderly, if agonistic, relationships.

The opposite of ambivalence, therefore, is not clarity (in the broad sense of certainty) but singularity of category: Something that is not ambivalent falls into one and only one culturally prescribed set. But where clarity may equate with being true to category in one culture, clarity in another culture may itself be equated with multiple possibilities. This is, I believe, true of Moroccan culture and perhaps that of the Arab world more generally. To Moroccans, ambivalence *is* clarity: It is the retention of inherent alternatives that keeps clear the field of action. It shows itself in the ethical and manly acts of constant choice among possibilities, it is made manifest in the constant quest to secure oneself and one's dependents against social chaos, it is confirmed in the recognition that in a world of elusive security flexibility of negotiation is of the essence of clearheadedness and is the lifeblood of social order. Clarity lies in multiplicity, not in singularity; ambivalence is the irreducible force holding the building blocks of society together; non-finality in mundane life is the way *of* the world and the way *in* the world.

To some extent we social scientists are all structural-functionalists: We seek in the societies and polities we study regularities that animate peoples' ways of living. But, as Levine has reminded us, there was a time when such studies were more attentive to forms of ambiguity and ambivalence than they are at present.[62] If, however, we begin with the hypothesis that these qualities are essential to culture itself—that the human capacity to create the categories of our experience is benefited by the retention of alternative ways of creating regularized patterns of thought and relationship—then we may begin to find ambivalence and ambiguity more often than we have. Whether it is understanding how the "power of the weak" can indeed constitute a form of power or how ambivalence may actually support, rather than undermine, the processes that make stable relationships imaginable, a focus on the cultural articulation of ambivalence may open up a host of interpretive possibilities, particularly in those parts of the world where it appears to be as fully developed as it is in Morocco and the Arab world. In the process, authority will be seen less as personal constraint than as part of a complex of power distribution, social roles will be seen to possess capabilities that depend greatly on network formation, and the multiple pathways towards the acquisition of power will be seen to be far more creative and variable for possessing just that quality of ambivalence which, far from being logically inconsistent with it, gives meaning to power in a number of contemporary Arab cultures.

What Is a Tribe and Why Does It Matter?

◠

Tribes get a very uneven press in both the popular and the scholarly imagination. Among some romantics—from Enlightenment philosophers to utopian nativists—tribes have been regarded as the locus of human contentment, that political form in which sociality and naturalness coalesce to near perfection. Tribes have also been seen in narratives of evolution as the crucible of physiological, social, and even moral promptings.[1] And for those who see the tribal context as the point of origin for our species' basic drives—whether sexual, aggressive, or altruistic—it is from the characteristics of tribal life that they derive explanations of current human behavior. To many commentators on the Arab world in particular tribes have been analogized as "closed circles" from which the people of the region are incapable of escaping, as the true form of organization propping up spurious states (depicted, in the title of one writer, as "Tribes with Flags"), or as the genuine (if undefined) basis on which any understanding of contemporary Middle Eastern politics must be erected.[2]

Scholars, too, have been vexed by the idea of the tribe—and have, in their own fashion, been subject to much of the imprecision and incomprehension that characterize accounts by popularizers and pundits. In the following essay I want to consider some of the theoretical and descriptive difficulties that anthropologists in particular have encountered with the concept of the tribe. Without belaboring the internecine disputes with which many analysts have occupied themselves, I want to show how we may have gotten to this state of affairs—particularly as it relates to tribes in North Africa (and by analogy to other parts of the Middle East)—and then to suggest, through several distinct metaphors, how we might more fruitfully think of these sociopolitical forms and how such rethinking may assist our understanding of the modern-day states with which they are both intertwined and, in some cases, constitutive.⁀⁀⁀⁀⁀⁀⁀⁀⁀⁀⁀⁀⁀⁀⁀⁀⁀⁀⁀⁀⁀⁀⁀⁀⁀⁀⁀⁀⁀⁀⁀⁀⁀

Much of early anthropological work focused on "tribes": Such units appealed to those who, from an evolutionary perspective, found in them the starting point of still-recognizable human communities as well as to the opponents of evolutionism, who saw in them the linguistically or politically bounded units through which a functioning system, unlinked to any determinate historical trajectory, could be analyzed as a scientific subject. Biblical scholars could find in such anthropological accounts the assistance needed to comprehend the context of Western religious systems; colonial regimes could find in them the structural accounts needed to organize an overarching administrative system. Indeed, the idea of the tribe was so firmly fixed in Western thought as a natural entity that attempts to capture it through precise definition seemed a goal that was both realistic and much to be desired. And yet, like that other elusive, seemingly self-evident concept that had lured so many scholars to a feckless end—the idea of "law"—the focus on what, at its most essential, makes a tribe a tribe often ended not in heuristic advantage but refined vagueness. Few could entirely let go of the concept, however, because as each new theory or governmental program came along there were new reasons to revisit the concept. Thus when the American government began to apply the Indian Claims Commission Act of 1946, which allowed any "band, tribe, or otherwise organized entity" to recover damages for injury (even moral injury) done to them by the federal government, it was anthropologists who were compelled to rethink the very meaning of the terms and theories they were to employ as witnesses in the resulting cases.[3] And when evolutionary thought took on renewed life in the 1960s, the taxonomy of band, tribe, chiefdom, state took on the naturalness of a nursery rhyme or sacred mantra from which the American wing of the discipline has, to this day, never entirely freed itself.[4]

Some of this history is reflected in those very definitional controversies. To get away from associations of ethnicity or political complexity—and the perceived threat posed by evolutionism—British ethnographers became increasingly vague. If, for example, one traces the definitions printed in the various editions of the Royal Anthropological Institute's *Notes and Queries on Anthropology,* one progresses through versions implying ethnicity and geography until one arrives, by the early 1950s, at the following vagary: "A tribe may be defined as a politically or socially coherent and autonomous group occupying or claiming a particular territory."[5] Some of those working in this tradition could, therefore, perpetuate the image of tribes as broadly lacking in history or larger interactions: Thus I. M. Lewis could write, in the "new" *International Encyclopedia of the Social Sciences* in 1968, that tribes are "closed" systems of thought, that they are "supremely ethnocentric," and that while they possess "closed horizons" their "political qualities are not always easily defined."[6] Like nature itself, tribes seemed to many anthropologists to be unavoidably "there," luring each successive theory to prove itself against this ultimate test.

While a few influential writers, such as W. Robertson-Smith and Edward Westermarck, had written extensively on Arab or Berber societies in the early part of the twentieth century—and both the French and British colonial governments had made extensive use of anthropologists in their conquest of tribes all over the African continent—the contribution to discussions of the nature of tribes made by work in North Africa and the Middle East only took on major new impetus in the middle and latter part of the century.[7] Two works in particular set the stage: E. E. Evans-Pritchard's work on Cyrenaica (itself deeply connected to his work on the Nuer of the Sudan) and Robert Montagne's work on the Berbers of Morocco.[8] Evans-Pritchard had described the Nuer as composed of a series of segments constructed by descent, a political form which, by means of a pattern of structured opposition, constituted an elegant system of stateless organization. However, even Evans-Pritchard suggested that this opposition of structural segments may, for the people themselves, constitute more of an idiom of self-description than a uniformly realized mode of governance. Montagne had found a similar structure in the High Atlas Mountains of Morocco, and even though early French ethnographers working elsewhere in the country had cautioned against reifying the structure of the country's many tribes it was Montagne's analysis, like that of Evans-Pritchard, that was to prove so important for later academic discussion.[9] That discussion gained its main impetus from the work of Ernest Gellner and from the alternative posed to it by several American anthropologists, most notably Clifford Geertz.

As in any organized body of scholarly discussion there are those issues and disputes which flare up and recede, which are more important to one side than the other, and which, in the course of "ordinary science," either run their course and, unable to produce interesting new ideas, simply get abandoned or, in the minds of some who cannot let go, remain so vital that no opportunity to recapture the terms of discussion may be ignored lest the impulse that brought them to this matter in the first place seem to have been misplaced. Such is the case with the notorious debate over segmentary structures. Like the drunk who searches for his keys under the lamppost not because that is where he lost them but because that is where he imagines the most available light to exist, the pursuit of "the truth" about segmentarity is ripe for disregard, the cutting of one's losses, and (as many long since have) moving on to other things. In drawing us back for a moment to this dispute, I do not wish to dwell on the matter because I hope to have the final word on the issue now that some of the protagonists have passed on or because I think it a very fruitful line of inquiry for future theorizing: To the contrary, I think the matter was settled some time ago. Rather, I want to ask some questions about the nature of tribal societies based mainly on my work in North Africa but also to some extent on my work as an attorney working on the legal problems of various North American Indian tribes. Thus by moving back and forth between my own views about tribes and certain debates in the literature, I hope to trace some elements of the history of this idea and the reasons why it has been so difficult to move the discussion of tribes, and their ongoing importance, in North Africa and the Middle East to somewhat more useful ground.

There are two features of Ernest Gellner's overall intellectual orientation that are indispensable to an understanding of his approach to the question of the tribe. Gellner had already had a distinguished, if volatile, career as a philosopher before he came to anthropology. Close to the work of Bertrand Russell and Karl Popper, he saw no redeeming qualities in the linguistic philosophy of the British academics of the postwar period. It was in his widely read book *Words and Things,* where he referred to the linguistic philosophers as "the Norodniks of North Oxford," that he made his most biting thoughts about the state of the discipline altogether clear.[10] Although he spent all but the last few years of his life in British universities, Gellner had been born and raised in Czechoslovakia, and he was at heart a Central European political philosopher.[11] It is not surprising, therefore, that when he moved into anthropology he brought with him one of the most fundamental questions of that tradition: How is anarchy possible? Although he claimed that he had not set out to demonstrate the validity of Evans-Pritchard's view of segmentarity, he did find in Montagne and in the mountains of Morocco the opportunity to test the reality of governance without central authority.[12]

The second thing to know about Gellner is that he was, by his own account, a "monist." That is, he believed that, in all things, singular rather than multiple factors usually were capable of accounting for the phenomenon under consideration: "I *am* a monist, or rationalist, and I do find the world unintelligible, and do seek to find a guiding light."[13] Although he recognized the limitations of this position ("Thus my commitment to monism is not altogether starry-eyed. One does appreciate the weakness of the position"[14]), he was, in this, as from so many other standpoints, more devoted to the idea than to its exceptions. Indeed, his hostility to pluralism figures largely in his rejection of many elements that are key to at least one alternative to his general stance in the discipline, namely the emphasis on the categories through which the people studied express their own comprehension of their world. To Gellner, this smacked of the same undisciplined and unrealistic pluralism on the basis of which the followers of the later Wittgenstein had misled a generation of British philosophers.[15]

Thus when he set out to study the people of the High Atlas Mountains of Morocco, Gellner was pleased to find a society in which the balanced opposition of largely kin-based groupings, mediated by saintly lineages who kept violence in check without wielding direct force, yielded an organized yet utterly decentralized political system. That, as we shall see, Gellner produced no circumstantial evidence to support the claim that the people he studied were in fact organized along these principles with any degree of consistency, that the exceptions (he called them "kinks") in his account devoured the rule, and that not one single instance has, before or since, been produced of any society that has operated on an enduring basis as a clearly segmentary structure is, oddly enough, irrelevant: As with Evans-Pritchard's "idiom" of segmentarity, Gellner and those attracted to his schema could always find some reason to claim that actual behavior was not the true test of segmentarity's validity. It was here, then, that the idealism of the monist and the intellectual proclivities of the Central European political philosopher so fully coalesced that nothing could shake Gellner's confidence that somehow segmentarity must hold the key to both anarchy and anti-pluralism.

Gellner's view of tribal organization, itself part of the larger view of the nature of Moroccan society, is not, of course, the only way that has been put forth for viewing the same data. Although we will return shortly to see how the debate sparked by Gellner's work played out in discussions of Middle Eastern tribal organization, I want now to place those discussions not in the context of the narrow debate over segmentarity but in the context of alternative models of the nature of the tribe as a political form. By using both a different set of images and testing them against what is known factually about tribal organization, one may be able to see the continuing intellectual fascination for this form of sociopolitical life and its implications for current affairs.

Scholarship, like life, often proceeds through an elaborate metaphor. Most of those used to understand tribes have been structural in nature: Tribes, it has been said, are constructed like a lattice or a grid, like a pyramid or a scaffold, like a nested set of balanced forces or a fractious array of fissioning and fusing units. Although some anthropologists have seen in these forms an element of the processual, the overwhelming majority have concentrated on structural form. They run into difficulty precisely because on a comparative basis the range of forms appears quite wide and, when history was finally taken into consideration by analysts, the form of any single tribe often appeared to be subject to rapid change. If one took the long view, as archaeologists and students of universal human history profess, the fluctuations could, depending on one's theory, be "evened out" and the broad course of evolution left unaffected by lower-order variation. If one took the particularistic view, the range of *structural* variation did not yield a simple characterization of tribes as a taxonomic unit for political or social analysis, and hence definitions became increasingly contradictory, vague, or unproductive.[16] Thus it is with some trepidation, tempered by some resignation, that one weighs in with yet another set of metaphors to supplement an interpretation that is part of my larger argument about Arab society in the sure and certain view that, as Samuel Butler said, "though analogy is often misleading, it is the least misleading thing we have."

Consider the amoeba. Scientists may know them as microscopic protozoans existing as masses of protoplasm, but for scientists, as in the popular imagination, this lowly organism is especially known for its capacity to change shape. Derived from the Greek word for "change," the term "amoeba" conjures up not the form it may take at any given moment but the capacity for shape-shifting, the changeling ability to form and re-form to suit current circumstances. If, then, one asks what is the shape of an amoeba, one has begun by asking the wrong question, just as it would be an error to assume that an amoeba has no regular and distinctive characteristics of its own. Rather, in understanding, at least metaphorically, what we mean when we speak of something as being amoeba-like, we must think of it is as a range of capabilities rather than one or more settled forms, a set of processes rather than a concretized structure, a quality of flexibility (without loss of identity) rather than a fixed pattern adapted to a singular circumstance.

Such a metaphor has much to commend itself as a vehicle for sorting out the problems that anthropologists have encountered in grasping the kind of political entity tribes constitute. For example, it has often been argued that tribes are really just combinations of bands, themselves extended family units producing and consuming together and often moving about until there is need for larger gatherings to exchange resources, engage spouses, or perform rituals. The classic example is the Cheyenne, whose need to hunt the in-gathered buffalo without any one band scattering the herds to the detriment of all is said to have precipitated such tribal-wide institutions as crosscutting voluntary associations, the unit that policed the hunt, and the chiefs who had to renew privately the resources of those they were called upon to punish for public infractions.[17] Connected to this image of the tribe as a collection of more fundamental bands were several additional theories: One argued that bands and tribes were part of an evolutionary scheme moving upwards to chiefdoms and states, while another held that language and descent bound the unit together through face-to-face interaction that is of necessity limited in scale. Evidence for the former was offered in terms of the increasing centralization of redistributive networks, while evidence for the latter was said to lie in the distribution of languages and the demographics of tribal groupings. Both of these theories failed to retain the confidence of even their own formulators, who began to see that the "evidence" was a function of each theory rather than produced by it, and every new example highlighted category shadings instead of clear-cut delineations.

Yet the very malleability of tribes often escaped emphasis. Rather, the elements that suggested such a quality themselves became the source for still more structural explanations—even when specific histories (as distinct from broad evolutionary trends) were added to the mix.[18] So, for example, it was argued that tribes did not precede states but were themselves precipitated by the rise of states: When a larger and more complex organization appeared on the horizon bands needed to coalesce in order to oppose them or to arrange accommodation on more favorable terms.[19] While this begged the question of how larger entities themselves came into existence, it did at least focus attention on the tribe as a political form whose very existence was neither timeless nor unaffected by interaction with other groupings. At one time Marshall Sahlins even argued that segmentary structures were a response to "predatory expansion": As related groups sought to move into new territories, they could effectively recruit allies from ever more inclusive (real or fictive) descent groupings while still retaining the independence, even opposition, incorporated in less extensive lineage alignments. In time, it was even argued that Evans-Pritchard may have inadvertently caught the Nuer at just such a moment in their history, and that had British ethnographers of the day not been so fearful that any consideration of history would lead back down the slippery slope of evolutionary inevitability, he and his contemporaries would have appreciated this point.[20]

As each theory and each ethnographic example was added to the literature, however, certain very important common features began to receive recognition. Tribes, for example, did not just lack centralized redistribution through inherited office: They possessed numerous institutions and practices for leveling the differences in wealth or status that might accrue over time to any one individual or faction. Everything from witchcraft accusations and joking behavior to patterns of avoidance and requirements for divestiture were aimed (in this very functionalist view) at diminishing economic and political centralization. Similarly, mechanisms were found that keep power from remaining in too few hands for too long a period of time: Individuals had to prove their capabilities before being granted recognition as holders of a particular status, or systems of rotation insured that power-holders alternated over the course of time. Although this emphasis on process helped to decouple the idea of the tribe from a limited set of closely related structural forms, and functionalism, despite its tendency to see everything as contributing to timeless maintenance of the working whole, helped focus attention on various connections of society to culture, even these insights could not shake most anthropologists, on both sides of the Atlantic, from their view of tribes as characterized more by form or stage than by process or variant.

The metaphors of the structural-functionalists, then, perpetuated the image of form and function over emergence and potential. The trick, as I have suggested, is, therefore, to consider some alternative metaphors for grasping the different aspects of tribal entities—metaphors that focus more on the malleable, changeable, fluctuating nature of the specific affiliations found in this political form and less on the structure that may appear to investigators to hold at the moment the group was studied. To see if such metaphors make greater sense of the data, we need to consider some of the features that everyone seems to acknowledge are important to the analysis of tribes regardless of one's overall theory and then see if the metaphors themselves help us resolve any inconsistencies in the available data. We can begin with three such features: the nature and role of opposed units, the impermanence of specific charters of identity and the variability of actual associations, and the moral stature of the respective components of the tribe.

Within any tribe there are subunits that stand in opposition to one another. These units may be extended families or mixed territorial/fictive kin groups, and they may (as in the case of North Africa) speak either Berber or Arabic yet still identify at some level as members of the same "tribe." But in whatever form, it is the oppositional nature of these entities that is quite striking. Whether their actions are cooperative or agonistic—or more likely both, in different contexts, moments, and under different leaders—their very existence depends in no small part on their identity *as contrasted with* some other unit. This takes many forms. Quite commonly, for example, the leader of any one unit is deeply dependent on the leaders of other units for his own acknowledgment as a legitimate leader: Only if potential opponents respect a man will his own group grant him recognition and support.[21] Moreover, since the enemy of one moment may very well be the friend of another, it is usual to pull one's punches: Instead of all-out destruction, one preserves the opponent not only as a potential ally in another context but because it is oppositional identity rather than complete triumph that constitutes the preeminent mark of successful leadership. The ambivalence implied in this relationship of power thus replicates the ambivalence towards power we have seen in other domains. This is true not only for various North African groups but for Saddam Hussein's Iraq,[22] the Ottoman Empire,[23] and modern-day Afghanistan.[24]

The changeability of the lines of affiliation in tribes and their constituent units is another clear theme present in virtually all accounts of tribal organizations. Initially anthropologists thought they had captured a sociopolitical form in which strict principles of descent defined the relevant groups, and comparisons of descent systems, kin-categorizing systems, and the mythological and ritual supports for these systems became a primary focus of the discipline. So much was this the case that when anthropologists began to work in places like New Guinea (rather than in Africa and North America) they found themselves hotly debating the applicability of the unilineal descent systems found elsewhere to New Guinean kinship structures rather than casting about immediately for some other paradigm. But like Lucretius's idea of nature— that if you throw it out the door it will fly back through the window—the tribe-like features that were noted appeared to demand inclusion in some view, however revised, of tribalism itself. Once again, the focus on form over process retarded theoretical innovation. In particular, that second feature of tribes— the very malleability of modes of unit identification—was only very slowly grasped.

Yet this feature is quite central to the whole analysis of tribes as political forms. Once attuned to it we see not an enlarged array of similarly structured and functioning units but a process that also makes sense in relation to other cultural features. We see, for example, that it is very common for the same terms to apply to different levels of inclusiveness. Thus, to take the Moroccan example, the apparent hierarchy of terms— 'a'ila (family), ferqa (fraction), qebila (tribe)—may be applied interchangeably, as individuals try to assert forms of attachment, degrees of importance, and elements of longevity that may support a particular ambition or confederation. Similarly, any given unit may have multiple names: The Middle Atlas Berber settlement that I have studied has, over the course of years, used at least four names simultaneously, each one suggestive of various qualities or affiliations and each deployed by individuals to various purposes in various contexts.[25] As with individuals, who may have so many names that occasionally a court document is sought to certify that they are all one and the same person, each nomenclature has its uses and each both represents and keeps open the flexibility of configurations that depend not on structuring regulations but on regularized and legitimate modes of forging attachments.

Seen from this perspective many of the "kinks" in the systems described by various analysts take on a very different appearance. Now the exceptions become part of a process. Now the fact that a "tribe" that at one time clearly identified itself as X but now identifies itself (e.g., for purposes of gaining access to a desired resource) as Y is part of the capability of the system and not a violation of it.[26] Now the way we read the past is not changed from a view that tribes have lost their currency or have been swallowed into the state or have lost contact with the adaptations that suited their form: To the contrary, now we can think about how these malleable, processual elements have qualities in their own right that are not fixed by momentary resultant forms. And other analogies may help us grasp this point: For if a tribe is, in a metaphoric sense, like, say, an amoeba and not a crystal, it may be precisely in its adaptability to changing forms in its environs that its fundamental qualities need to be sought. Without reifying the analogy, we may think of this as a highly adaptive structure, one that can come in and out of existence as context suggests and can survive to another day in ways that more complex or rigid forms cannot. When, therefore, it was said in a legal case involving the Mashpee Indians—who were seeking recognition as a tribe under U.S. law—that (as the jury found) they were a tribe at certain times but not others and therefore were not a tribe for purposes of the statute because they were not a tribe at all times, the whole point of this type of structure may have been lost: Tribes, like amoebas, are sociological changelings, and a definition based on form is far too fixed to capture these most enduring and variable of forms.[27]

This pliable quality may also relate to other features of tribal cultures. In the Near Eastern context, for example, it is clear that even the overarching body of Islamic law (*shari'a*) is actually superseded by local custom, itself conceptualized at the popular level as being Islamic law rather than something separate from it.[28] And just as a portion of the legitimacy of a tribal leader may rest in the hands of his opponent, so, too, the role that women play in tribal forms remains enormously varied and understudied. Women, for example, often are crucial to the good opinion that men have of themselves, and in past times the fact that, in many areas, they would follow men onto the battlefield and shame them if they were insufficiently brave, or that it was they, in addition to or in

place of men, who placed their offspring in crosscutting voluntary associations, fits very well with the image of the tribe as a contestable yet locally definable set of processes that produce and reproduce a range of locally recognizable resultant forms.[29]

A third factor common to tribes has to do with their moral stature. This
may seem an odd feature to emphasize but it really is quite crucial, for it is particularly characteristic of tribal systems that no one unit is regarded as morally
superior to any other. That is, no section or fraction of the tribe stands, inherently or permanently, above any other in its worth, its potential, or its supernatural merit. What Paul Dresch says of northern Yemen is equally applicable
elsewhere: "The morality all tribesmen recognize is infinitely fragmented into
separate spaces. Whether movement is temporary or permanent, it represents
an avoidance of any absolute judgment, a kind of moral particularism or pluralism."[30] Small wonder, then, that conceptions of time commonly lack a consistent chronological narrative or that each set of events, like the beginning of
a new round in an ongoing game, focuses more on the range of maneuvers
than on the discovery of some implied direction. As a type, tribal systems
maintain their flexibility, their capacity to allow individuals and groups to
form and reform within the parameters of recognizable processes, in no small
part by being linked to cultural conceptualizations—from those involving religion and myth to human nature and the shape of the cosmos—that recapit-
ulate this moral equivalence.

Moral parity is also consistent with the capacity of tribes to exist concur-
rently with other political forms. As anthropological accounts became increasingly structural and functional or evolutionary in the postwar years, the
appreciation by some earlier scholars of this element of tribal flexibility managed to get lost. Jim Boon, for example, reminds us that Robert Lowie had argued that tribes co-exist with numerous other "sodalities" (i.e., crosscutting
voluntary associations), and that no single element of organization—descent,
territory, dialect, or cult—captures the totality of their social and political organization: "[Sodalities] reveal a tribe's capacity to sample alternate social
forms, without necessarily adopting them as the central components of its social machine. Each tribal population appears almost to toy with patterns that
are fundamental to its neighbors."[31] A number of earlier scholars of North
Africa came to a similar appreciation.[32] Indeed, if one traces the history of particular groupings, one encounters numerous alliances that linked specific
groups for a period of time (like the fraction pairings, or *uṭada*, of the Middle
Atlas), to say nothing of the numerous *zawias* (religious brotherhoods) that
also crosscut kin and locality.[33] As the Moroccans are still wont to say: "Your

neighbor who is close is more important than your kinsman who is far away." Those who still rely on the American cultural evolutionism of the 1960s continue, however, to ignore both earlier findings and later theories. For example, in his Pulitzer Prize–winning bestseller, *Guns, Germs, and Steel,* biologist Jared Diamond, in his search for the "ultimate factors" underlying broad-scale human history, while noting that tribes "shade into bands at one extreme and into chiefdoms at the opposite extreme,"[34] accepts the idea that "[s]maller units do not voluntarily abandon their sovereignty and merge into larger units. They do so only by conquest, or under external duress,"[35] that "societies of thousands can exist only if they develop centralized authority to monopolize force and resolve conflicts"[36] (something both Gellner and most of his critics argue against), and that societies "evolve" through "stages" such that "tribes conquer or combine with tribes to reach the size of chiefdoms, which conquer or combine with other chiefdoms to reach the size of states."[37] But there are some serious difficulties with this view.

Leaving aside the fact that the anthropologists Diamond cites have long since recanted their earlier evolutionism, and notwithstanding any questionable claim that a "science of history"—particularly one of "ultimate factors"—calls for a different level of explanation than lower-order occurrences, it can at least be argued that only reliance on misguided views of the nature of tribal systems can produce such easy evolutionism. If, by contrast, we see tribes not as stages and appreciate that they co-exist with other types of political systems, the step-like evolutionary scheme—whatever its merits in other regards—does not fit with what we know of this particular sociopolitical form and may, indeed, call into question the widespread Western assumption that the narrative of human history must work through the tribal "stage."

In fact, the ethnographic evidence suggests that tribes do not simply lead to states or come into existence with the state or stand opposed to the state: They may do all these things—and more. As systems of limited power their interrelation with other types of political forms is not set by structural elements but, as we have been arguing, by their flexible yet well-defined capabilities. Whether one chooses to approach these qualities through the metaphor of the amoeba or analogize them (without the negative connotations) to viruses (in that their partial nature allows them to connect to other entities for momentary completion), or whether one chooses to see them as constructed like wallpaper patterns designs (rather than a geometric form) such that large portions of them may be lost to disease or conquest yet the underlying pattern survive to another day—whatever the choice of metaphor, those that focus on the tribe as idea, as process, as repertoire, and as a range of recognizable moves go much further towards accounting for what has otherwise been seen as a series of contradictions to be denied or aberrant results to be defined out of existence through unrelentingly structural or evolutionary views.

The idea of power implied in tribal forms also has a direct connection to each of these concerns. To many the tribe has, as we have seen, been regarded as existing as against some other form, primarily the state. But this may be to mistake a propensity for a target. For as we have been suggesting tribes may be compatible with—or at least may be able to adapt themselves with some success to—alternative political forms. It is their generalized mechanisms for diversifying and disseminating power that may be central to these qualities. Thus when Pierre Clastres speaks of tribes (or stateless societies) *against* states, we are confronted with what is only one among many possibilities now presented as the sole pattern. Clastres may be right to sense that tribes "had a very early premonition that power's transcendence poses a mortal risk for the group."[38] But he wrongly sees the space and speech of the leader as dutiful palaver that does not work to convert personal force into political power, and he romanticizes the tolerance of the tribe and its aversion to power as proof that "it is not possible for the State to arise from within primitive society."[39] Yet even Clastres is correct to suspect that tribes are not stages in development and that their survival may, ironically, have depended on their antipathy to placing too much power in too few hands for too long a period of time and on their possession of mechanisms to level potential power and hence assist in adapting to surrounding political necessities.

We can now return, briefly, to see why the formulation of tribal structures in the North African and Middle Eastern context as primarily (or ideally, or archetypally) segmentary has failed to bear fruit. Given the anti-pluralism of Gellner's formulation and the constant search for some other structural explanation when each proffered one came up against incontrovertible contradictions, segmentary theory became an almost classic instance of ordinary science unable to recognize newly presented paradigms. On the one hand the ethnographic record is now quite clear: No cases have been presented that show a society in which segmentary organization operates in accordance with the theory offered over a significant course of time. Gellner's own *Saints of the Atlas* actually contains no data—no circumstantial cases that follow over time the applicability of the theory—and numerous instances have been presented, from North Africa to Pakistan, to show that the idiom of segmentarity is quite separable from practice.[40] Supporters have suggested that empiricism is no disproof: Thus Kraus claims that Gellner's was "a formal model of logical relations which does not claim to *describe* social reality"[41]—a statement which is not only contrary to Gellner's thesis but one that leads Kraus to misconstrue much of the debate, denies any possibility for assessing the issues on the basis of specific case studies, and leads to the proposition that the "underlying formal model" provides us with "the key to understanding the ambiguities" Gellner presents without in any way providing us with standards for assessing alternative readings of the situation.[42] That actual relationships may for a time track segmentary idioms only demonstrates, as several of the commentators of various persuasions have failed to grasp, that segmentarity may serve as one among many templates which a strong individual may add to the sources of legitimacy that ratify his personal web of obligations, a process which, as one traces actual instances, nevertheless occurs on so irregular a basis that the principles at work cannot be reduced to those of mechanical structures or vague notions of some "logical" model.

Equally faulty are assertions that somehow a more cultural/interpretive model is but a continuation of the Orientalist perspective or is so vague as to be unworthy of serious attention. Charles Lindholm, for example, simply reduces all such perspectives to the maintenance of a colonial mentality, concluding with the casually slanderous assertion (clearly referring to Geertz, the present author, and others) that "most writers have been unwilling and *morally disinclined* to take up the challenge of developing a new theory"[43]—without ever citing, much less understanding, the works that demonstrate such alternative theories. When the evidence against his theory (and the broader Khaldunian theory to which it was attached) became overwhelming, Gellner himself went so far as to suggest, albeit rather ambiguously, that even a faulty theory was better than none at all—as if no alternative had been presented![44] Similarly, the idea that what is really going on is not a structural form but the ability of tribesmen to be rhetorically persuasive, as Caton suggests, simply begs the question of how this process works—its connection to multiple resources for building followings, why the same style may be effective in one instance and not in another, etc.—and how speech might be connected to the segmentary idiom.[45] Even those who understand full well why segmentarity is an inadequate explanatory scheme let their antipathy to certain interpretive approaches show through with such clarity as to call into question their ability to entertain alternatives in an appropriately scholarly fashion.[46] Obviously, these attacks are part of a larger assault on what some of these critics wrongly lump together as "interpretive" approaches, but the inability of many of them to see the arguments for what they are and to address them concretely further demonstrates not only how wedded some are to models they themselves know are inadequate but how their own antipathies interfere with the scholarly requirement to entertain new possibilities.

Indeed, as one thinks through the proposition that tribes are predominantly a conceptual order whose particular shape—and even whose timely manifestation—can be accommodated to changing circumstances, it becomes more possible to consider how various aspects of tribal ideology remain of considerable importance to the understanding of current political and social principles in the modern Middle East. We have seen that tribes are not forms of organization that, under some law of political physics, cannot occupy the same space as any other political entity: To the contrary they may or may not co-exist—symbiotically, agonistically, or indifferently—with states (as in Libya, Jordan, Iraq, or for that matter the United States), and they may or may not appear and subside as circumstance and force of character come into play. What they do entail are those cultural elements—among which are included oppositional concepts, leveling of power, and moral equivalence of parts—that may flow over into their members' orientations towards and involvement in other institutional forms that carry culturally distinctive elements of their own. The result is a kind of cultural and political mélange, a hybridization, that is sometimes attributed to the residual aspects of a preceding stage of organization but is far better regarded as part of a distinctive cultural orientation that, rather than being reducible to certain forms with which these cultural features may be, or may have been, associated, is in fact another shift of the kaleidoscope of cultural elements, aspects, and overtones that inform ongoing social and political relationships. It is the range of variation, not the typological form, that must receive attention.

Seen from this perspective one can consider some of the variants that continue to have force in the Middle East. For example, it may be useful—without, again, allowing taxonomy to become the reductionist focus—to think of some contemporary regimes as more like paramount chieftainships than like states. Unlike monarchs, whose power comes from above, paramount chiefs get their power from below—from other chiefs. If these chiefs must themselves demonstrate that they have the characteristics ideally associated with leadership, rather than an entitlement to it through inheritance, the paramount chief among them is subject to similar constraints on his own legitimacy. There are certainly people in the Arab world who are called king or sultan, but when the Qur'an itself refers to kings as "the destroyers of villages," when the claim to power is as much (or more) a claim to in personam rather than territorial jurisdiction, when Islamic law conforms to the political structure of dispersed and localized power, and when challengers are legitimated by virtue of their ascension to power, the qualities are perhaps more those of paramountcy than of the impersonality of stateship. In the range of contemporary polities that may possess these qualities, "tribal" cultural orientations can certainly continue to play an ongoing role as commonsense support for attitudes towards legitimacy, power, and the moral stature of the constituted authority. Once one separates tribe from fixed form and concentrates on it as a cultural process, images like the closed circle or tribalism as an example of cultural survival fall to the wayside, and the features that cohere as a range of variations begin to take on more definition and explanatory utility.

Moreover, the very idea of "tribe" becomes a more useful test of anthropological theorizing than when it was a question of trying to capture its precise essence, like some specimen to be found in pristine form in the field and set in formaldehyde or a taxonomic chart for all to witness and acknowledge. A more adequate view of tribal qualities tests our ability to think not of pure forms but of arrays, not of fixed modes of mentality but orientations that have no less specificity for being variable, not of idiom or template or grid or principle as mutually exclusive but of malleable yet distinctive orientations that challenge our paradigms to be as resilient as the subjects they seek to comprehend. Our questions, too, can grow more refined: Does the potential for anti-authoritarianism one may attribute to tribal cultures actually reinforce political personalism, such that the latter emphasis in Middle Eastern polities continues to draw some of its propulsion from the tribal orientations that prevail in other aspects of the overall political culture? If we recall that even Ibn Khaldun specifically spoke about tribalism as not being incompatible with urban life, should we formulate our theories so that we more rigorously separate tribal aspects of culture from those forms of living with which our theories—but not necessarily the people themselves—have assumed mutual exclusivity?[47] And if, in a sense, all politics in the Middle East can be said to be if not local then personal, can we reinterpret the forces that constrain power so that even where power seems to be intensely concentrated in a dictator or president for life, we need to look more carefully at the interpersonal level to understand just what and where power has spread beyond the apical point to which our assumptions and analogies direct our foremost attention?

&

"We're still here," say many American Indian tribesmen. And indeed tribes—or the style of cultural orientation we might call "tribism"—will be with us for a long time to come. Indeed, it may lie dormant, mutate into related orientations, or tease up our attention at just the moment we had thought it had subsided into irrelevance. The challenge presented by the idea of tribe is as politically and culturally real as it is manifestly important to our understanding of the range of ways in which human beings fashion their relation to the problem of power. If we are as supple in our own means of grasping these orientations, if we are as flexible in our choice of metaphors and our willingness to listen carefully to forms of theorizing that are not immediately consistent with what we have come to assume, we may be able to catch the scent of these most fascinating of subjects in ways that are closer to their capabilities and hence to our own realization of their ongoing importance.⟳⟳⟳⟳⟳⟳⟳⟳⟳⟳⟳⟳⟳⟳⟳

Constructing Institutions in a Political Culture
of Personalism

∽

From time to time over the years I have had occasion to mention to the people among whom I was working in the Arab world the decisions rendered by two justices of the United States Supreme Court. In both instances, I explain, the judges upheld the constitutionality of the death penalty even though each expressed his personal opposition—even deep moral revulsion—to its imposition. Justice Frankfurter, faced with re-imposing the death penalty after the first effort to electrocute a prisoner failed, had said:

> One must be on guard against finding in personal disapproval a reflection of more or less prevailing condemnation. Strongly drawn as I am to some of the sentiments expressed by [the dissent] . . . I would be enforcing my private view rather than that consensus of society's opinion which, for purposes of due process, is the standard enjoined by the Constitution.

Similarly, Justice Blackmun wrote:

> Cases such as these provide for me an excruciating agony of the spirit. I yield to no one in the depth of my distaste, antipathy, and, indeed, abhorrence for the death penalty. . . . [W]ere I a legislator, I would do all I could to sponsor and to vote for legislation abolishing the death penalty. . . . [Judges] should not allow our personal preferences as to the wisdom of legislative and congressional action, or our distaste for such action, to guide our judicial decision in cases such as these.[1]

How, I would ask my informants, might someone in a position of authority in their own countries handle such a conflict between the requirements of the office and the promptings of their individual conscience? Almost without exception, the response has been a distinctive mix of informational and rhetorical questions through which my interlocutor was clearly seeking to correct my version of the stories.[2] Who is this man, they ask—where does he come from, who is he connected to, with what party is he affiliated, has he or someone close to him ever been subjected to a violent attack, how do those with whom he is connected benefit by his ruling? The thrust of these inquiries soon became clear: The instances I posed were not examples of separating person from office but of insufficient knowledge in my rendition of the story—particularly in my own store of information about these men—to be able to determine, by the full context of their situations, the consistency between who they are, in the broadest sociological sense, and why they oppose the death penalty. If I just knew this indispensable information, my interlocutors were saying, I would understand that there is no separation of the judges' situated place in society and the "real" meaning of their decisions. It is the closest I have felt to the experience of Elizabeth Bohannon, who relates how, when asked to tell a story from her own culture to the people in Africa among whom she was working, she proceeded to tell them the story of Hamlet, assuming it to be universally comprehensible—only to find her listeners correcting her in the light of the kinship structure and religious beliefs through which the world makes sense to them.[3]

In the West we are accustomed to thinking of the Arab countries in terms of individual leaders—Nasser or Sadat, Qaddafi or Bourguiba, King Hussein or Saddam Hussein. We may even have read books or seen films about lesser tribal leaders famous in their day—the Pasha Glaoui of Morocco, the Mahdi of the Sudan, the Rifian bandit/rebel Raisuni, the "warlords" of Lebanon, Yemen, or Somalia. In each instance the image is that of a single leader, rather than of a polity composed of institutions which stand separate from those who operate or manipulate them at any given moment. We may even see the absence of democratic institutions in the Arab countries as a function of this failure to create depersonalized positions in the political order and hence find expectable my interlocutors' disbelief that Supreme Court justices could separate their official positions from other aspects of their selves. In trying to understand just how this common sense of the person and the nature of personalism in the structure of the polities of the Middle East may operate, I want to consider how the individual is constructed in these societies and to see in what ways this pattern connects with a rather different sense of institutions than is characteristic of Western political experience and theory. Bearing in mind that one cannot generalize for the whole of this part of the world and that the differ-

ences are, depending on the level at which the analysis is posed, very significant, I nevertheless want, in a theme and variation sense, to try to consider
why, for my Near Eastern informants, the retelling of the story of Justices
Frankfurter and Blackmun might take the shape it does.◌◌◌◌◌◌◌◌◌◌◌◌

I have often thought of the culture of the Arab world as being set about ten degrees off from that of the West: While it looks remarkably similar from the outset, the further you go along its path the more imperceptible divergence becomes inescapable difference. This is well-illustrated in the idea of the person.
In the West, the idea of the self being divisible has very deep roots. Beginning
with the Greek concept of the persona as a set of distinguishable roles, through
the twelfth-century Renaissance, with its "discovery" that people have an inner
state separate from their overt acts and utterances, and coalescing with the Enlightenment acceptance that individuals can fashion their own identities and
values, the idea of the self in the West has incorporated the idea of its divisibility.[4] By comparison, among the Arabs the person is largely envisioned as a
unity of character traits and situated encounters bounded by the limits of Allah and subject mainly to each person's capacity to fabricate advantageous ties
without needing to create a subjective world focused inside oneself.[5] While
this view of the self may seem reasonably familiar to the average Westerner, the
differences, when drawn out over a course of religious, political, and interpersonal trajectories, become increasingly unfamiliar. Thus, to know a person's
connections is vital to knowing both his character and how to form your own
ties with him; knowing someone's background tells you what he intends by his
acts; knowing how he has dealt with others in the past tells you how he deals
with others now. These perspectives, again not really strange to the Western
eye, nevertheless take on unusual implications: In law, judges have been known
to disguise themselves and encounter an accused in a similar infraction in order to establish the latters' misdeeds in the case under consideration; in common perception people say they can always tell what is in another's mind because deeds and statements correlate quite precisely with intent; in economics,
a contract is not formed until a present relationship affecting both parties' networks of obligation has taken on public visibility; in language, truth does not
inhere in utterances concerning relationships but occurs only when appropriate validation brings the remark into the world of relational consequences; and
in politics, legitimacy inheres not in a set of positions but in the capacity of the
individual to marshal alliances that establish his actions as having profound
implications for others' bonds of interdependence. What begins, to the Western observer, as a recognizable form of "individualism" becomes, as we shall

see, a view of the person as an indivisible unit composed of sociological features so reinforced by religion and customary law as to produce a very distinctive view of how the political order itself is comprised.

As we begin to unpack the Arab view of the person, this emphasis on the features of one's character as a set of situated and negotiable encounters with others becomes quite central. There is a rich Arabic vocabulary of character traits and, notwithstanding variation over time and place, common themes to their deeper qualities and modes of assessment. S. D. Goitein, remarking on the "almost unlimited amount of synonyms for the idea of character and character traits" in medieval Islam, says: "[T]he profuse richness of the Arabic language in words for character and character traits proves the ancient Arabs had a keen eye for human nature—or, to be more exact, for the personality of an individual with whom they had dealings—and that they also possessed the gift to express in words what they had observed."[6] This remains true to the present. For example, there is the old wheeze that every term in Arabic means something, its opposite, and some feature or delight of a camel. But if the vitality of naming camel parts may have declined, the more important feature remains vital, namely that, as Goitein himself notes, "Arabic characterization [has been] aimed [at] an understanding of men through their contradictions."[7] Thus as each person encounters others and establishes a web of indebtedness through which he has a hook in the others' behavior and through the totality of his situated ties becomes known, the very range and behavioral antonyms that others must learn about are simultaneously settled by the shared vocabulary of possibilities and rendered immensely flexible by the combinations of their implementation. As Gilsenan says of the Lebanon: "One does not hide, then, behind various classificatory masking devices as in Bali. Rather one steps forward, differentiates oneself, invites judgment, and strives to establish a significant social biography. . . . In my experience there is a high degree of consensus on readings of individual character in our sense of the term."[8] Small wonder, too, that often in Arab-Islamic culture the image is encountered of a game, one in which the rules need not change for the allure of the play to seem endlessly creative and totally consistent with the true nature of human beings.[9]

We can see the shared vocabulary of person appraisal and the centrality of developing the capacity to know others from their worldly consequent connections in diverse realms: in the emphasis given as early as classical times to the written biography and its exemplification, as Franz Rosenthal has put it, that for Muslims "history is biography";[10] in the *shari'a* (Islamic law), where the key factual determinations are based on the testimony of a certified "reliable witness," one whose own ties are so intertwined with those of others that he will ideally resist jeopardizing the willingness of others to deal with him by engaging in perjury;[11] in the marketplace, where there is a constant quest for information, prices being unfixed, values and quality dependent on personal client/patron relationships;[12] or in kin relations, where every tie is negotiable, rather than prescribed, and the multiplicity of names by which a person may be known gives evidence of the sources that reveal and shape one's possibilities.[13] Even time in this system becomes a series of situated encounters so that the truth of a man is not revealed by the unfolding of his acts over a defined period but by the nature and range of his ties to others regardless of their chronological order.[14] In every instance one's web of indebtedness demonstrates the dynamic relation between the norm and the individual play given to it.

As in any cultural system indications of where these norms lie is suggested not just by their everyday implementation but by those instances in which they are specially heightened or ritually reversed. North African saints, for example, must personally demonstrate that the spiritual powers they claim are effective in the world of human relationships, knowing all the time that their claims are themselves dependent on attributions accorded to them by their fellows. Only their own efforts—reinforced by their uprootedness (when being attached is so crucial to the ordinary man's well-being and identity) or their inversion of time (usually defined as situated encounters but now represented as independent of momentary indebtedness)—demonstrate that very ambivalence which is so typical of all human relationships.[15] Similarly, the stranger reinforces the norm by his exception to it: A Jew, for example, can become a closer emotional alter than a fellow Muslim because the impossibility of full reciprocity—converting an economic tie to a marital one, or a relation of informational exchange into an electoral debt—highlights the principle that "normal" relations always incorporate the idea of convertible obligation. Even poetry, where new relationships may be created by capturing the terms of reference in some distinctive fashion, demonstrates the importance of the interpersonal precisely by being a form in which manipulable reciprocity appears to be negated to the benefit of pure emotion—only to depend in turn on the reader's actions. Like prayer itself, such utterances, by their very reversal of the everyday, reinforce the central criteria of Arab personalism—that the ties among sentient beings incorporate an expectation of reciprocity, that the configuration of one's bonds of obligation define who a person is, that the self is not an artifact of interior construction but an unavoidably public act which even those seeming exceptions—the saint, the poet, the stranger—reinforce by the elements of their heightened ambivalence and the risk and challenge of their apparent reversal.

Such an emphasis on the situated person creates an intriguing problem when one adds the no less significant emphasis on the collectivity—the "community of believers," or *umma*—to the equation. Ideally, the umma, even more than lesser inclusive groupings based on kinship and territory, takes precedence, for it is not possible to fulfill many of the requirements of Islam—collective prayer, for example, or the performance of certain duties by some on behalf of all—without the existence of the umma. Whether it is the fundamentalist who has seen this as the indispensable unit of socioreligious existence or the Arab socialist who has romanticized and secularized the community, the precedence and indispensability of the group has been seen by many as central. One modern Lebanese writer "compares individuals in society to grapes which have become dislodged from the bunch, and she expresses skepticism about the ability of any laws or belief-system to reassemble these individual grapes into bunches."[16] In fact, at the same time that reference is made to the umma, the ambivalence that applies to all relationships and the qualities of maneuverability they imply colors the very relationship of individual to group.

The relation of person to community is, perhaps, another example of reinforcement through reversal rather than an expression of an unalterable norm. That is, it calls for the submission of the person to the whole at the same time every cultural artifice calls for the assertion of personality. Like prayer (though less intensely), which demands the complete suspension of individuality into a mass of believers prostrate before their God, attachment to the umma is more of an emotional than a sociological bond.[17] It is the dependent variable—dependent on personalism—just as submission to God is intensified by that same ambivalence towards power that allows individual challenge to kinship, gender, and those who control access to knowledge. To forego personalism and immerse oneself in a group is not, therefore, simply to be incorporated into the collective but to be set apart: To submerge oneself into the group is to give up on the normal course of negotiated ties as a way of uniting chains of persons together and presupposes the rejection of commonsense social life as it is reinforced in so many domains. Thus to choose Western-style individualism, on the one hand, or, ironically, submersion in fundamentalism is to cut oneself off from the familiar sources of sociability and hence to take a radical departure from the supports of everyday life. Even for modern theorists of the Muslim polity—whether the socialists for whom, as Malcolm Kerr put it, "it is not privacy but sociality that must be promoted,"[18] or those heirs to classical Islamic thought who see in the Qur'an's constant concern with social chaos (*fitna*) the fear that backbiters and unbelievers might undermine the umma—the idea of the community is rendered deeply ambivalent by the constant counterweight of person perception and the actuality of person-centered networks of attachment.

These orientations may be closely attached to the nature of tribal organization and power, to which, in no small part, they are linked. As we saw in the preceding chapter, there are aspects of tribalism, as practiced in the Near East, that are compatible with, indeed reinforce, the stress on personalism. Near Eastern tribes disperse power as each individual seeks to garner a set of dependents of his own. With each tribe or fraction thereof standing on an equal moral footing with any other, with (as Dresch has put it for the tribes of the Yemen[19]) tribes being characterized by "fragmented answerability" and an "indefinite divisibility" of units, intense personalism is reinforced at every point. Identity comes, in no small part, from those to whom one is opposed, and indeed each leader needs his opponent to both define his situated existence and his qualities of character.[20] Political matters get pushed down to the level of interpersonal associations, the constraints of such interdependent ties being managed at higher levels of organization only if they mirror the style of the personal. When an individual's pattern of associations accords with those said to be valued by the collectivity, it is not because the "rules" of the game lead to prescriptive social results based on filling a set of given positions but because some individual has been able to cumulate added legitimacy by rendering his networks consonant with the template valued for the larger group. All politics could be said to be local in the sense that it is dispersed, but it would, perhaps, be more accurate to say that in this part of the world all politics is personal.

Thus each individual, to greater or lesser extent and success, must create his own voice, his own concatenation of attributes and affiliations that define his place. There is no unified narrative to which he may attach himself: Whether it is in the medieval style of collapsing a wide range of occurrences into a single instance centered on a noteworthy individual's ability to take action with his recruited supporters,[21] or in the fabrication of a poetic or oratorical voice that so captures the terms of discussion that reference may long be had to the overtones attached by this one person,[22] the belief that men rise and fall on their abilities, rather than that the universe depends on any settled distribution of powers and resources, calls for a story of relationships that depend on a single person. Kinship may reinforce patrimonialism but it cannot be said to produce it: The Arab leader is not called "father"; the ambivalence contained in the challenge of disciple to master or the need of each son to break with his own father in order to ingratiate himself in his own name is too great and too common to risk the inflexibility that may come from equating position and identity, and the hope held out of rising or falling on one's sociopolitical merit is too great to yield to a structure that focuses on differentiable roles rather than cumulated obligations.[23]

The implications of these elements of political culture for the type of state that may result are enormous. The Arabic word for "state" comes from a root that means "to change periodically, to rotate, to move up," a root that also yields "to give ascendancy," "to hand each other something," "to circulate or negotiate."[24] It is a fitting image for this kind of personalistic state, for not only do leaders alternate but, in many instances, the elites circulate as well—both as categories and in their content—as the individuals at their negotiated centers rise and fall. Such a state, for all the autocratic power of the ruler at its center, rarely controls the details of everyday life with direct intensity: More commonly it is, in another of the ironies that comports with this style of person-centered governance, a minimalist state. It must assure overall safety from outsiders, but from within, (1) it largely stays out of the way of its citizens' maneuvering for advantage, (2) it is so identified with the ruler that he may take large portions of the public domain as his personal property, but, even in so-called socialist regimes, governments support the idea of private ownership which is so central to personal identity, and (3) in conformity with the Islamic idea that, as the Qur'an says, "no man bears the burden of another," the state expects individuals to be responsible for their own well-being and does rather little (the occasional services and centralizing of some charities aside) to guarantee the average citizen against his or her own failings. What keeps this from simply looking like a Republican's view of the way governments should always be—protecting vested interests, fending off foreign forces, and punishing criminals with death or imprisonment—is, of course, just how much, at any moment, all this depends for its specific implications on the capacities of the king or president or dictator at its center. What Clifford Geertz has said of one such state is thematically true for most of the Near East: "Not quite an anarchy and not quite a polity, the Moroccan state had, with its endemic particularism, just enough reality to persist."[25]

Given this configuration it is not surprising that some commentators would see Middle Eastern states as ones in which the very idea of legitimacy is constantly undermined. Daniel Pipes, for example, has argued that Islam has not only included the ideals of the state in its concept of the community of believers but has set those ideals so high that no government can ever achieve them and hence be truly legitimate.[26] To the contrary, I would argue that each leader is by definition legitimate if he succeeds in forging the kind of following that allows him to grasp the reins of power.[27] The expectation is, as in all other personal ties, that the relationships of reciprocity having been successfully constructed the relation will be one of a leader to dependents whose ties must be constantly serviced: Reciprocity defines ties among people, but the state— as an impersonal entity—is unreciprocity incarnate. The state, therefore, can have no legitimacy because it does not, in a very deep sense, exist independent of those who fill it out; hence the whole question of legitimacy is misplaced by Western observers if it does not focus on the nature of personalism.

Similarly, the authoritarianism of Near Eastern states is sometimes attributed to their being rentier states or said to be definable by sectoral analysis. The former holds that the receipt of money from "rents" (usually oil income) paid from abroad means that governments do not have to be responsive to or expect much productive effort from their own populations, while the latter says that being so dependent on a single source of income, leaders need only watch carefully over this resource and can be free to ignore other issues. Both, again, fail to see that legitimacy is dependent on the construction of personalistic ties and that in the Arab countries the resources for building such alliances are so diverse that challenges can come from virtually any direction.

It is also argued that the state is weak because of the depredations of colonialism. Undoubtedly, colonialism intruded on the course of indigenous political life, but there is neither some inevitable course that "development" would otherwise have taken nor any reason to believe that structural change was itself short-circuited by the arrival of Western powers. What is clear is that in many Arab countries there had long existed a kind of internal colonialism, in which locals were subject to many of the same processes of indirect rule that reinforced local authorities under colonial regimes. Therefore, without in any way downgrading the specific impact of Western colonialism on the polities of the Near East, it is worth considering, in the light of our argument about personalism and the state, how two factors in particular played into the colonial situation, namely, the concept of the person and the community as legal entities, on the one hand, and the relation of colonialism to the existing structure of customary law on the other.

Islam, it is often noted, has no concept of the legal person.[28] If by this it is meant that one cannot separate different aspects of the person from one another and give public recognition to some aspects and not others, this is precisely what we would expect. Having culturally fractionated the self, Western polities can more readily ask whether an arbitrary age or ritual passage marks one as capable of contracting, or whether a mental disease or defect renders one immune from liability for various harmful acts. In Islam, by contrast, the focus on relationships and consequences yields, most commonly, an emphasis on who people are in relation to others, rather than where they are in a set life structure, and what consequences have befallen others by their acts. Thus even a child may be held liable (in its assets) for the harm it accidentally causes another (e.g., by knocking a pot off a window sill that strikes someone down below).[29] Similarly, the idea of public space—in the sense of an area "owned" by everyone—is largely absent in the Arab polity. People feel no responsibility, for example, for public streets or sidewalks: They assert their presence on areas that become theirs in some usufructory way but quite without any belief in shared responsibility for the parcel, and they may move onto another's property knowing that, as the saying goes, if a person is absent his rights are absent, and that if such rights are not asserted the intruder's presence will become ratified. In each instance, it is the personal (in the Arab sense of that term) that defines the situation, not the (rather unimaginable) construction of a legal person some of whose features can be divorced from others and fixed within an institutional frame.

Customary law is another domain that underscores the structure of personalism. Elsewhere, I have argued that Islamic law is best seen as a kind of common law system inasmuch as it disperses power through a number of localized institutions and draws on changing local practice through the direct absorption of local custom and opinion.[30] Indeed, both indigenous Arab governments and colonial regimes employed a mix of direct and indirect rule, in which some emphasis was given to recruiting an elite while simultaneously building up local authorities. Customary law became a crucial element in this pattern, for it served not only as the mechanism for allowing change to occur in a controlled fashion (since it was filtered through state-certified legal forums) but supported local sensibilities by being meshed with the system of personalistic rule so characteristic of local authority.[31] Whether it is a matter of the Ottoman Empire or the contemporary Palestinian Authority, it is important to realize, as Haim Frisch has said, that "[d]iscussing customary law solely in organizational terms . . . misses the personal nature that pervades it."[32] By pushing many decisions down to the local level and by not centralizing control through unified law but through the indirect legal mechanisms built into Islamic law itself, the very features of personalistic rule are retained and reinforced across yet another domain of political life.

The legitimacy of the ruler, then, and his style of asserting that legitimacy rest on his ability to consolidate support in ways that are culturally recognizable and which, from the perspective of everyday commonsense, can no more be separated from the totality of a person's connections and character than each of these elements can be compartmentalized in any human being's nature. Usurpation confers legitimacy if it is successful—that is, if it is created by personalistic webs of obligation that result in the cumulation of power in the hands of the winner: Trying to move the personal to the archetypal is to contravene commonsense about how power is acquired and arrayed. Many Muslims, particularly those of Egypt, envision Pharaoh as the quintessential tyrant, but it is noteworthy that common sayings in this regard ("Oh, Pharaoh, how did you become Pharaoh? No one opposed me.") stress that there was no one who stood as a successful counterweight, rather than that the ruler was restrained by any institution or role.[33] Tyrants are not natural forces, unpredictable and utterly detached from the societies that legitimize them: To the contrary, they are the momentary expression of a system of person-centered networks that may dominate the center even as they are vulnerable to the legitimacy of any who successfully challenge them.[34]

The styles of such personalistic rule vary, of course: Hafez el-Asad or Saddam Hussein may destroy a city to remind his opponents of his raw power, Nasser or Qaddafi may play to the rhetorical grasp of the situation, Bourguiba or the Algerian crypto-socialists may try to render the purposes of Islam compatible with Western practices. Each may also envision his mode of employing his networks in different terms: Hassan II of Morocco used to say: "Power is a millstone: If you rub up against it adroitly it stimulates you in return, but if you lean on it too strongly it rolls away." And again: "Moroccans are sometimes difficult people to lead . . . My father—God bless his soul—always told me: 'Morocco is a lion you must guide with a leash—he should never sense the chain.' So, we spend our time adjusting: When he pulls too much, I slacken, and when he slackens, I pull a little."[35] Hassan's style of royal arbitration, divine right, and preeminent manipulation of relationships and gifts may have differed in its subtlety from that of some other leaders but, again in a theme and variation sense, the common thread is clear: Personal networks, however rationalized by descent or control, constitute the basis for both the legitimacy and the specific content of any regime, and to change the presuppositions on which this is based would require a change in both the perception of persons and the commonsense vision of how, as a part of divine order, human beings and their world are constructed.

Given this pattern the kinds of controls one has on the authoritarian ruler are also rather differently imagined than in the West. As noted earlier, I have, on a number of occasions, been struck by people saying to me, for example, that "bribery is our form of democracy." When I express some confusion, they explain that if the big man says "do such and such," but I can bribe one of those he depends on to carry out his orders, I have in fact a way of limiting the ruler's power. We had earlier seen how, in reaction to rampant corruption (itself envisioned as the failure, within the "Limits of God," to share whatever largesse comes one's way with those with whom one has forged ties of dependence), people repeat the saying about staying close to the tyrant or play on the ambivalence about power generally. What matters is not whether these mechanisms are effective methods of control but that they are consistent with the overall assessment of persons and powers as centered on the ties—even the choice of whom to defer to or depend upon—through which the view of human nature to which they have entrusted themselves is construed.

In what we take to be the great age of information, the power of such autocrats is said to be more readily converted to control than at other times in history. But even here the pattern of dispersed power which must be cumulated in one person's hands to be legitimate is of critical importance. For knowledge in this kind of system does not simply consolidate power; in fact it disseminates it, in the sense that it both derives from and must be communicated to multiple sources which may themselves constitute the seeds through which the existing power figure's control is built. As with all other aspects of this system of political organization, one is only as good as one's last performance, one's ability to constantly service one's network to advantage, at the same time that every resource upon which alternative bases of power can be built is constantly subverted by being dispersed and subject to constant reconfiguration.

It is against this background that we may try to understand the place that democracy and institution building occupy in the Arab world. Indeed, in many respects the common forms in which the questions are themselves posed is, I believe, somewhat misplaced. Why, ask many Western editorialists and political scientists (as well as many Arab intellectuals), have democratic institutions not developed in the Arab countries? Answers have ranged from some nebulous *goût de l'absolu*, to the supposedly endless cycle of feud and violence, to the claimed fantasies about an idealized past which present realities can never recapture.[36] But this is not the most helpful way to put the question. It would be more fruitful to ask: What kinds of institutions have developed in the context of the personalistic orientation of Arab society and cultural life, and how must analysts approach the kinds of institutions connected with this style of governance regardless of what shape we might personally wish them to take? Seen from this perspective it becomes possible to study what has happened rather than to assume some sort of failure as against a Western standard.

If, as we have been suggesting, one begins with the concept of the person, one can, perhaps, make greater progress in understanding these issues. We have seen that in Arab culture the self is not divisible as in the West, and that as a result one cannot speak of a series of roles which somehow stand either separate from that which is properly called the self or which can be taken on, as masks of the self, allowing the performance of tasks that may contradict other aspects of one's overall identity. This quality is replicated in innumerable domains of social, religious, and cultural life: One sees it in the folk support of the Qu'ranic idea of the *jnun* (or genies), that netherworld of human-like beings whose attributed acts in this world constitute not an aversion to human responsibility but a cultural sense that the self cannot be split and hence it must be some other entity that at times may speak through an individual human;[37] it is displayed in the absence of that type of drama in which people literally play roles different from who they "really" are and in the correlative absence, except in very limited ritual reversals, of using masks to bring out an inner self or to heighten, rather than merely overlay, one's undifferentiable identity.[38] It is also manifest in the fact that personalism trumps class such that any attempt to fix the order of society by social categories invariably finds the unit dissolving in rapid order as the force of personality reestablishes itself at every juncture;[39] and it is imminent in the ways that time itself is marked, each moment being envisioned as the story of a set of person-centered networks whose consequences for the relationships of others mark off a packet of time as an instance of almost magnetic coalescing.[40] Justice, power, and institutions may, then, be seen as domains that are defined and drawn together around this mode of constructing the person and the universe.

Justice—that most vital of concepts for the Muslim—is really the distribution of reciprocal ties among sentient beings who by their very reason must find ways to equilibrate that which may be essentially unequal. No human can establish with certainty the basis for equilibrating essential differences, for that power lies only with Allah. Whereas, in the West, one may create the criteria of equalizing or claim to have found, in the natural world or natural law, the just price, the true value, the exact correspondence of one thing to another, in Islam traditionally there was not even an appellate level that could render such judgments since no human could ever claim ultimate certainty. An unresolved contradiction actually reinforces the ambivalence towards power and hence the ongoing process of seeking relative advantage: On the one hand, no human can have unlimited power since no human can establish a perduring standard of judgment, and, on the other, the fact that no one can break out of this pattern to establish evaluative criteria of human design keeps all relational ties constantly in play.

Moreover, justice is simultaneously an attribute of the person and of the times in which one lives. Justice therefore occupies a middle ground between the public and the private. For while it is possible that a man may be just (ʿadl) and the times unjust, it is thought that one needs just times in order for this personal possibility to be most fully realized. The fractionation of the self in the West made possible the division between a public and a private persona, a self-fashioned moral stature distinct from being an actor on the public stage. Muslims, by contrast, believe that in the absence of a non-chaotic community of believers the quality of justice is almost impossible to achieve since, by definition, it depends of the good opinion, the proven trustworthiness born by a network of consequential social ties, the common design that is forged with other believers. This contributes to a distinctive relation to the ruler and the state. One needs good rulers to be completely just, but in the face of a bureaucratic state—which lacks the interpersonal reciprocity and dissolves the personalistic into disconnected, meaningless encounters—it is well-neigh impossible to gain a sense of oneself as ʿadl. Thus people feel they are forced to live with injustice, unable to rejoin their quest for unifying social bonds with their pursuit of those discriminating interpersonal relationships which together constitute the very fountainhead of their moral and social sensibility.

The felt sense of injustice, so strong in Arab sentiment and rhetoric, is not, therefore, some inability to grasp reality but its very opposite: the attempt to grasp the world when it is at base almost impossible to balance one thing against that which is basically dissimilar. In such a cultural logic, justice is the construction of precisely those networks of obligation that provide some degree of certainty and predictability in a world of potential chaos (fitna), thereby turning the whole sense of the worldly order back upon the personally forged ties of social consequence.

Power, too, accords with this view. For not only does it inhere in persons rather than in events, external forces, or the whim of chance occurrence, but power is utterly dependent on the repercussions it evinces in the realm of interpersonal relations. It does not abide in institutions (as depersonalized positions) or even in divine ordination (for one must still demonstrate through worldly acts that it has taken effect in one's own case). And it cannot, in the Weberian sense, be charismatically routinized since every claim to its continuance is not a duty laid down on the follower by divine injunction but is itself an attribution that flows from acknowledgment and ratification by those who will be called upon to entwine their actions in its terms. In this respect political legitimacy is consonant with the cultural pattern that relates to spiritual legitimacy as well. For saints are not only dependent on the opinion of others but, as John Waterbury pointed out, the political system that provides for and sustains them constitutes "a permanent process of originating charisma."[41] One way in which this is demonstrated in contemporary times is by the means through which an individual leader connects to the masses.

On its face it may seem odd to suggest that control of a nation-state could be possible if based on personally forged ties of interdependence. How, after all, can one leader connect to millions of people with whom, in this purported style of governance, face-to-face relationships would appear indispensable? The answer may lie in the style of communication itself, a style which, just because it uses modern electronic media, does not suggest that such devices or the messages they carry hold the same meaning as they do in Western societies. Specifically, the leader must rely on those events and mediating structures through which a kind of virtual personalism can be enacted. Gamal Abdel Nasser of Egypt is a particularly cogent example of this process.[42] According to Yoram Meital, Nasser made effective use of the symbols of collective memory—and particularly the reinforcing role of the great singer Umm Kulthum—in the years after the 1952 revolution.[43] Umm Kulthum showed that through the radio, used as a "live" medium, real-time connections could be made even at a distance yet still in highly emotional and personal terms—indeed, in ways that affected people's views of themselves and hence their "reality." Nasser built on this form of creating a personalistic attachment to the masses via the bridge made recognizable by Umm Kulthum. Moreover, as the anthropologist Mohammad el-Zein used to say, Nasser would use words in such a way that no one could use them again without the overtones he had captured for them. The result was not unlike that of the classical Arab poet: Nasser's "real reality" mimicked the virtual reality of the artist, partaking of the legitimacy of the one at the same time he made unique connections of his own. These latter consisted in touching the lives of ordinary people so that his contact implied many of the features of a personal relationship. His choice of the Aswan High Dam, for instance, was especially apposite for it literally affected the lives of every single Egyptian. And when it came time to celebrate the completion of the initial stage of the project, who should be beside the leader on the platform but Umm Kulthum. Nasser thus cumulated sources of legitimacy— in what might be called the strong version of the Arab game of maneuvering we have discussed—and though he did it in quite a different way than, say, the Alawaite dynasts of Morocco (who combined Prophetic descent, saintly powers, and kingship), Nasser amassed the resources of power in a way that touched the relationships of all the citizenry. Only the shock of losing the Sinai and the Suez Canal in 1967 could fracture this impact, through the failure of security, boundary maintenance, and retention of a definable zone of mutual benefit.

In such an environment "institutions" is not a term that can be defined in quite the same way as in the West, where they imply the very impersonality that is absent in the Near Eastern concept. Certainly there are numerous positions which perdure as individuals who occupy them change, and certainly there are duties which someone is required to perform on behalf of all if the community is to be a proper one in the sight of Allah. But there is very little structured separation of occupant and position, or of the powers that inhere in a post and those that its momentary occupant may bring to bear through it. Nor is there intense cultural support or personal training through which role segregation is practiced and reinforced. To the contrary, all of one's ties and traits come into play in the way in which one enacts any position one holds, and the result is one in which it is difficult to segregate office from occupant. I have, for example, never heard a phrase used in Arabic that would translate, however idiomatically, as "the system failed"—whether it be applied to the legal system or any other part of the political structure. Indeed, the idea of institutional failure is virtually unimaginable when persons (again, in the Arab concept of the term) take up all the space of institutions. Institutions are attributes of the person, not the other way around; they are the garments one may wear, not as part of a distinguishable role or persona, but as part of one's overall attributes. To treat them otherwise would, given all the supports of religion, law, and common culture for the personally forged ties of connectedness, quite literally make no sense to members of these cultures. Counterbalance, as we have seen, resides in the threat that any individual may align his or her affiliations so as to render another's powers nugatory, and since the other's success will be legitimate for having partaken of the rules of the game through which those attachments were achieved, the ever-present threat of someone else's success colors the evaluation of any position they may presently occupy.

Small wonder, then, that the claimed separation of person from position I thought to be exemplified by my stories of Justice Blackmun and Justice Frankfurter should call for correction by my listeners. Neither statute nor constitution, living sainthood or bureaucratic notice can be viewed independently of the whole scheme of relationships that defines who a person is. The social atom, the validated self, has never been split in Arab culture: Its enduring strength comes from its replication and reinforcement in every domain of social and cultural form; its persuasiveness comes from its "obvious" reflection of what human beings are seen to be really like. Democracy, whether in the Middle East or elsewhere, may, therefore, require either the fractionation of the self or, ironically, its deep embeddedness in the collectivity, where a sense of contribution to the whole is constructed through a revised conceptualization of consent. Democracy may, in this regard, have found more fertile ground in parts of sub-Saharan Africa or the Far East in recent times, whereas neither the idea of the person nor that of a community of believers (*umma*) achieves either of these goals in the context of Arab society. Middle Eastern personalism may not yield the sorts of checks and balances Westerners take as reasonable given their view of the person as divisible by roles and duties, but it is imperative that, far from being a perverse rejection of Western values or a flawed system for containing human failings, the culture of personalism that characterizes much of Middle Eastern political life be understood as one that has enormous resilience and merit given the premises and accomplishments upon which it remains so firmly based.

PART TWO

Memory Worlds, Plausible Worlds

Contesting Sainthood

The Romans listed among the pantheon of divine figures the god they called Rumor (Fama). In the temple built to this god, sacrifice was made in acknowledgment of one of the most powerful and elusive of godlike abilities—the capacity to communicate without demonstrative origin or personal attribution.[1] Indeed, to anyone who has heard news of some occurrence and then been asked how they came by it—and who was then unable to recall its precise origins—the way in which word spreads does indeed seem like the work of an unseen hand. And to have a rumor that has been obtained from one source confirmed by another is to convert the merely insubstantial into the incontrovertibly concrete. A social theorist might say that it is an example of a cultural concept being spread over enough domains and actors to bind a social and cultural world into a meaningful whole. A skeptic might just quote the old saw that when two fools agree on something it takes on the air of objective truth. By whatever means the process works, rumor always needs verisimilitude for credulity to become credibility. The question is not only how word is spread but why a given story is believable to some people while other stories that depart from the same circumstances are believed with equal force by others.

In what follows we see how the account of a Moroccan Muslim saint's posthumous encounter with the Jews of the city of Sefrou was related by different sources. Like Kurosawa's classic film *Rashomon* or Lawrence Durrell's *Alexandria Quartet*, no single version of the story can be said to be true for all viewers. Whatever the "facts" it is the stories that are "true," each revealing a great deal about the context that makes it believable to one person or another, one portion of the population or another. The stories thus test not the limits of the true but the bases of the credible, and in doing so reveal more about the viewers, their circumstances, the changes that have occurred in their society, and the ways in which they have come to construct a believable world than could be learned from pursuing some singular truth that might be thought to lie at the heart of events.ᑐᕥᑐᕥᑐᕥᑐᕥᑐᕥᑐᕥᑐᕥᑐᕥᑐᕥᑐᕥᑐᕥᑐᕥᑐᕥᑐᕥᑐ

"Have you heard the news about Sidi ʿAli Bouseghine?" Omar's voice over the phone from New York in the spring of 1998 was somewhat less excited than bemused. Perhaps for that reason my unspoken reaction was a touch irreligious: How much news could there be about a Moroccan saint who had been dead for several hundred years? I knew that to people of the region saints are regarded as still alive in their tombs, able to serve as intermediaries for those who come as supplicants in search of restored health, the birth of a child, or assistance in some trying moment of life. I knew, too, that people often made symbolic prestations to the saint in an attempt to conduce his favorable response, and that the material gifts presented at the shrine were shared among the contemporary descendants of the saint. But if (continuing my faintly sacrilegious tone) the saint had proved himself still living by rising from his sarcophagus, throwing off the green cover that marked his resting place, and strolling out to see how the city receiving his benefaction had grown over the years, I assumed that I would already have picked it up on the nightly news.

Of course, the name applies not only to the saint himself but to the site of his shrine on the hill overlooking Sefrou, the city in central Morocco where I had done research for many years and from which Omar had emigrated to the United States. Perhaps, I thought, some additional construction is going on around the site, like the building of a hotel to house pilgrims that had occurred some years earlier, or the alteration of the roads now that the old French fort on the adjoining hill had been abandoned by the Moroccan military, and easier access might be had from the side of town facing north towards Fez or to the tribal regions of the Middle Atlas Mountains to the south. Or maybe Omar was going to tell me that the descendants of the saint were involved in yet another lawsuit concerning the division of the gifts brought to the shrine, or even that a group of pretenders were, as is so often the case with such holy sites, challenging the present line's very legitimacy to control and benefit from the pilgrims' contributions. Knowing a good deal of the history of the shrine and a number of the current descendants of the saint, my mind raced through a host of potential grounds on which renewed squabbling might arise. But Omar's response to my simple utterance that no, I had not heard the news, truly caught me by surprise.

"Well," he said, "the King has declared that Sidi ʿAli Bouseghine is not a Muslim shrine at all, but a Jewish one!"

Now Omar had my undivided, if still somewhat bemused, attention. The idea of the posthumous conversion of a saint was rather endearing, and the distress this must occasion for the argumentative descendants, not all of whom are regarded by the people of the region as the reified essence of personal humility, could not but peak one's interest and delight. In one sense I could immediately see the plausible nature of this stunning news: It was quite common in Morocco for Muslims and Jews to share saintly shrines. Indeed, one such saint, situated along the Fez road and variously called Sidi Daoud or Kaf El-Yahudi (referring to the cave in which the shrine is located), is still visited by Muslims and Jews.[2] Omar's story seemed reasonable, too, because Sefrou had had a substantial Jewish population for centuries, and it was, therefore, conceivable that King Hassan II had simply decided to reconstruct the religious identity of the saint—whether out of annoyance with the litigious descendants or as a further gesture towards the Jews of Morocco, whose visits from abroad and whose investments in the country he had encouraged.[3] I recalled, too, that, in a speech to the nation's architects some years earlier, the King had singled out Sefrou as an example of a formerly beautiful town that had been spoiled by bad city planning and worse urban architecture. He had announced at that time that he would not visit the city again until its appearance was improved, thus prompting the city fathers to a series of desperate and rather amusing responses, ranging from repainting the whole town first one color and then another, to building an archway at the entrance to the city that looked straight out of a Disney version of Moorish delights.[4] But as Omar continued his account I was brought back to the particular aspects of the story that were of obvious importance to him.

Apparently, said Omar, some excavating was going on around the site of the saint's shrine and various Jewish artifacts began to be unearthed, as a result of which the King declared the site itself to be a Jewish one. I readily appreciated why both aspects of this account were very plausible, especially to Omar. The idea of hidden treasure is a common theme in Moroccan myth-making: Practically everyone has some story to tell about how there is a treasure hidden near the area they come from and how various relatives and neighbors, having searched for it or stumbled across it while plowing a field, were frustrated, quite often by a genie, from obtaining it. Folktales and common conversation are full of references to such buried treasure as well as to the creatures of the parallel world who figure so prominently in the Qur'an, guarding this wealth and dispersing it to those they favor. Indeed, there is a well known saying, itself a metaphoric warning to those who might fail to note the ambiguity that lies at the heart of temptation: *kull l-kanz fiha l-khanz*—over every treasure there stands a genie.[5] I recalled, too, the story of a rural friend who, with several fellow villagers, went looking for treasure supposedly buried near their settlement. Each wore a Qur'anic phrase in a leather sack around his neck to protect him from the genie guarding the treasure. They sprinkled barley around the site and where it seemed to collect the treasure was said to be buried. But as one of the men began digging he suddenly dropped his shovel with a shriek and said that he had been hit hard on the forearm, doubtless by the genie. They all decided to retire until they could get a Qur'anic scholar to write other phrases strong enough to protect them. Sometimes, too, these genies are thought to be amenable to the manipulations of Jews, old women, magicians, and religious scholars, hence the connection of the genies and the Jews is doubly plausible. Indeed, in an account given by another man that was very similar to Omar's, the excavating was said to have been undertaken by Soussis, emigrants from the Moroccan south who have a reputation for being clever about matters of money and who are thought to be aided by the power over certain genies exercised by the patron saint of their homeland.[6] To Omar and others, then, the image of a treasure guarded by the creatures of a parallel, if hidden, world—creatures who figure prominently in the Qur'an itself—is both culturally plausible and religiously tricky, since denial of the existence of genies might seem to deny the explicit description of them in sacred text.

The second leg of Omar's account also lent it considerable plausibility, namely the supposed action of the King in regard to the identity and legitimacy of the saint. As descendants of the Prophet and Commanders of the Faithful, Moroccan kings, since before the inception of the present dynasty in the sixteenth century, have reserved to themselves the power to certify saintly lineages. In the Sefrou region itself the story is well-known, for example, of how, when the man who was to become the patron saint of the Berber tribe of the region managed to subject one of the most powerful of Moroccan sultans to his request, his primary demand was that the sultan certify the saint's own prophetic descent.[7] For a contemporary king to withdraw the authorization of spiritual descent from Sidi 'Ali Bouseghine's heirs would, therefore, be at once a reassertion of the spiritual power of the monarch and a potent demonstration of the need to remain on the right side of the King in matters mundane. That Omar himself felt it was wrong for the King to take their saint away from the Muslims of the city in no way masked his appreciation of just how forceful a demonstration of the King's power and legendary cleverness such an act would be.

But was it true? Did Omar's account accord with the "facts"? I was planning a trip to Morocco that winter and decided to try to track down the story, the conversion of a saint being a matter of significant anthropological curiosity. When I arrived in Morocco, therefore, I began to inquire as to what had actually happened. But what I heard, instead of a single truth that was more or less fully known by those who were closest to its source, were several quite different versions of what had happened. Indeed, I never did find out what "really happened" in some ultimate sense, but I learned something that is a good deal more interesting, namely several distinct accounts each of which bears sufficient verisimilitude for those who related it to me such that it could constitute for them an entirely convincing account of what transpired. Each story was believed by its teller, each partook of that store of associations relating to the saint, the city, and the memories of times near and far so as to render the account subjectively believable. That I never located "The Truth" did not matter: What counted was how each version, each rumor, made sense to those who related it to me. Far from being an instance of mindless postmodernism, whether found *in situ* or born of my own imagination, the stories of the saint of Sefrou became a test of the ways that culturally plausible accounts make sense to their respective adherents, a marvelous example of how multiple worlds of meaning may exist side by side in a single culture, lending comprehensibility to some even in the absence of complete agreement among all.

When I arrived in Morocco in February of 1999 I immediately headed up to Sefrou with a Moroccan colleague to see what we could find out at the site itself. When we arrived the shrine was open and a few people were going in and out while others sat on the low wall at the edge of the hilltop enjoying the view over the town and countryside beyond. I had forgotten that just below the hilltop site were a series of grottos that had a dug-out look to them, an area that could certainly support images of pot-holing and unauthorized excavation that might indeed turn up the odd artifact. The adjacent site of a hotel also gave the appearance of a digging operation that had been put on hold, and I was later to learn that renovations on the hotel had been suspended for some months.

There was a small shop selling food and cigarettes attached to the shrine itself. My Moroccan colleague approached the man behind the counter and a man who was just standing there and said that he had seen something in the newspaper a while back about some digging that had been going on around the shrine and was wondering what it was all about. Both men denied that anything was going on, but the way they avoided direct discussion, the way they smiled and giggled evasively, left us with the overriding impression that their halfhearted and bemused avoidance was prompted by the desire—or the instruction—that they not discuss such matters. My colleague then approached another man by the parking lot and got the same reaction, thus confirming our sense that their bemused denials were indeed covering some story.

From others living in Sefrou or having connections to it I began to hear several different versions of what had happened. All seemed to involve some sort of friendly visit by Moroccan Jews now living in Israel or Europe; all seemed to involve some question about the religious identity of the saint or the shrine. No one but Omar mentioned that the King himself had actually made a declaration about the religious identity of the saint, but others did suggest that the King's earlier displeasure with the town and his eagerness to receive Jews returning to Morocco to visit or invest, along with his role as an important intermediary in Arab-Israeli negotiations, was wholly consistent with nostalgia for the local Jewish population so many of the Muslims believed vital to the economic well-being of the area. Altogether the whole business was regarded by most people as being of no great moment, but everyone with whom I spoke was confident that their version of things was essentially correct. Each version centered on some aspect of the religious status of both the Muslims and the Jews of Sefrou, and each, therefore, reflected as much on the society at large as on the individual teller.

For many years I had been well-acquainted with a man who had once held an important judicial post in Sefrou but who was now retired to Fez after a career of the highest distinction and probity. I asked him about the rumors. He had not, he said, heard of any particular dispute about the saint but then went on, repeating points he had made to me on earlier occasions, to explain why such a story would come as no surprise to him. He recalled how, during his own years in Sefrou, some members of the Arabic-speaking Beni Azgha tribe claimed to be the true descendants of the saint in question. Their claim was rejected by local officials. Thereafter, the Beni Azgha told anyone who would listen that the saint was actually Jewish. My informant was one of those Fassis who often characterize the people of Sefrou and its hinterland as converts from Judaism, and who cite everything from the large concentration of Jews in the city until recent times to the Muslim Sefrouis' accent, cuisine, and occasional intermarriage with Jews as evidence that the people of the city, like the Berbers of the hinterland, are only lightly Islamized. Thus to him the plausibility of Omar's account was quite high since it combined both the disputatious nature of claimants to saintly benefits and the image that people from Fez attribute to people from the Sefrou region as being Judaized Muslims. These background factors clearly played an important role in each of the specific versions of the events that I was to hear.

The next full account of the events surrounding the saint was obtained from a professional scholar who also lives in Fez but comes originally from the village of Bhalil, an Arabic-speaking settlement located just off the road to Fez. "Oh yes," he said, when I asked if he had heard anything about a dispute concerning the saint, "I can tell you exactly what happened. About two years ago," he said with alacrity and conviction, "an Israeli scholar—probably of Moroccan origins—requested permission to dig for artifacts at the saint's shrine. He was prompted to do so because the name 'Bouseghine' is actually a Jewish name. Although he was refused permission he nevertheless did a bit of digging and came up with a necklace that had some sort of Jewish symbol on it. The government then forbade any more digging of any sort at the site. As a result the site remains open to pilgrims but no one is allowed to do any excavating in the area." When asked, he discounted any involvement by the King and assured me that, as one with some interest in the archaeology of the region, he was certain that this was the whole story of the matter.

In this account several important factors are added to Omar's version of events. For while this second story made no direct mention of the King's role in legitimizing a saint, it did emphasize that through excavation, whether authorized or not, evidence might be obtained about the "true" identity of the saint. This was of obvious interest to a scholar, but like many other accounts I collected it stressed the possibility that (a) there is some truth to the claim that the site, if not the saint, is really Jewish, and (b) that this might be determined on the basis of excavation rather than princely dictate. This point was further underscored by another story the scholar told me involving yet another excavation, in this case one conducted by professionals whose credentials and excavation permits were unchallenged. In the course of working on other matters their investigations suggested that a saint who is related to the royal line may have initially been buried at another location before his remains were moved to the site of his present shrine. Soon after delivering a lecture in which these results were mentioned, the lecturer received a visit from officers of the local gendarmerie. They told him that under no circumstances was he to go around suggesting that the saint in question might ever have been buried in some other place than the site of his present shrine. The importance of certain saints, the prerogative of the King to determine saintly legitimacy in every respect, and the relation of the symbols of dynastic legitimacy to contemporary political power were brought vividly home by this encounter. To those who relayed the story of the Sefrou saint along these lines, their story gained credence from their larger understanding of the role played in the control of saintly identity by the modern, and not just the historic, Moroccan state.

A third, and no less circumstantial, version of events came from Si Muhammad, a highly educated member of one of the oldest families of the city of Sefrou, now living in Meknes, who claimed not only to know what almost certainly had happened but (and here he was even more sure) why. His story was far more elaborate and depended on a broader appreciation of some of the familial relationships that adherents to this version believe important to the structure of Sefrou society.

About a year ago, said Si Muhammad, a group of Jews who were originally from Morocco but now live in Israel came back for a visit. They arrived in Sefrou on a bus that was decorated with banners proclaiming their welcome. When they pulled into town they stopped at a café. There was a Muslim seated in the café, a man who (Muhammad surmised) must have been drinking or smoking *kif*, who said in a slurred but not aggressive voice, loud enough for all to hear, that these Jews, like those of an earlier time, must be here to take *their* saint away with them. It was this comment that began to get around. Muhammad then went on to explain that the man's remarks undoubtedly referred to the time when the Jews of Sefrou were allowed to reclaim the remains of a saint, Lalla Sitti Messaouda, who, though regarded as a Muslim by the majority of the city's inhabitants, was actually Jewish. The story, he said, goes like this:

Back in the earliest period of the Islamization of Morocco, in the days of Moulay Idriss II (the saintly figure who brought Islam to the country in the late seventh century A.D.), Sefrou had a substantial Jewish population. The Jews wanted a cemetery, and for this purpose they purchased a piece of land just outside the walls of the city. A Jewish woman, Esther Messaoudi (both parts of whose name are recognizably Jewish), was one of the first to be buried in this new cemetery. But soon after she was interred the Muslims asked the Jews to move their cemetery farther away from the town, to the area along the road to Fez, near the site of the present Kaf el-Yahudi. The Jews agreed, or were compelled, to do so. But since it was regarded as a sin to move the bodies of the dead, Esther and the others buried at the initial site were left where they were. The graves of these others became neglected, but, owing to her reputation as a wonder-worker, the Jews still came at night and secretly lit candles at Esther's tomb. Indeed, quite a number of miracles began to occur in association with the site. As a result, the Muslims, too, began to revere Esther. Eventually, they came to regard her as a Muslim, built a dome over her grave, and called her Lalla Sitti Messaouda.

Meanwhile, Muhammad continued, the head of the Jewish community at that time, the Grand Rabbi himself, had been stealing from his own people: He had been putting the titles of Jewish communal properties, like the original

Jewish cemetery, in his own name. He had also been misappropriating funds, it being the custom in those days that craftsmen would bring their assets to the Grand Rabbi, who would, in turn, invest and redistribute the income on a regular basis. This rabbi came from a family known as the Nas Adlun, whose original name, said Muhammad, was Azoulay, a name, he assured me, that is not only a Moroccan Jewish name but is found among Jews in the Arab east and Israel. When the Grand Rabbi realized that he was about to be unmasked by his co-religionists he rushed to Moulay Idriss and converted to Islam. The formula he used for conversion, however, is highly significant. He approached Moulay Idriss, who was seated on his horse, and said, "I convert *bin rejlik*," which literally means "between your legs." Whether he was referring to the sainted figure on horseback or to the horse itself is not clear, but it was not only gauche and potentially salacious—the correct metaphor being *bin iydek*, "between (or within) your hands," an utterance that should be accompanied by prostrating oneself—but suggests more a request for personal protection than an act of religious conversion. The Jews cried and raked their nails over their faces until blood ran down their cheeks, but once the rabbi had converted there was nothing they could do to get their money back.

Having converted to Islam, Muhammad continued, the former rabbi proceeded to marry a Muslim woman and build a house outside the city walls. As the family expanded over the years, several branches began to diverge. One branch returned to its original Jewish identity; another received a document from the ruling sultan of the day declaring them to be *shurfa*, descendants of the Prophet Muhammad. This divergence of lines, he said, explains why the same name is found among both Jews and Muslims and how the Nas Adlun quarter of Sefrou came to be located adjacent to the *mellah*, the old Jewish quarter. More importantly for the present story, it later transpired—Muhammad did not know exactly when—that a branch of the Adlun family who had remained Jews came from abroad and presented the local Moroccan officials with documents showing that Lalla Sitti Messaouda was actually the Jewish woman Esther Messaoudi. On this basis they were allowed to reclaim her remains and take them away with them. So we come full circle—to the man in the café who started the rumor that once again the Jews had come to retrieve one of their saints, in this case the patron saint of Sefrou, Sidi ʿAli Bouseghine.

There are many reasons why, for Muhammad and others, this account makes sense. For them the story breaks down into two separate though related parts—the story of the Jews who have returned to claim a local saint as their own, and the story of the Adlun family. To take the latter part first, it is necessary to understand the role of this family in the life of the city, at least for people of Muhammad's background and generation. The Adlunis had long been the wealthiest, and in many respects the most powerful, of the families who claimed to be "originally" from Sefrou. Throughout the postwar years until his death in the 1970s, the scion of the family, Moulay Abdesslam bel Larbi el-Adluni, was a figure to contend with in all matters relating to the city and its hinterland. The family owned substantial properties in the city and country-side and Moulay Abdesslam was for years the elected representative to the Agricultural Chamber of the national parliament. But the family—and par-ticularly Moulay Abdesslam—had a reputation for being autocratic, ungener-ous, and quick to take offense. Each of these factors played a role in the credi-bility of Si Muhammad's version of events.

It was, for example, commonly believed that much of the Adluni property had come into their hands through their close association with the late nine-teenth-century administrator of the region who was notorious for appropriat-ing the lands of those he opposed and selling them to his own clients. More-over, as we saw in the comments of one of my other informants, Sefrou has long been regarded, especially by the haute bourgeoisie of Fez, as a Jewish city many of whose Muslims are either converts from Judaism or insufficiently Is-lamized, or both. While this is less a matter of deep-seated suspicion than an example of those intercity rivalries that are common to Morocco, the Adlunis have long been sensitive to such implications. This is even more the case as it concerns their claim to be descendants of the Prophet in the line of the ruling dynasty. Si Muhammad, in his own remarks, had pointed out to me that Moulay Abdesslam would get very angry if someone did not address him by the title *moulay,* which indicates one of such descent, and that he even sued people who, by failing to address him in this fashion, called into question his professed entitlements. It was with great pleasure that an upstart Berber once defeated Moulay Abdesslam in his bid for re-election as agricultural represen-tative, the general glee being short-lived, however, when, with the aid of some of the highest officials in the country, Moulay Abdesslam managed to block his opponent from ever taking office.[8] And there were many who were eager to tell me the story of how, in the 1970s, Moulay Abdesslam gave money for the con-struction of a mosque (albeit one that was to bear his name) and, having finally accomplished one reasonably selfless act, had the good grace, on the very day the mosque was completed, to drop dead.

Si Muhammad, like other "old Sefrou" family members, was wary of the Adlunis. To many people like him the idea that the latter were "really" Jews was a dig at the overall influence and, as they saw it, the hubris and lack of gen-erosity of the entire Adluni clan. To join them to the issue of Sidi ʿAli Bouseghine through the questionable comment of a café-crawler of dubious propriety was apparently a narrative temptation of irresistible proportions. But their historic antipathy lent credibility to the first part of the story—that the Jews had come to retrieve "their" saint—and helped make the second part—the history of the Adluni's questionable conversion—seem to have continuing import. The whole story then not only reasserted the role of the Jews in Sefrou in the very positive terms with which the Jews are quite commonly described but, in a characteristically Moroccan turn of ambivalence, also allows the story of the Adlunis to be re-told in a way that calls their claim to noble descent once more into question.[9] If, to Moroccans, power is not always where or what it may seem to be, and if the telling of events is one way of reasserting this broader truth, then the version told by Si Muhammad conjoins many of the themes that are central to Moroccan perceptions of power, identity, and religion—and does so to very contemporary effect.[10]

There are, then, many features that all three versions share in common. Stories about Muslim saints are never static, nor are the claims of those who stand to gain by asserted proximity to the saint permanently uncontested.[11] Indeed, Muslim saints are often in competition with one another, and since their wonders are associated with them while living—either during their actual lives or because they are regarded by many as still alive within their tombs—the sense of their continuing efficacy in this world is very pronounced.[12] And while Muslim shrines have long been the focus of income for those associated with the saint, it is indeed arguable that in recent decades, as Marcus has argued: "Saints may still be sources of revenue, but they are no longer sources of power."[13] This commercialization is quite evident in Sefrou both as it applies to Sidi ʿAli Bouseghine and to the Jewish cemetery on the Fez road: The construction of a new hotel at the Muslim shrine and the careful restoration of the Jewish cemetery (with attendant *hilloula* [celebration] each spring centering on the tomb of a local rabbi) are both regarded by people in the city as significant sources for touristic income.

It is also generally true that Jews who originated in Morocco—including a number who are now Israeli citizens—have been paying visits to Morocco to tour the sites of their family homes and local saints. These guided tours do indeed arrive by bus and sometimes there are banners welcoming their visit. Sefrou is one of the stops on these routes and the presence of Israeli Jewish returnees was a given in each of the versions of the stories told about the saint.[14] André Levy also argues that for a number of these visiting Israelis a kind of reversal of power ensues, in which the Israelis, having long felt that their families were put in an inferior position by the local Muslims, comport themselves quite differently since it is now the Muslims who must deal with Jews who are not subservient to them.[15] Although the visiting Israelis generally hide this sense of inverted power and relations to the Muslims are cordial if distant, their very presence may underscore the change in their status and with it the changes each of these stories reflects.

There is also the idea, present in each of these accounts, that the Jews have indeed sought to return some of their sainted predecessors to the Holy Land. And there is some truth in this. On several occasions the Moroccan government has quietly granted permission for just such transfers, and given the general lack of publicity surrounding such events, other unsubstantiated claims that Jewish remains have been successfully repatriated are rendered more credible. For example, in the 1980s the scion of one of the most noted of Moroccan Jewish families, descended from the famous saint Rabbi Haim Pinto, claimed to have brought back to Israel the remains of several saints, one of whom he implied was a woman.[16] Hence the idea, present in each account, that the Jews may be seeking to repatriate yet another saint, as they are asserted to have done with Lalla Sitti Messaouda, was a shared and credible element of each version of the events surrounding Sidi ʿAli Bouseghine.

But each story of what "really" happened concerning the saint also may represent significant differences among the people who heard and relayed one or another version of events. For those who spoke of the King's intervention there was, perhaps, a displaced criticism of the monarch in general. In the last few years of his reign, Hassan II had been the subject of several symbolic protests—from the removal of his portrait in many shops in the early 1990s, to opposition to his joining the West in the Gulf War (which was mainly a protest against the King's more domestic actions), to limited riots over everything from the price of bread to the absence of jobs for college graduates. To say that the King had even gone so far as to declare a Muslim saint to be Jewish was precisely the kind of symbolic assertion that some found credible both as a criticism of the King's attention to outsiders' sensibilities and as a way of arguing by exaggeration that the King was losing sight of what was central to Moroccans' own needs.

To those who were taken by the emphasis on the quest for treasure associated with the saint, the story involved, on the one hand, the classic struggle for control of descent from the saint and the income generated by his shrine and, on the other, a symbolic reassertion that fortunes may rise and fall with great rapidity and that "the game" is still afoot notwithstanding the fact that new-found sources of wealth and power may be more limited than they were in the past. As a story of the uncertainty of resources the version of the saint's identity told in this regard finds particular favor with those who expect from such symbols the reinforcement of their view that their own fortunes may, in an increasingly restricted environment, suddenly take a turn for the better.

And finally, for those to whom the most believable version goes right back to the sources of identity of one of the richest and most powerful families in town, whose very origins may be based on a suspicious conversion prompted by a venal predecessor escaping the justified wrath of his own people, the story becomes a parable of the structure of society and the contestable power of anyone regardless of stature. Now the saint's identity is tied up with the legitimacy of those who presently possess financial power, and the very structure of their claim to wealth and moral superiority are undercut by this version of the story. Like all the other versions of the story, this one has its adherents as much for the sheer beauty of being able to recount through it a long list of historic exceptions to the behavior of the rich as for its ability to summarize so many of the values on which their own claims for identity and status are founded. Each finds, in rumor and in fact, the believable tale that he seeks.

Rumor has its own house in every culture, the place where it lodges most comfortably. It may be in the baths or the agora, it may take shape in the airwaves or in the pamphlet, it may gain credibility from the style of its presentation or simply from the reinforcement of the social position of those who capture its terms. In Morocco, the premier lodging places have classically been in the contestations over genealogy or wondrous occurrences, recounted in the privacy of conversation, religious lodge, or public marketplace—and particularly where all such elements converge, in the telling of a saint. The rumors about Sidi ʿAli Bouseghine show the continuing vitality of this forum for grasping the real, even if what is now "real" is itself as uncertain as the other truths that surround each version of its telling.

Three stories then—but are they three versions of the same events, three stories in search of an event, or three stories about stories that only require some event to have an excuse for calling up, yet again, the world of contestable concepts? Perhaps what matters most is not "the truth" as something positive to be grasped but the ways in which verisimilitude itself is constructed, the ways in which the plausible is developed such that it can be applied to the situational. To understand why we accept something as true we may, as the case of the contested saint of Sefrou suggests, need first to place belief in its larger sociohistorical context and then watch, in all its circumstantial detail, how those who entwine their lives with such orientations transform the latently credible—fraught with both rumor and fact—into something each may, for a time, accept as manifestly true.

∾ 6 ∾

Memory in Morocco

How will we know it's us without our history?
JOHN STEINBECK, *Grapes of Wrath*

∾

Social scientists who have studied memory, whether collective or personal, have tended to focus on the ways in which events are reconstructed at some remove in time. Whether it is the re-imagining of social identity or the reassessment of experiences occasioned by a major disruption, the refurbishing of past glories or the reinterpretation of the causes of decline, the reconstruction of myths for current ends or the use of "time past . . . in time present to control the future,"[1] studies of such phenomena give us an extraordinary sense of how people reconstruct the past in the light of current needs or expectations.[2]

But there is another aspect of memory that, quite remarkably, has received very little consideration, namely the ways in which the categories of cultural experience may have changed over time and with them the ways in which, as a matter of commonsense, past events are now described and explained.[3] We do, of course, have excellent studies of how, at a given moment, the structure of memory accords with other elements of social organization—from accounts of structural amnesia, by which the collapse of genealogical levels draws contemporaries and ancestors into greater affinity, to the recasting of national identity in the light of changing concepts of race, ethnicity, and human nature. But even these analyses are quite different from studying the ways in which, at the very time they are occurring in the lives of ordinary people, changing conceptualizations of persons, causation, relationships, and external circumstances lead to a new set of orientations by which the past itself is being captured.

In this essay I want to ask whether and in what ways, over the course of the three decades I have been working in central Morocco, any shifts in cultural concepts have begun to manifest themselves and how such changes affect the ways in which people now relate and assess events as compared to the way they did twenty or thirty years ago. Put somewhat differently, the question arises whether it is possible to detect any fundamental alterations in the categories people use to understand their past, quite aside from any differences in the way in which the past is used in the present.[4] In approaching this question it will be valuable, first, to consider some of the categories by which time itself is marked out: In what ways have these markers changed over the course of a generation, and how do such changes bear on the structure of contemporary relationships? To test some of the possibilities that present themselves, consideration will then be given to three particular domains where the reconfiguration of memory appears to be at work: reflection on the period of French colonialism in Morocco (1912–56), the relation of local versus national history, and the recollections concerning the all but absent Jewish population of Morocco. Finally, it may be possible to draw some general suggestions about the relation of conceptual alteration to the reconfiguration of memory itself.⊙⊙⊙⊙⊙⊙⊙⊙⊙⊙⊙

MARKING TIME

Kan wa ma kan, fi qadim azzaman.
[It was and it was not, in a past long ago.]
TRADITIONAL OPENING TO A STORY[5]

If the times are just, one day is for me and one day is against me.
MOROCCAN SAYING[6]

In the late 1960s the image of society that Moroccans constantly projected was one in which each person, through the careful construction of a number of negotiated arrangements with others, could build a network of reciprocal obligations into as large or small a constellation as his or her circumstances and force of character would allow.[7] This "game" had its rules—a series of customs and conventions by which ties could be formed and recognized by society at large—but like the moves in a game of chess, the skills involved and the outcomes of the moves were seen as infinitely variable and endlessly creative.[8]

Connected to and supporting this dynamic view of social maneuvering was a view of time as composed of sets of relationships, packets of interrelationship whose movement over the course of months or years was far less important than their internal dynamics and implications. Thus for purposes of understanding others it was not movement across time that revealed what was true about persons but how they formed networks of obligation at any given moment. What one remembered about another was not couched in terms of duration, linear unfolding, or cyclical replication but sets of situated relationships; what was remembered about events were the persons whose networks set the context within which one's own actions were themselves placed. Two markers helped to denote this concept of occurrence, one emphasizing the conjunction of particular persons and time, the other their disjunction. Thus, in the first instance, an entire period might be referred to as "the days of so-and-so," the big man whose own negotiated network affected an array of satellite arrangements. Consistent with this is the Arab saying that "men are more like their times than their fathers," an idea that emphasizes the amalgamative force any current set of arrangements can have in the formation of the units of memory.[9]

The flip side of this concept marks those moments, of whatever duration, in which "the times" are not under the nominal effect of a superordinate power and in which, therefore, the very arrangement of interpersonal obligations is subject to society-wide alteration.[10] Asked to relate their own historical memories people would often refer to moments when the existing sets of dominant relationships were in a state of uncertainty or upheaval—when the possibility existed for the board to be swept clean and a new round of the game could begin. Thus one would be given such markers as the year when, following the killing of a powerful local administrator, the disorder (*siba*) that threatened extensive social chaos (*fitna*) led to the wholesale reconfiguration of personal attachments; or people would cite "the year of the ration coupon" (1945), when the introduction of a new monetary form disrupted existing obligations and made whole new sets of arrangements possible.

Similarly, the terms by which events were placed in the past mirrored the emphasis on the relational. Events that had occurred even a rather short time before were characterized as *bekri* ("early") if some element of the way present networks had come to be arrayed were attached to them, but as *zaman* (a unit of time divorced from continuing social life, "ancient") if no clear connection to present obligational bonds was attributed to the bounded packet of relationships in question.[11] In such a conceptual scheme some very recent occurrences could be regarded as *bekri* and ones only a few years earlier as *zaman*, and people might seek to characterize their attachment to various networks by the way they manipulated this historical taxonomy. Thus people may contrast the present to the past by saying that previously people acted "with *niya*," a term that not only means "intent" but implies an openness, even naiveté, through which honesty and belief are discernible.[12] Or they might say of such a time that people "had *asel*," a term that conveys not only a sociogeographic point of "origin" but a predictable set of associations to which one could now seek a basis for one's own connection. In both cases, however, these terms were applied to periods still described as *bekri*, thus suggesting that they are not entirely in a separated past but do, or might, hopefully or actually, continue to exist in the present social world. Such emphases reinforce the spirit of the Qur'anic assertion (57:19) that "the present life is but a sport and a diversion," such that memory operates by focusing on person-centered networks of obligation and when the latter cease to exist in recognizable form those "person-events" recede from collective awareness.

Confidence that the rules of the game continue in effect has, however, eroded quite noticeably over the years, and with it some of the conceptualizations through which memory is constructed. Whereas through the 1960s one's foundational security was said to rest on *ḥbab* (kinsmen), and later, in the 1970s, on *saḥab* (friends, connections), now, people say, everything depends on *flus* (money). A clear sense of uncertainty exists about whether the rules of the game have changed; the concern is that if one cannot ante up to the new game by getting access to money, one cannot as easily use family or connections as in earlier times—maneuvering within relationships, converting obligations of one type into advantages of another type, ingratiating oneself into increasingly favorable alliances.

Indications of this uneasiness began to show up in the 1980s in a variety of linguistic emphases. For example, people began to use the Arabic word *mes'uliya* as never before. The word comes from a root that means "to ask," "inquire," "request," "demand," or "claim." It is commonly used to mean "responsibility" in the sense of adhering to the forms of etiquette through which responsive interactions, the obligatory prelude to possible ties of interdependence, could be developed. *Mes'uliya* thus implies that very "civility" that seems to so many now to be lacking, the forms by which predictability can flow from the rules of the game to each of its moves. It is, I think, not nostalgia for an imagined past that leads many Moroccans to reflect differently on what they know of the past. Rather it is that present circumstances have led them to become more conscious of the category of civility and its role in network formation now that they find it more difficult to get others to attend to these as the terms of the game.

Similarly, Moroccans' own sense of self may be undergoing reorientation. Moroccans, I suspect, never saw themselves as "witnesses in spite of themselves" (to borrow Marc Bloch's phrase): As quintessential participant-observers Moroccans qualified as reliable witnesses to relationships precisely when their own networks of attachment, and the information that flowed through them, put them in touch with what for them constituted "events," namely person-centered interactions. But as the game has itself changed both one's reliability and one's power to choose one's dependencies have begun to shift. Now when one recalls the recent past the terms are less those of networks and obligations than of gaining wealth first and then being able to use it to create dependencies.

Such a reorientation may also connect with a subtle shift in ideas of causation. Where previously it was believed that in human affairs it is mainly persons (and other sentient beings) who cause things to happen, now events can cause other events to occur in chain-like fashion without a conscious agent being the point to which one must trace all chains of causation. From this viewpoint one searches for causal explanation not in terms of persons but of forces—whether of nature, types of institutions, or professional or educational status. A description of past events that once was couched in terms of who did what at each point may now be couched in terms of what circumstance, position, or scientifically determinable connection has given rise to what follows. Farmers who, a generation earlier, attributed the advisability of using manure as opposed to fertilizer through a chain of relaters to a respected authority now focus on direct observation;[13] the failure of a government education policy years earlier is not explained now, as it was then, as due to the misdeeds of specifiable officials but as the result of broader forces of population growth, economic turmoil, and faceless corruption. Uncertainty of person-specification has yielded, at least in part, to tentative explanations that depend far less than they did on chains of persons for their explanation.

Thus as contemporary cultural shifts occur the terms by which the past is captured take on a different cast. The period of the French Protectorate is characterized as *bekri* where current social ties are traceable to that era, but for others who envision their ties as built on a different base it is characterized as a bounded past, *zaman*.[14] The nostalgia Arabs take as a given throughout most of the Middle East plays almost no role in Morocco, where the taxonomic emphasis on current relationships squeezes out the regretted past in favor of an existent or nonexistent impact in the world. Indeed, there is no real speculation as to how things might have been different.[15] This is not, as Westerners sometimes assume, simply because of the Prophetic injunction against idle speculation, but because event consciousness stresses whether things happen or do not—and hence whether an account of them is true or not. These all-or-nothing cultural emphases—relation-bearing or not, occurring or not, true or not—are, however, subject to being recast as confidence wanes in the ability of all to participate in network formation and as an emphasis on the etiquette of play combines with a discourse of probability and impersonal forces to displace the knowable person with the impersonal event.

These emphases may account for the diminished use of marker years of the type referred to earlier. Such markers have been used to indicate the break in existing networks of attachment and their placement in one or another level in the attic of memory—*bekri* if they held resonance for current ties, *zaman* if they did not. But since Morocco gained independence in 1956 events have not led to fundamental changes in social ties as a result of a single cataclysm. Neither attempts on the life of the late king, Hassan II, nor local rebellions, which may have had such an effect in the past, have implied such moments of structural disruption.[16] Whereas previously, varied social resources (connections of family, access to influence or wealth, strength of arms or clever alliance) made it possible to create climactic moments or served as the tools by which one could dramatically ratify one's newfound networks, now the centralization of state power and diminution in alternative means for building a power base allow change to go unmarked. Those moments of climax with power—whether precipitated by setting up a base for ingratiation separate from one's father, or by being sharply identified politically, economically, or militarily by the person one opposes—have been blunted by a regime and an economic environment that render events inchoate, impersonal, unclimactic.

Into such an unshapeable environment of personal obligations the idea of probability can express the lack of joinder, impersonal causation can bespeak unformed association, and circumstantial evidence can uneasily displace the once knowable person.[17] Each new cultural emphasis, however, lacks full amplitude, a sense of connectedness across cultural domains: Each conceptualization remains an aspect of a limited domain, rather than a force that unifies a new cultural paradigm by its replication in every area of life. For such linkage to occur, for the explanation of the past to become part of a new commonsense, perhaps the concept of time itself would have to change: New markers would be needed to validate new concepts. Until then, with only a vision of time as a function of ongoing relationships, themselves now rendered uncertain, the past itself goes unclearly marked, like a faded signpost, and the past, the present, time itself go unmeasured, unjoined, without convincing force. The result—a kind of approach to the vague, where concepts and their linguistic embodiments are very much in flux—shows itself in several specific domains that bear consideration, namely the re-telling of the colonial past, the reconfiguration of local versus national history, and the vision of the role of the Jews in Morocco's past now that they are largely gone.

PASSÉ SIMPLE, PASSÉ INDÉFINI

The past is a foreign country, they do things differently there.
L. P. HARTLEY, *The Go-Between*

"The French did that," said my companion. We were walking through the extensive garden the French had laid out alongside the river that begins upstream of the city of Sefrou, criss-crosses a small irrigation canal that carries water around the center of the town, and comes to an end at a swimming pool formed by a small dam. "The French did that," he would repeat, pointing to the layout of the paths, the plantings, the benches. My companion, a worker who had picked up only a smattering of French while growing up during the middle years of the French Protectorate that lasted from 1912 until independence in 1956, spoke in a wistful tone, neither ironic nor envious, as if pointing out a natural phenomenon, like a bird flying or a flower in bloom. And yet, like so many similar comments made by others of varied background in the late 1960s and 1970s, the utterance was also accompanied by a tone of mild astonishment— 'ajub, they would often add, a word that means "wondrous," "admirable," and "amazing" as well as "curious," "strange," and "odd"— a recognition of something peculiar, even distinctive to a moment,[18] something that was true of these foreigners that was not true of their own everyday lives.

The Moroccans have a great many sayings about how one should deal with power: "It is the tyrant who does the asking," says one; "Hold on tightly to the oppressor," counsels another. In each instance the nuances of the Arabic and the ambiguity of the structural form suggest the deep-seated ambivalence of the utterance. Thus in the first case the term that translates as "asking" can also indicate, in various verbal forms, "to demand," "beseech," "invite," and "search for," as well as "to constitute a problem," while in the latter saying the term I translate as "to hold on" can, in various transformations, not only mean "to take away," "fight," "contend with," and "avoid," but also "to desire," "yearn," "pine for," "tend or incline towards," and "take over."[19] These multiple, seemingly contradictory meanings, though often sorted and disambiguated by context, are here left deeply ambivalent, their multivocality partaking of that tradition of common perception and high Arabic literature (*adab*) in which, to quote once again Franz Rosenthal's way of putting it, in "the Muslim view . . . all matters human have a positive as well as a negative side."[20]

This ambivalence towards power occupies a central role in the way the memory of the French presence has been played out over the course of the past thirty years. The French, as powerful figures, were regarded like other such rulers—as people you had to cleave to (in both senses of the word), staying close enough to them to predict and influence their actions without allowing that proximity to limit other attachments that may be of use. Such association carries rather little in the way of lasting implications of being a collaborator, however much it involves taking one's chances of being caught on the wrong side at any given moment. Indeed, by hedging one's attachments—whether by placing one son in one political party and another in the opposition, or working for a Frenchman but helping freedom fighters in their fund-raising—one could try to keep a foot in each camp. This willingness to adapt to the situation of the moment shows itself, in the particular case of the French period, in a number of circumstances.

In rural areas French indirect rule during the Protectorate took on the form of using and modifying tribal organization for French administrative ends. Thus sheikhs were often appointed who crosscut prior local divides, or superordinate administrators (*qaid*s), overseen by *affaires indigènes* officers, were organized within the French bureaucratic hierarchy. At the same time, however, tribal attachments were re-forming around the French presence, taking on revised configurations in response to the foreign incursion.[21] Tribes would disperse into constituent fractions so the French could not claim land was unoccupied or to cloud the useful knowledge garnered by a Protectorate-appointed sheikh. Indeed, as we have seen, it is a characteristic feature of tribal organization generally that tribes possess a certain amoeboid quality, shifting their shape to fit changing circumstances. So, for example, fractions might recast their histories or genealogies—and hence their access to resources or apparent subservience to a new administrative charter—as old pathways become less favored in the light of the ruler's actions affecting market routes, grazing permits, and new infrastructures. Reciprocal change occurs as the tribes and their constituent parts reshape their momentary form, if not their overall bases of forming attachments, even as the conqueror imagines himself the arbiter of all change.

This adaptability has several distinct features that run deep into Moroccan political history. Michael Brett notes that throughout Berber history tribal leaders have sought recognition even by their enemies as the legitimate leaders

of their own groupings.[22] Conversely, Moroccan administrators interviewed
in their Middle Atlas domains in the late 1960s repeatedly claimed either that
people in their region never really resisted the French or that they did so initially but then saw the value of the French system of administration and took
positions within it.[23] Whether, as Abdellah Hammoudi argues, tribal structure
lost its fluidity as the French (and later independent Moroccan) administration gained unprecedented control over communications and resources, or
because local leaders gained in their oppressive powers over fellow tribesmen
as the latter lost bargaining powers vis-à-vis the new state, the recollection of
this period bears witness to the changing concepts by which power and causation, process and momentary networks are themselves subject to contestation.[24]

Put somewhat differently, one can see a contest between two different views
of the past informing memory of the Protectorate period as it has played out
over the last several decades. On the one hand there is what might be called the
official (or, perhaps, more accurately, *officials'*) view of the past. This view sees
the past as a story of the state absorbing the tribes: Local resistance gives way
to an appreciation of the structural benefits of new administrative forms,
which in turn leads rebels, as a kind of legitimizing enemy, to accept positions
within a system to which the newly independent nation's own administrators
have fallen heir. The opposing view is that the tribes have absorbed the state:
As so often in the past rural people have engulfed the new power, stayed close
to it in order to know it, involved themselves with it without sacrificing the
techniques by which interpersonal obligations are formed, and adapted themselves, their genealogies, and even their names as circumstances suggest.[25] Ur-
banites, too, partake of this popular view, seeing themselves as cleaving to the
oppressor to contend with him, moving through an urban-like labyrinth of
pathways forming beneficial ties without loss of self-esteem, and envisioning
time as nested relationships that operate by long-familiar criteria of human
nature and opportunity. The past may, of course, come in for revision—as, for
example, when a man who might once have felt shame for his father's failure
to actively resist the French now sees that period as a context of force and violence that required more adaptive strategies. But the overall theme of official
incorporation versus local absorption forms a large part of the repertoire by
which that past is envisioned and put into play.

Time, in this paradigm, plays tricks—old tricks. Whereas in the decade after the end of colonialism people often spoke of the colonial era under the category of *bekri,* that earlier context of relationships that still bears some con-

nection to the ties that exist in the present, the colonial period has now slipped into a kind of persistent ahistorical moment, that perduring realm (often referred to by the classical Arabic term *dahr*) signifying the operation of common forces of personality and social connection but without a distinctive tie to current arrangements. Since chronology does not reveal the truth of persons (as situated relationships do), and since many of the relationships formed under the French—whether actual interpersonal ties, adaptations to their particular presence, or associations made possible by their technology and infrastructure—no longer have currency, the Protectorate actually becomes a reinforcement for the categories of time and relationship they once confirmed, quite differently, by their interruption. The French grammatical forms—the *passé simple*, the *passé indéfini*—blend into the Moroccan system of time demarcation where moment-to-moment passing losses distinctiveness as completed packets of relationship, no longer differentially relevant to the pre- and post-Protectorate periods, get increasingly mingled in the storehouse of memory.[26]

"The French did that," my friends used to say. But the garden we walked through is now open only intermittently to the public: too much to care for, too expensive, too full of people lying around, say the town fathers.[27] But there was always a conceptual disjunction. Public space, in the sense of space for which there is shared responsibility, barely exists as a concept in the Middle East; unoccupied space, whether it be a field or the sidewalk, is land not (yet) identified with someone and hence land that is identified with no one, land waiting to gain meaning by being associated with someone's nurturance and connections. The state may control space, but the state is not a person. You cannot have a negotiated relationship with the state: The state is unreciprocity incarnate. Time and memory, where the state is involved, are dependent variables; where human relationships are involved they are marks of engagement. The Protectorate has become a test—indeed a confirmation of the paradigm of bounded pasts divorced from present relations and perduring moments of interdependence, even as it has served as a catalyst for breaking the paradigm of personalized pasts and emphasized impersonal causation.

The garden is mostly closed, like a moment that never quite fit, an odd instant when absorber and absorbed, cleaving and cleaved never achieved resolution. It is a past that can be stored as a package, deeply relevant to what came after yet increasingly overlaid by other packets. The memory of the colonial era remains part of the vocabulary of power—indeed reinforces rather than disproves its central terms. But for many it has largely been superseded by the

ways in which local and national history have come to be entwined in more recent years.

LOCAL HISTORY AS NATIONAL HISTORY

The most difficult thing to predict is not the future, but the past.
RUSSIAN PROVERB

Two Encounters

Bouderbala—August 1967   A historian friend and I interviewed a ninety-
four-year-old Berber leader in his home in the Middle Atlas Mountains. In his
day he had been rather famous for having entered the sultan's palace in Meknes to convey the countrymen's threat that if the sultan did not remove the
French intruders he and his fellow tribesmen would see to it that the sultan was
himself dethroned. When the Protectorate began our elderly informant took
to the mountains and held out against the invaders for seven years. He then ca-
pitulated and took a post under the local French administrator. One of the
things that was so remarkable about our conversations was that one of the old
man's sons, himself only in his late twenties, sat with us. He was wide-eyed
throughout and later told us that he had never known about many of the things
his father had done in the pre-Protectorate period and was only learning of
them for the first time during our discussions.[28]

The Medina of Fez—July, 1991   Walking through the old walled section of
various Moroccan cities in 1991, I am struck by the absence of portraits of the
King from all but a tiny handful of shops. In the past stores always seemed to
have a picture of the King, or at least of his father, on display, but now they
were, quite simply, gone. As I walked through the old city of Fez one day with
a well-known traditional jurist and his son-in-law, I pointed out this absence
of royal pictures. The son-in-law was quite surprised and replied that he simply
hadn't noticed it before. With a wry smile and an appropriately indulgent tone,
the older gentleman responded by saying: "If you want to see pictures of the
King nowadays you'll find them in the offices of the major corporations."

These two anecdotes may be taken as indications of a shift that appears to
have occurred in the relation of local to national history, and with it the way in
which category shifts affect memory. In a very real sense the old Berber chief-
tain's history was not his son's—not just in the sense of it not being his personal history but because for the son's generation the history of the new nation
of Morocco displaced almost all local history. Indeed, national history was local history. It was not just the difference in age of more than half a century or

the formal distance Arab men often keep from their fathers that accounted for their differential orientations. It was also that what the father was relating had never had to be heard because it did not define still-relevant relationships and with them the relevant memories for the son's generation.

By contrast the absence of the King's picture in the early 1990s signified an alteration in the nature of local history that could be seen in a number of other ways as well. For it symbolized less a protest against the monarch than a displacement of national history as the preeminent historical basis for one's own identity. It was true, of course, that a great many people had been put off by the long drawn-out war in the Sahara and the King's demands for money for the building of the huge new mosque complex in Casablanca, and they were still more prone to blame his ministers—rather than the King himself—for the surge in corruption that, as we saw earlier, is believed to have undercut civility and negotiation. But the King was not overtly excluded from their shop walls by way of protest. Rather he was rendered symbolically irrelevant as previously he had been regarded as symbolically central.[29] Disappointment in the use of education as a vehicle to a good job, hope for employment in the burgeoning private sector as opposed to reliance on public service jobs, and increased access to communications that transcend national boundaries had all contributed to an environment in which one's identity was less tied to the national course of events than had been true for the generation that remembered the days of the Protectorate.

This partial reversion to local history in place of national history manifests itself in various ways. In the 1960s, when I discussed history with men who came of age during the struggle for independence, they often spoke of the past using verbs of the imperfect tense, thus suggesting an ongoing process with which their lives were deeply entangled. Even much older men spoke in this way as they united their actions against the French in the early years of the century with contemporary national history. But in the 1990s the same men were speaking more often in the past perfect—of acts that are completed, acts that do not continue into the present.[30] Some of this may, of course, be a function of aging: Psychologists who study memory are largely in agreement that memories from one's youth have a particular stamp on memory in general.[31] But the choice of tenses literally configures the past, and it now does so in a way that perhaps indicates a deeper structural de-linkage—like the barely noticed departure of the King's image in the shops—among those elements of one's identity that were once so entwined with that of the state.

Earlier in this chapter I noted the partial shift—a kind of mild entropy—by which the ability to focus on the person as the fundamental unit through which negotiated ties are forged may have been undercut as the rules of the game itself began to change. This point connects with local versus national history/identity in another way. Commonly, among members of the Arab and Berber-speaking tribes of the Middle Atlas Mountains, settlements—like individuals—were known by several names, at least one of which was usually derived from the name of some noteworthy predecessor. During the course of several decades I could trace shifts in the way people referred to a given rural settlement. Thus in the 1960s one Berber fraction (*ferqa*) of the Ait Yusi tribe (*qebila*) was usually called I'awen (a name of apparently geographic origin, used by two other related lineages farther up in the Middle Atlas Mountains). By the early 1980s people sometimes referred to themselves by the name of one of their leading members, a big man in the making. The reference was sometimes made jokingly in his presence, sometimes with serious admiration when he was not around. (A similar settlement-name usage had occasionally been used for a predecessor big man, but when he became senile and childlike in his old age the usage quickly declined in favor of the younger man.) By the 1990s, however, dominant usage was concentrated on a third name, Boukherfan (Berber for "the sons of," or "the ones characterized by, the practice of herding sheep")—a name that had long been present in the array of names and one that emphasized the village men's success as dealers in sheep all over central Morocco.

These shifting emphases of name suggest that, as broader alliance is displaced by local figures and they in turn by activities that define the person more than does the constellation of power of their leading figure, the choice of names from an existing repertoire may vary. Moreover, memory itself begins to rely on somewhat different categories of perception. Where once one could get genealogical explanations for attachments among groups, now one gets statements about the economic ties that linked people to one another; where patterns of transhumance were described by real or imagined kinship, now trading patterns are more likely to be said to have derived from financial partnerships.[32] Such altered emphases obviously reflect current perceptions cast back into earlier times. But they also affect the way one tells the past, the categories through which particulars are kept in one's memory or edited out. Throughout the struggle for independence and the consolidation of the present monarchy as a modern bureaucratic state overseen by a master of political legerdemain, Moroccans could displace local history with national history, or at least elide the two. But as "the times" marked by the reign of Hassan II lasted for nearly four decades, and as the regime (first under the French and then under an independent government) became more centralized, an ironic possibility began to appear: though more centralized not all the occurrences could be attributed to the

King.[33] As a result, alternative explanations for events have had greater scope, and, in combination with other developments in the culture of explanation, the local could, for very different reasons than at earlier times in Moroccan history, begin to compete with national history. Put somewhat differently, as the routinization of the state and its limitations have increased, local history has once again begun to displace national history, or at least to render the national comprehensible in terms of the local.[34] It is not simply a case of *plus ça change*. Rather, the contest between local and national history underscores the gradual movement towards less certainty in interpersonal relations, less confidence that new relationships will perdure if worked out in terms of national attachment, and an increased sense that one's well-being and safety will have to be worked out locally with whatever means are now available.

ABSENT PRESENT: THE CASE OF THE JEWS

In memory everything seems to happen to music.
TENNESSEE WILLIAMS[35]

Rabat, Morocco—July, 1991   A Muslim friend takes me to a café operated by a Jew who has converted to Islam. Late in the evening the café owner sings old Jewish songs which the people who come to the café, all of them Muslims, know well and join in to sing. On each table sits a bottle of "Rabbi Jacob" wine (marked kosher for Passover in Hebrew on the label), and the food consists primarily of Jewish delicacies such as brain, tripe, spleen, and kidney. The songs are mostly laments for lost loves and tragic affairs of the heart. At the back of the room sit a couple of heavyset men in tight-fitting jackets. My friends say they are government agents who always come, whether to see if there is anything political in what is being sung or as a form of government protective presence. No one is intimidated by their presence and when I look over at them I notice that, inadvertently or not, they too are tapping their feet in time with the songs.

What is one to make of this brief encounter? There is, of course, a certain nostalgia involved in all of this, a kind of cultural curatorship exercised by Muslims who view Jewish culture as part of their own, now absent, environment. The presence of the Muslims may be a sort of affirmation of their own capacity for multivocalism—a more appropriate term perhaps than toleration—an attachment to the sheer pleasure of contemplating multifarious relationships when hearing multiple voices. Whatever else was true about them as desirable business partners, for many older Muslims the Jews were of considerable psychological importance. One could have a kind of emotional attachment to a Jew that was less possible with a Muslim, given the absence of full reciprocity with the former and the ever-present sense of obligation whenever dealing with fellow Muslims.[36] It is a relationship fraught with ambivalence—the quintessential test of Moroccan cultural assumptions about power, gender, circumstance, and personal ability. Everyone at the café knows that the owner's conversion to Islam is a fiction, but it is a shared fiction, like those forms of wordplay in which one is free to say things without literalness forcing rejoinder or confirmation.[37]

But it is also an odd sort of memory that attaches itself to a people who are all but gone. And it is, not surprisingly, a form of memory whose terms may have undergone some change as other categories by which the world is rendered comprehensible change. Jews were often spoken of in the 1960s, when there was still a significant number present in Sefrou, as a kind of limiting case: One remembered their still larger presence for the relationships they made possible and the proof their presence added to the general rules of relationship. Thus if there was no rainfall and the Jews performed a ritual, not unlike that of the Muslims, God (the Muslims said) would answer it because if even the Jews were praying the drought must be serious indeed. (I heard a similar attitude expressed by a medicine show quack in 1991 who thumped his naked chest and showed proof of his concoction's curative powers by claiming that "even a Jew aZicted with intestinal gas would be able to get rid of it with this medicine.") This use of the other as the limiting case that proves the main proposition— what Bernard Lewis has characterized more generally in Arab rhetoric as a trajetio ad absurdum, rather than a reductio ad absurdum argument38—signaled the way a stranger could serve as both mirror and verifier to the cosmological order and the Muslim's own sense of identity.

Jews were also the embodiment of mediation between and among the categories of the everyday. Precisely because they "did not count" in the sense of fully interchangeable reciprocity, they could stand between entities, drawing them together without actually mixing them together. When they were a significant presence in the population, Jews could pursue such trades as the working of metal or gold—because having a Jew enter one's home to fix a pipe was not as threatening as allowing a fellow Muslim to see the intimacies of the household, or to guess at the level of one's finances and commitments through the sale of jewelry or valuables. When the Jews departed, comments by Muslims about their absence often implied the loss of mediation: In Sefrou I have heard it said that since the Jews left the river no longer has as much water as it used to, while another told Clifford Geertz that with the departure of the French and the Jews "we have lost both our brains and our pockets."[39]

But by the 1990s, when younger people in particular had virtually no experience of the Jews, the terms had shifted. The Jew was seen, in contemporary and historical terms, less as a relational figure, a particular kind of person in the overall scheme of Moroccan person perception, than as a role, a placeholder, a category outside of direct relational and obligational bonds. Their presence in Morocco was retold not as the loss of valued trading partners and confidants but in a vague, diffuse, non-person-oriented way—as if the features of an acquaintance, even a real friend, had begun to fade with time. Muslims had never been obsessed with Jews, neither as test nor proof of their superiority or their religious truth,[40] and the functional role of the Jews, as intermediaries and confidants, largely fell into disuse as the "need" they once fulfilled became a need no more. Identification with international Arab politics muted the local recollection; the Jew as a local figure was being lost to sight. Whether it was in the people who mused on the absence of the Jews but could no longer regard them with specificity, or the audience at the apostate Jew's café, singing their songs but no longer visiting in their homes, a fog of unremembrance had begun to cloud any specific way of recalling the Jews. They have become a phantom memory, the felt presence of an absent limb. Like other aspects of personhood that have been undermined by the mundane forgetfulness of social displacement or the malign aspects of corruption, incivility, population displacement, and economic malaise, the picture of the Jew could not be called up with clarity when once meaningful categories, by which memories themselves are organized, no longer have persuasive force, when the only present is, to borrow the telling form of a Hebrew verb, an "absent present."[41]

LAYERS OF MEMORY

Remember the future, imagine the past.
CARLOS FUENTES[42]

> She laughed and told him a story about Degas, who was a firm believer in memory drawing. In Degas' ideal painting school, the first-year students would set up their easels on the first floor, where the model posed. The second-year students had their easels on the second floor, the third-year students on the third. The second- and third-year students would have to run down the stairs, study the model, then run back up the stairs and paint what they had seen. The more advanced the student the longer he would be required to remember his last glimpse of the model.[43]

The Arabic word for mankind is *al-insan,* "the forgetful ones." The reference is, of course, to humankind's capacity to forget the message brought by the

Prophet, as proved by those unbelievers to whom that message was brought (as tradition says it was brought to all peoples) but who subsequently forgot it. However, both memory and forgetfulness are differential: They depend not only on the justification a later age finds in recasting the past but on those subtle shifts by which experience is categorized and comprehended, which in turn affect the way in which the process of collective memory itself proceeds.

To some extent the Moroccan case recalls Bergson's notion of "habit memory" inasmuch as ruling conventions may edit out a part of one's cognizance and, by sheer force of replication in a variety of domains of life, lead individuals to downplay the forms of memory that accompanied earlier ways of recollecting.[44] But in Morocco it may not be change of habit that is at work. A better image may be that of a repertoire, or even of a set of sedimented layers, in which different cohorts and different circumstances may govern the choice of explanatory emphases that get applied to history as to other contexts. Certainly everyone does not remember the same, as memory-bearing sectors of the population die out or are displaced and "memory holes" begin to appear.[45] The operative community of memory in Morocco, however, is not a "community of memory" in the usual sense—bound together by memorial sites, rituals of remembrance, and reference to common sources of cultural stability.[46] Instead, the memory is that of the repertoire, the procedures for forging ties, the process of creating webs of indebtedness. In such a system details are constantly forgotten as each new alliance becomes the repository for remembering the rules of the game: Clever moves of the past are not remembered as such but serve as confirmations for the ability to maneuver in the present. Like the amoeboid structure of tribal organization itself, memory, by remaining diffuse, covers its own holes of specific forgetfulness within an overarching emphasis on the processual.[47] But when "civility" seems to die, when the rules of the game become unclear, when the ability to adapt is blocked by external factors, memory, as it were, backs up, becomes a memory of separable events or timeless values rather than a merged confirmation of the viability of the game. Then, as in Borges' *Funes, the Memorius,* people "may become incapacitated for rational deliberation and principled action by a surfeit of memory."[48] The signs that one may be entering a condition where memory operates under conditions of uncertainty are thus often linguistic and conceptual in nature.

Whether it is in the use of multiple names for a person, place, or group, the quest for multiple attachments to hedge against uncertainty, or the use of multiple vantages on the same situation to grasp its unrealized possibilities, the language of remembrance becomes open to the same contention for control as is true within any other domain of Moroccan life. If, however, people are beginning to speak a language of probability where before they spoke a language of authoritative opinion, or if causality is becoming detached from agents and beginning to be attributed to forces of nature, the marketplace, or political constructs, the way the past is framed by the same people over the course of a number of years can hardly be expected not to display some changes. My argument here, however, is not that such wholesale change has become regularized, much less institutionalized, in Moroccan life but that a shift in emphasis in the repertoire has begun to appear—more notably in the field of memory than in any other domain—and that this shift, affecting each cohort differentially, is at once characteristically Moroccan and potentially quite new.

In Moroccan culture, history is made at points of attachment (*ribaṭ*), those junctures of relationship where network formation, centered on a particular person, draws from a latent repertoire to become manifest in a social form. As the sense of control over those repertoires fluctuates, the sense of being able to partake of "the game" is jeopardized, and the past becomes not solely a revised vision of a present difficulty but a field on which new explanations of what people and actions are really like can be explored, contested, and rethought. Personal memory has not, as some have argued for the workers of France, been confiscated or diluted—the history of something like a labor movement having displaced national memory and become a kind of official memory.[49] Even the diminution of identifying oneself with national history in favor of local memory is not a full-scale eradication of the former from the repertoire of alternatives. But as the structures of cultural perception shift it remains to be seen—as perhaps the case of the Jews suggests—whether new habits will leave certain structures so attenuated that they will have little to attract people to their use. This may occur when, as we have seen, those person-centered points of attachment so central to Moroccan cultural expectations are undercut by bureaucracies admitting of none of the networking save that which money alone can buy.

This may help to explain why some of the markers of time—those that conjoin person with period, as well as the layering of packets of time depending on their bearing on current relationships—may themselves be subject to alteration. Unlike earlier breaks, where social disorder threatened and old alliances came under intense pressure, recent events seldom involve cataclysmic breaks. It may have been that people created opportunities for such breaks in the past, but it was precisely King Hassan II's extraordinary ability to play individuals and interests against one another that has rendered such climaxes almost nonexistent in modern Morocco. The advantage to authoritarianism is that, being brittle, it is possible for breaks to occur: A cunningly benevolent form of authoritarianism, however, leaves people "tied up" (*thqaf*, as the Moroccans say: "powerless, immobilized, unmanned") so that no new set of arrangements can take place.[50] Ideas of probability and shifts in notions of causation or responsibility may occur, but until they become institutionalized, until they reverberate across a number of cultural domains, until, perhaps, the very notion of time itself is altered, the markers of sharp breaks will lack real force and amplitude—like a gun that is jammed or only fires blanks—and markers for such opportunistic change will not be noted.

One very important consequence of the emphasis on a repertoire is that, at least thus far, Moroccans do not seem to feel they have lost control of their own history. Nostalgia for some glorious Arab past is not part of the Moroccan sense of memory: Even ceremonies of collective memory are few in number and of rather little importance by comparison to the standard holidays of the Muslim calendar.[51] In a sociopolitical system that focuses so intensely on the person, attempting to turn the personalized into the archetypal would be to undermine the very foundations of legitimacy. To the contrary, many cultural forms conduce to an emphasis on contemporary relatedness: Cemeteries may be re-used after forty years since few people still go for meals among their dead after that, old victories or bargains are not incessantly related, saints are regarded as alive within their tombs hence relationship is possible with them, and the simple profession of faith can insure that the Prophet will include the deceased among those for whom he vouches on the Day of Judgment. Tales told in the marketplace or around the hearth or café are not so much exemplars of "principled irresolution"—instances of structured incoherence—as the proof of process, moments of disambiguation, when moral precepts and personal cleverness draw from the pool of available ties to give effect to a moment of consolidated power.[52] "Screen memory," if such a thing exists at the collective level, condenses to the present game: Old victories or deals are compressed and inserted into the results of the next sequence of relationships, and one is only as good as one's last performance, not the one before last.[53] The cultural emphasis falls quite squarely on the currency of relationships as the key index for the categorization of events in compartments of the past.

Change, of course, can be very subtle—as when one is no longer able to attribute intentions on the basis of knowledge of another's background, or where responsibility is loosed from agency and attributed to outside causes. Cohorts may differ in the ways their interpretations of the past are affected by the changing structures of memory; individuals may recast their versions of past events less to fit the present to it than because a revised common sense has shifted the sense of what human relations are like or how events are connected.[54] Memory, always at work under conditions of uncertainty, here becomes both creator and result of the struggle for ways of grasping experience. Watching the same people remembering over the course of many years and watching them grapple with the very concepts by which memory is captured and revised constitutes a critical test of the range and validity of ideas by means of which a people seeks to understand its own sense of identity. It is indeed difficult to determine at the moment of its occurrence whether the change signaled by alterations in terminology and recollection is indeed fundamental. What is, however, somewhat clearer is that, in Sefrou as throughout Morocco, memory itself is one of he crucial domains in which the struggle for a sense of contemporary reality is very much in play.

Have the Arabs Changed Their Mind?

The concepts a culture may develop concerning the nature or accessibility of another's interior state can never be seen entirely in isolation. However refined the language for the discernment of intent, however erudite the claims made to its apprehension, the very concepts of intent and motivation are embedded in a series of related conceptual domains with which they share certain implications and constraints. If, then, one asks whether ideas of intentionality in a particular culture may be undergoing significant change, one has to face not only the difficult issue of how to recognize change while it is actually occurring but also the issue of how changes in intentionality relate to those in connected realms.

In some societies, the domains of religion and sociopolitical life may be demarcated precisely by the projected impenetrability of another's mind, thus making it difficult for those one does not trust—questionable neighbors, centralized powers, or the unpredictable promptings of one's own emotional states—to gain access to some deeper self through one's motives or intentions. In other societies, however—those of the Arabs among them—domains such as intent are so deeply connected to the concatenation of conceptual domains through which a person is known that whatever happens to one set of concepts is likely to affect many others as well.

It is for this reason that the present essay questions whether anything has led the Arabs of Morocco—and perhaps those in other parts of the Arab and Muslim world—to change their concept of intent in recent decades, and it does so by moving the inquiry outside the realm of intent alone to consider whether similar shifts are also taking place in the concepts of probability, causality, and responsibility. If concepts of intent are redefined by profession-alized groups, if the metaphors by which the minds of others are said to be grasped turn on new and changing images, or if the presuppositions on which trust among members of a family or tribe is based come to be eroded, then the discernment of others' mental states may be expected to show systemic alter-ations. But if existing concepts appear able to absorb change without them-selves being changed, how are we to know whether any fundamental shift has really occurred—and how are we to think about the ways in which concepts such as intent operate when change itself is rendered problematic? ๑๑๑๑๑๑๑

Social scientists who are interested in the process of cultural change have a number of serious problems with which to contend. Lacking a suitable taxon-omy of the multifarious forms of cultural change, and lacking good theories to help us discern change while it is actually happening, we find it difficult to dis-tinguish deep, fundamental conceptual shifts from mere variation, evanescent alteration, or misleading occurrence.

As the sources for our understanding of history and social process have moved from the acts of potentates and politicians to the rituals of impover-ished peasants and the cosmological musings of the illiterate, the study of fun-damental cultural change—whether it be called "the history of *mentalités*" or "the archaeology of knowledge"—still leaves anthropologists with some feel-ing of envy of their historian colleagues. For as difficult as it may be to recon-struct the past and discern order in its many strands, a no less daunting task confronts the student of contemporary society when he or she asks whether what is still taking place amounts to a fundamental shift in the culture under study.

These difficulties have been exacerbated within the discipline of anthro-pology itself, which has long eschewed any claim to predictive power and has been guarded in its approach to history, lest present structures appear as de-terministic ends. It seems that in the study of sociocultural change, as in their encouragement of it, anthropologists tend, as Lévi-Strauss once quipped, to be radicals at home and conservatives abroad.

And yet, in the course of the last two decades, as I have watched the social and cultural life of Morocco and, indirectly, of the Arab world at large, I have found myself asking whether any of the things I have observed amounts to a fundamental change in the culture of this region. One can, of course, point to all sorts of major developments: the staggering growth in population, the movement away from extended-family residence patterns, the increasing com-mercialization of agriculture, the impact of widespread migrant labor and relative depopulation of the countryside, the widening gap between rich and poor. Such changes are undoubtedly crucial, and their importance cannot be underestimated. But that is not quite what I am after.

What I want to know is whether there has also taken place any significant alteration in some of the basic concepts by which many people in Morocco and elsewhere in the Arab world view others, comprehend the nature of their ties to one another, and envision the ordering principles by which a coherent social life is rendered possible. I want to know whether, in the face of so many changes in their political, economic, and social lives, they have also come to think differently about why things happen the way they do or what it is that people really must be like. I want, in sum, to know whether things that once seemed obvious have come to lack persuasive force—whether what was once a matter of common sense is giving way to a different sense of what should be considered true.

It is not, therefore, revolutionary change that concerns me—the wholesale alteration of an entire worldview. Instead, I am concerned with changes in that difficult-to-define middle level of culture—the level that lies above the range of individual variation yet below that of cataclysmic reconstruction, the level in which the categories of ordinary experience perform their everyday work. On a number of occasions I have wondered if I was indeed confronting intimations of such deep-seated change.

I have particularly thought about this in regard to a series of concepts that have seemed to cry out for notice in Arab culture, concepts that may be taken up (at the risk of resembling the chapter headings of an introductory philosophy textbook) under the categories of certainty and probability, causality, responsibility, and—most importantly for purposes of this essay—intentionality. Because each label fits readily the categories employed by Arabs themselves, and because each bears a definite relationship to the others, focusing on these central concepts can provide a worthwhile test for the telltale pulse of change in the culture of the modern Arab world.

PROBABILITY AND RELATED CONCEPTS

How people describe the world and how the discourse of description is itself composed are intimately connected to what people largely assume to be certain or likely and to the way in which various levels of assurance about the world can be gained. Throughout these essays we have been seeing that, in the case of Morocco and perhaps of the Arab world at large, these concepts are deeply intertwined with a view of human society as personalistic and contractual. This orientation suffuses assumptions about human nature and social order, personal character and individual psychology, time and the calculation of what is possible. What is central to the entire system is a repertoire of concepts and relationships all grounded in the assumption that human beings are essentially proprietary and contracting creatures, that a person's social identity is determined by the relationships the person services and creates, and that to deal in the world one must try to know as much as possible about others' relationships and how they may be fit into one's own network of associations.

Everywhere one turns in Arab culture, one encounters an emphasis on the person as the embodiment of a distinctive set of situated qualities and relationships: in the idea that God only punishes sins when they become so public that they have adverse effects on social networks, in the constant need to organize the community against the threat of chaos born of unchecked passion, in the differentiation of men and women for their inherent capacity to acquire knowledge, and in the belief that the harm one does—and the punishment it deserves—increases as the scope of one's network of affiliations expands within society.

For the Arabs, as we have seen in various contexts, the person is not, as he or she is imagined in the West, a self-fashioned entity, an individual who possesses both the capacity and the right to formulate moral concepts or for whom the privacy of thoughts and values may be treated as sacrosanct. Rather, for Arabs the person is the amalgamation of a complex and shifting set of attachments to others, by virtue of which his or her own qualities, forms of interaction, and basic affiliations may be known to others.

It is for this reason that in stories, chronicles, and ordinary discussions people are described predominantly in terms of the situations in which they have been involved—what they have said and done—rather than what they think or feel, the composition of their individual psyches. Seeing others like gems turned in the light, one knows them from their situated encounters, not from some set of abstract qualities. And because humans exist only in social context, it is not chronological time that reveals the truth of persons but persons who reveal the truth of events. Stories therefore often shift back and forth in time, focusing less on serial order than on showing the varied contexts of action and relationship that reveal the attributes and connections of any person.

It is in the light of this cultural emphasis that the concepts of certainty and probability take on a particular shape. For Arabs, the acquisition of knowledge is supremely valued, but knowledge is seen less in terms of what is known than in terms of who knows it. The Qur'an delineates only a few unquestionable verities. Moreover, like the authoritative traditions that describe the actions and utterances of the Prophet, the Qur'an specifies the outcomes of many endeavors but leaves open both the means for their accomplishment and the exact features that favor one or another result. The quest for certitude where God has not spoken leads inevitably to individuals who demonstrate by the successful fabrication of their social networks that they indeed possess knowledge of spiritual and worldly matters.

Numerous examples support the proposition that knowledge is always perceived in relationship to the person who knows it. Thus, the value of a Prophetic Tradition depends upon the chain of relators of that tradition, whose garnered respect gives credence to their transmission. So, too, the believability of news depends on the reputation the speaker has earned through his connections with others. And the accuracy of any description of facts depends mainly on the reliability of the witness. Truth in ordinary affairs is pragmatically defined: The emphasis is on what works, what vitalizes ties among men, what acts and deeds circumscribed by social convention yield up human sociality and freedom from social chaos. To know whether something is so, therefore, it is necessary to consider persons more than occurrences. It is the one who notices, not the thing noticed, that counts; it is not a "fact" that comes to one's attention, but someone's attention that is drawn to a fact.

It is against this background that people speak about the likelihood of events. When Moroccans refer to events, they tend to speak in binary terms of occurrence and nonoccurrence. In calculating outcomes, they speak in bold antitheses: crops succeed or they fail, allies remain faithful or prove unfaithful, the times are just or they are not. And answers to the question "What happened?" are couched in terms of persons: "He said" and "he did" are the common focuses of description, rather than sequences of events. Probing into the complexities of this traditional mode of thought in domains such as medicine, magic, politics, and sexuality, the anthropologist looking for signs of change may quickly encounter seeming evidence of significant alteration. Several examples may serve as illustrations.

A number of years ago I accompanied an old man with whom I had worked for more than a decade on a visit to a garden he owned just outside the central Moroccan city in which he lived. I had been in the garden many times, but it was only after I had come to realize that my old friend was not, despite his traditional style of dress and his politics, opposed to the use of Western technological innovations, that I was prompted to ask why he used manure on his crops rather than the readily available and, as he himself acknowledged, perfectly affordable fertilizer. His answer—one I was to hear from many other farmers—was that "fertilizer burns up the earth"; it necessitates greater use of water for the crops, and once it is employed one cannot easily convert back to using manure. How, I asked, did he know this? His answer was couched not in terms of his own experience but by reference to the opinion of others whom he respected. For him, the crucial piece of information was who else said it was so. It was not that he would deny the evidence of his own eyes; rather, such "facts" had to be authenticated, rendered capable of being comprehended, by being linked to what particular others told him or what came through a chain of relators in whom he had confidence because of the nature of their own social links. For this man, the question that had to accompany even what he could see for himself was "Who says so?" Infinite regress is stopped by finite persons of reliability; personal forcefulness is accommodated by mustering a network of social obligations such that others will regard oneself as a reliable opinion holder.

The way such matters are phrased—and the change in their phrasing over time—is significant. In the past, colloquial Moroccan Arabic usage of terms such as *imken* and *warrabemma*, usually translated by Westerners as "likely," "possible," or "probable," did not substitute for statements of relative frequency. Instead, they generally appeared in contexts in which the source of authority for a statement was unclear or in which the speaker had not yet marshaled opinion through ties of obligation, so that the speaker was reluctant to make an unqualified assertion. Events were either asserted sharply or denied, for the intermediate qualities of what Westerners call likelihood were but signs of the imperfection of a claim; they signaled the nebulous quality of an assertion to which the consequences of claimed truth were not attached.

And yet for my old friend, as well as for many younger men and women, the concepts by which outcomes are calculated may be undergoing a significant change. Whereas in the past the discourse was largely one of occurrence versus non-occurrence, there have begun to appear overtones of the possibility for increasing the chances for one or another result. Speaking of agricultural success, people used to say that three or four years out of every seven would be favorable. Now one hears more reference to what can be done to increase the frequency of positive outcomes. Similarly, in politics and law, reference is made more explicitly to the connection one event may have to another and how the arrangement of the sequence may affect the results.

Now the everyday Moroccan use of the Arabic terms *imken* and *warrabemma* appear in contexts where claims for the truth of something are less sharply dichotomized. People speak of a situation as being "maybe" so or "likely" as a way of addressing how often it turns out a certain way. What "may be" is expressed in terms of what affects the distribution of its occurrence—

surrounding events, world conditions, the acts of unknowable others—and not just in terms of whether it is so. The question thus arises whether some "frequentist" concept of probability is beginning to creep into Moroccan culture, either through outside influence or through a reconfiguration of indigenous conceptions. In addressing this question it may prove useful to keep in mind the process by which Western ideas of certainty and probability shifted during the seventeenth century.

In Europe before the seventeenth century, the idea of probability—the likelihood of events—was identified with the idea of authoritative opinion. As Ian Hacking has shown, not only did the word "probability" generally mean the approval of an opinion by a noted authority, but also, because there was no developed concept of evidence as something that could be provided by things, even the testimony of one's senses depended for its credibility on the observations of recorded authority.[1] During the seventeenth century, however, these concepts began to change. In a host of domains, from religion and rhetoric to law and science, the concept of certainty began to become more relative and complex.

As Barbara Shapiro has argued, a shift in the categories within which knowledge itself was defined made it possible for contradictory perceptions, varied interpretations of scripture, and alternative demonstrations of legal proof to be embraced in a language that maintained a sense of cosmological orderliness even as it introduced a new basis for discussing that order. Whereas true knowledge had once been a unified concept coincident with absolute certainty, now a continuum that ran from "mere opinion" through "highly probable" to "moral certainty" allowed forms of knowledge to acquire the stature and standards by which they could be applied to a wide range of phenomena.[2] In time, the boundaries between moral certainty and probability as well as those between knowledge and opinion began to erode. Investigations in all fields of knowledge gave rise to a preoccupation with matters of fact and to the consequent diminution of the equation between what one could reasonably believe and the opinions of wise men. The direct assessment of things themselves became an increasingly common orientation.[3]

There is, of course, no reason why Moroccan or Arab cultural history would have to follow that of the West, and notwithstanding outside intrusion the meaning of any altered concepts may not be truly consonant with their meaning in Western culture. Indeed, there is every reason to believe that the elaborated Arab concept of probability is largely an independent development rather than one borrowed from the West: Arab cultures have always shown an emphasis on the way things interact with other things, even though the preeminent meaning drawn from such interactions is couched in terms of the relationships among people that result from relations among things.[4]

Whether it is in the greater tendency in courts to hear circumstantial evidence, or in talk among farmers about what must be done to assist new strains of seed, an elaborated language of events can be discerned in the Arab world that may presage a turn from opinion to observation, and with it a shift to images of probability that have certain parallels to those found in Western culture. Thus one hears events described in terms of the relationship of one event to another and of the "likelihood" of various events occurring in combination or sequence. What appears at first sight to be missing from these discussions and comments is reference to who says this is so. It is as if the referent for that which "may be" is not a particular person's evaluation but the nature and frequency of physical occurrences irrespective of their human assessment.

If such a change is taking place, however, it is unlikely—or so the common assumption among theorists of cultural change would appear to hold—that it would occur in conceptual isolation. Before suggesting whether a shift in the idea of probability is indeed under way, let me turn to the second of my categories, namely, causality.

Truth, certainty, and the assessment of outcomes, it has been argued, have, for the Arabs, traditionally been seen in intensely personalistic terms. So, too, it appears, has their basic conceptualization of causal relations. Elsewhere I have invoked the image of the marketplace in describing Arab society as a set of negotiated encounters shaped by family, circumstance, and personal vigor.[5] Just as in the market, where a price means nothing until it is accepted in a recognizable way, utterances about relationship come into the realm of truth only when that quality is added to them through their pronouncement by a reliable witness, their validation by a holy oath, the performance of an act of ritual constraint, or the recognition that new ties have been formed in reliance on another's representations. The world is thus seen as quintessentially relational, as being described by the ties among sentient beings that bring still further relationships into existence. Causality is largely a matter of agency, of the actions of reasoning beings, and thus a proper explanation of what happened is incomplete without considering who was involved in its occurrence—both in initiating the event and in experiencing its consequences. What is downplayed is the sense that events cause other events.

This does not, of course, mean that Arabs are unaware that heat melts ice or fire burns wood irrespective of who is around at the time.[6] Pushed to it, Arabs will usually avoid the troublesome issues of the nature of essence or the logic of infinite regress by asserting that even ostensibly physical events have their immediate or ultimate cause in divine action. It is as if common sense had largely come to accept not the Aristotelianism of an Avicenna—that even God acts through a necessary set of causal relations such that things possess qualities that affect other things—but the view of a Ghazzali—that all acts ultimately require the imposition of will, and even repeated events gain their apparently mechanical regularity from the beholder's knowledge of their normal habits.[7]

Modern medicine could, therefore, be readily assimilated to existing beliefs because it is Allah who grants a physician the knowledge to see a regularity that may cure a patient. For the same reason, courts of law assume it is normal for mothers to be good custodians of their children, place confidence in competent contracting parties, or consider people to be ignorant, say, of house values unless they have specific knowledge of that sector of the market. Certainly in matters that affect the formation of networks of obligation, and even in the commonsense assessment of ultimate physical causation, it is the element of will, of agency, of reason itself that forms the keystone to the discourse of causation.

And yet here, too, change may be at work. People may now be more willing to see events as causing other events without needing to posit the intercession of human will at every stage. Thus the rhetoric of economics, of the patterned force of events, and of the structural consequences of one or another ideology may now be found in political discussions alongside the argument from personality or the claim to more effective networks that can be turned to the benefit of one's constituency. Judges, too, seem more prepared to hear circumstantial evidence rather than rely exclusively on proof by witnesses, oaths, or presumptions about human conduct. Whether in Morocco or in Saudi Arabia, judges have been known to cite the Qur'anic version of the story of Joseph and Potiphar's wife (Sura 12:23–29) in support of their use of such evidence. For unlike the Old Testament version of that tale, in which Joseph is imprisoned when the rebuffed wife falsely accuses him of assault, in the Qur'an the woman's own kinsman proves her story false when he notices that Joseph's garment is torn from behind, which could only have occurred if he was trying to escape the woman's advances rather than attack her.[8] I recall quite vividly a trial I watched in a Moroccan court in which a man was accused of striking an old woman at a shrine. The court, which might otherwise have moved quickly to the use of a decisory oath,[9] first weighed the woman's observable injuries against the man's claim that she had tripped, and then found that the man's account of the events did not fit the perceived injuries. If, for whatever reason—Western influence, dissolution of traditional social bonds, the erosion of confidence in reliable supporters—there is beginning to enter Arab culture a view of causation that grants less centrality to persons than to things, the first signs might be evident in just such instances as this.

What may be true for causality could be true for the concept of responsibility as well. It has been a central tenet of Islam that, to borrow Franz Rosenthal's phrasing again, "man was seen . . . as the center of action in this world."[10] This position depends heavily on the belief that humans are reasoning creatures and that it is within human power to control the tendency towards forgetfulness and misguided passion that threatens all society with chaos. (Indeed, as we have seen, the word in Arabic for human beings, *al-insan,* means "the forgetful ones," that is, those who easily stray from what God has told them.)

This emphasis on reason, will, and the responsible exercise of choice is readily discernible in a number of cultural domains. In literature and storytelling, repetition is used to demonstrate that at each point a full assessment of circumstances remains incumbent on each rational person and that replication and habit are matters of choice and hence demand responsible attention. In the Arab concept of time, each moment, identified as it is with the individuals whose acts describe it, is the enactment of the choice—and the responsibility for that choice—that yields the attachments by which a person is known and the times are made just. This same emphasis on responsible action is also evident in the constant assertion that it is not people who change—who fashion their own psyches or beliefs—but the situations of relationship in which they place themselves. By putting oneself in the company of wise teachers, good leaders, or honorable compatriots, the possibilities and constraints inherent in human reason may be shaped to the requirements of a true community of believers.

As we have seen, these propositions gain further meaning when the cultural logic of their implications is traced more fully. To the Arabs it follows, for example, that if men can increase their stature and security by acquiring the knowledge that creates useful relationships, then the more extensive one's networks, the more harm one's actions are capable of doing. When people who are more learned and well-connected go astray, they should, therefore, be punished more heavily than those who are less knowledgeable because the damage they do, in fact and as exemplars, is necessarily greater. So, too, the range of excuses for a person's actions is in most instances quite limited, because what one is held responsible for is not what lay behind a deed so much as what it led to.

Arab culture thus places a strong emphasis on the consequences of actions, not on their antecedents. Responsibility goes not to the question of causation—the interplay of persons and "facts"—but to that of outcome—the interplay of situation and result. Kinsmen may be held co-liable and individuals may be held to a standard of strict liability, all without contradicting the idea of responsibility, because what one is responsible for is the enactment and repercussions of one's situated personhood in the scheme of interlocking obligations by which society constitutes itself against chaos.

But may not all this too be changing? The diminution of co-residential, kin-based bonds, with their capacity to insure individuals against unforeseen burdens, the introduction of legal codes that restrict the range of excuses—for example, in cases of wife beating—and the geographic movement of individuals that makes perception based on social background and connections more tenuous could be contributing to a shift from responsibility as a calculus of consequence to responsibility as a coincidence of motive and event.

Again, the clues lie predominantly in the realm of language. Where once it was enough to specify a person's kinsmen, place of origin, and customary practices, now people grope for descriptive terms that will adequately suggest how and why individuals act as they do and hence what can be expected of them. What once could be embraced by the shorthand reference of a name or physical symbol—and with it, a sense of assessing persons by assessing a knowable set of attributes—may now be so uncertain that when people speak about what a man can be held responsible for they focus on indicators of wealth and occupation rather than social background. Thus, as the indicators of a man's identity change, the ways in which harm and responsibility are appraised could be shifting as well.

If alterations are indeed occurring in the domains I have already discussed, signs of their impact might also be expected to appear in the last—and, for present purposes, the most central—of my four cultural categories, intentionality. The Arabic word for intention, *niya,* means not only "will," "volition," and "plan," but, because it is said to come directly from within a person and may express unimpeded devotion, niya also means "simple," "naïve," and "sincere."[11] Each prayer begins with the statement of the niya, the intent of a devout act, just as, in ordinary discourse, people speak of the state of mind that informs another's deeds.

But whereas in the modern West intent is regarded as separable from deeds and capable of being analyzed as an internal dynamic or a source of moral standards, in Arab culture another's mind is regarded as directly evident in words and acts and therefore as neither significantly private nor inscrutable. A judge in Saudi Arabia can write that "just by looking at a suspect [the judge] should be able to tell what the man had concealed in his testimony."[12] A Moroccan merchant can say that if you know a man's background you know his niya too. For purposes of interaction, all that matters about another's mind is available in his record of situated acts—his origins, associations, and range of knowledge—which is as readily understandable to the experienced eye as is the blush on the skin or the tremor in the pulse to the Western observer of emotion and intent.[13]

But as relationships and concepts change, this interpretive scheme may itself be giving way. If background and past affiliations are unknown, the capacity to impute intent—and, no less crucially, the ability to instill it—may weaken. Where once Moroccans said that "if you know a man's background you know his niya," one hears that "now even people who have real social roots (*asel*) lack niya." In the markets, cafes, and legal proceedings stereotypes of others often fill gaps in the information once vital to assessing others. Niya is still the dominant word, but whereas people twenty years ago were comparatively inarticulate about what went into its recognition (because it was so much a matter of common sense), now the discussions evoked by the word seem more self-conscious, effusive, and evaluative as its interconnected meanings seem less tightly integrated, known, and shared. The calculation of outcome, the analysis of causality, and the attribution of responsibility may be changing as the centrality of the person is itself subjected to forces of profound and unforeseeable implication.

CAPTURING CHANGE

And yet is deep cultural change really occurring? I think the answer is no. This answer is limited both by our factual knowledge of the Middle East and by the uncertain state of our theoretical apparatus, and my argument will, therefore, be made with somewhat greater force than conviction. But I think it will be useful not only to state my reasons as sharply as I can but also to suggest what might be necessary for such a transformation actually to occur and what all this may mean for the way we think about the nature of cultural change.

Fundamental change in the concepts that inform a culture can come about (among other possibilities) either by a true alteration of their referents (and, by implication, their connections among existing concepts) or by their actual replacement. The shift in meanings and implications that etymologists and philologists may note in a language exemplify the former; the repercussions of a social and political revolution, the latter. In the Arab world, neither has occurred in recent times. Indeed, the Arabo-Islamic system of thought has proved enormously effective in absorbing and amalgamating conceptual shifts without giving up its characteristic structures or modes of incorporation.

Consider once more the concepts with which we have been concerned. Studies by philosophers and psychologists of lay judgments of probability show that, for Westerners, statements about probability are really claims about "something out there," representations of an objectively verifiable set of facts. For the Arabs, with their equally varied vocabulary of likelihood, chance, expectation, and possibility, the point of reference is not what is said but the reliability of the person saying it.[14]

In the West, propositions about probability have looked increasingly towards short-range sequences and reflected a diminution of the specifics with which we describe ultimate results. Whether they forecast the trends in our markets, the state of tomorrow's weather, or the trajectory of our moral life, ordinary statements of probability are played out against a limited sequence within which any calculations of certainty can be composed. By contrast, the Arabs, emphasizing the largely unchanging character of human nature and only the broad outline of divinely ordained results, insist that the likelihood of particular occurrences is dependent on the exercise of someone's free will. To calculate the probability of short-term events, it is not sequence that is crucial but the types of relationships that are involved.[15] And the typology of attachments itself exists not as an abstract set but only as living embodiments in particular lives. The result is an enormously supple conceptual system. The claim that the Qur'an is not only God's unaltered word but includes reference to all events—from the advances of modern medicine to the landing of men on the moon—coupled with the discourse of situated persons that pervades all areas of social life, gives the Arabs a powerful instrument for analyzing both near and distant events. And because the rights and obligations God leaves to men to arrange among themselves are not seen as standing apart from the claims of the Almighty but as embraced by—as an essential part of—His own powers, there need be no discrepancy between most human acts and their determinate results. Knowing that the likelihood of occurrences is assessed by assessing individuals, the replicated contexts of their interaction, and the knowledgeability of men of high repute, it comes as little surprise that the predominant word in Arabic for "probability" (*muraja*) means not only "likelihood" but also "repetition" and "authority."

Moreover, the common Western idea that statements of probability work predominantly to qualify or guard our assertions need not play so major a role in Arab culture. For if utterances may, like a price in the market, be offered without truth attaching to them until they receive separate validation, much of the need for guarded probability statements is preempted.[16] Similarly, it may be because they see no disjunction between the ordering principles of the world of men and that of the supernatural that Arabs could envision this world as subject to regularities of bargaining and alliance building that have been assigned to humanity, rather than seeing the world, as did the ancient Greeks, as ruled by irregular forces for which even an incipient mathematics could not dare to calculate probabilistic occurrence.[17] For the Arabs, the metaphors of the marketplace and the contract have proved to be powerfully absorptive vehicles by which authority and attachment could prevail over images of frequency and impersonality.

This resilient and incorporative scheme, with its stress on persons and networks, also leaves little need for a different vision of causation. R. G. Collingwood's assertion that we distinguish causes from mere conditions when we can exercise control over results is, notwithstanding the fact that we often seek causes for matters we cannot affect, a useful distinction:[18] It underscores the fact that people may attribute causes differently if their levels of control vary. In the Arab case, the emphasis on persons as causal agents is so well integrated with the concept of social and cosmological order that relatively little room is left for a causality based exclusively on a vision of underlying, mechanistic forces.

The Arabs, as we have seen, place great stress on face-to-face relations. In its Moroccan variant saints are said to be alive in their tombs and to respond to direct contact, news is believable if a chain to an eyewitness can be fashioned, and strangers construct a set of personal linkages rather than probe for occupational or economic indicators as they try to grasp who another is.[19] For Moroccans, like many others in the Middle East, those who come before or after in time may establish Collingwood's mere conditions, and those contemporaries we never meet may shape the contexts of our interaction, but only those we encounter face-to-face or through an imagined chain can have consequences that affect our own network of ties. Typologies and particulars merge as classes of events are distinguished not by whether sentient beings are somewhere involved in their course—for even the most "impersonal" events involve an ultimate act of God—but by the distinctiveness of the enactor. To know, therefore, that things are linked causally is, in this scheme, not to drive out the role of the actor but to amalgamate the person and the event by asserting who it is that knows this to be so and whose relationships this instantiated knowledge will affect.

The Arabs have not, therefore, had to accept or refashion a concept of evidence for themselves: They can continue to employ the evidence of men and relationships even for events. Consider again the story of Joseph and Potiphar's wife. Westerners might take the point of the Qur'anic version to be that linkages among physical facts may reveal a chain of events and hence the truth. But the Qur'an draws quite a different lesson from the tear in Joseph's cloak, namely, that women are by nature a perfidious lot and men must not be misled even by their own kinswomen. Similarly, whereas in the West circumstantial evidence of this sort would go to the question of physical causality, it is employed by contemporary Arab judges to cast further light on the modes of relating to others that characterize the parties involved. Even in the case of the injured woman mentioned earlier, the judge was not satisfied to stop his inquiry with an assessment of the physical injuries. He returned immediately to asking who these people were—where they were from, to whom they were attached—because he obviously felt more certain of his ability to assess them as persons than he did to evaluate the circumstantial evidence.

It is true, moreover, that for the Arab world, as for premodern Europe, the stress on opinion entails certain assumptions about both evidence and assent.[20] But whereas for Europeans the evidence that was obtained began to challenge concepts that were unable to contain and assimilate new claims, for the Arabs the contradictions have not been so unavoidably presented. If each person is different and the difference is knowable, then it is possible to judge people without recourse to an objective standard like that of "the reasonable man." If everyone knows that atheism yields chaos because it means the abandonment of reason and reason's grasp of God's articulated scheme, then it is possible to use the denial of atheism to reassert that what man knows is always attached to reason. And the test of reason, the proof of its existence, is not deductively producible results but the garnering of support in recognition of one's knowledgeability. For Arabs, the merging of knowledge, person, network, and opinion serves more to maintain than to shift paradigms. And it has thus far maintained them in a fashion that absorbs substantive propositions by making them meet the test of socially forged opinion.

Sir Hamilton Gibb once characterized the Arabs as possessing a quality of double-mindedness, the ability to hold two contradictory propositions simultaneously—like saying everything is in God's hands and here is what we are going to do about it.[21] No doubt one could say of any Arab, as Thoreau said of people generally, that each man's life is a mass of contradictions. It would be folly to attempt to reduce any culture to a pristine set of logically consistent propositions. But if one tries to grasp why something that appears contradictory in one culture poses no such problem in another, one cannot help but note that in many Arab societies the resources needed to build networks and garner reliability are multiple and diverse. One person may build from inherited ties, another by capturing rhetorically the terms of discussion, and a third from the acquisition of worldly goods. The patterns and results will be distinctive because the modes of attribution and formation are culturally distinctive. What matters for our present purposes is simply that because these resources are so diverse, it is difficult for any one person or group to capture them utterly and thus difficult to envision society as limited, fixed, or zero-sum in nature. Arabs are no more double-minded than they are single-minded. They have so far simply managed to maintain a set of assimilative concepts and their attendant institutions with sufficient success that they have been able to avoid altering at least the fundamental concepts discussed here without eliminating some of the new information that alternative concepts have presented.[22] Another way to see this point is through the Arab metaphor of the game.

If there is any image that comes to mind when thinking of Arab culture it is that of an elaborate game of skill. "Know ye," says the Qur'an (57:19), "that this world's life is a sport, and pastime, and show." It is a theme that has run through the whole course of Islamic thought. In the earliest days of Islam, scholars debated the nature of this pastime, and their choice of image carried vast theological implications. Adherents of a game of chance called *nard*, apparently played with dice, argued that it was both permissible and desirable as a pastime because it coincided in its form with the Prophetic vision of the world as wholly determined by God. The game's dependence on pure chance, its outcome determined and known only to the Almighty, was similar to the submission and trust that humans must place in God. Proponents of the game of chess, however, argued that their pursuit relied on human choice and ingenuity and, within the framework of limiting rules, proclaimed that God intends for man to benefit by his reason and to triumph over his opponent. The result of this debate, as Franz Rosenthal has said, is that "the Muslim case against nard has always been stronger than the one against chess," and contemporary Arabs are quick to point to the enduring symbolism of chess in human affairs.[23]

For the outside observer, too, the game image is a useful one when contemplating the capacity of Arab culture to absorb and thus rebuff certain forms of cultural change. For if one sees Arab social organization and its attendant conceptual structure as one in which individuals negotiate within and through a series of informing conventions, then, as in a game of chess, one can see how it is possible to be caught up in the endless variety of play without ever feeling the need to change the basic rules. The "Great Game" in Arab culture crosscuts politics, religion, family life, and art, linking them as elements in a structure that can contain every level of ability and a deep-felt sense of incorporation. The image of the chess game is not only a metaphor for life employed by the

Arabs themselves but an analog for that cultural resilience by which creativity is engendered and contained and the present world made consonant with the world beyond.

If the particular bases for uncertainty have changed for many Arabs, the expectation of social uncertainty has not. Attitudes and institutions that have garnered staying power over the years have been based, in no small part, on the assumption that the world is uncertain and only the careful coalescence of strategic attachments can fend off potential chaos. Intention, like other fundamental conceptualizations, thus continues to turn on the relationships formed by the expectations of inner thought; attributions of purpose and direction continue to be comprehensible only to the extent that some basis can be found for the discovery of the inner through the socially consequent.

But if fundamental cultural change has not been occurring in the Arab world in the concepts I have discussed, why, it may fairly be asked, might one ever think that it has been, and what does this misapprehension say about the anthropologist's stance, the status of our theories about cultural change, and the prospects for fundamental conceptual change in the Arab world?

It is noteworthy that most of the signals one might take as indicative of deep change are linguistic: People seem to use words and phrases implying intent or cause differently, more often, and to more varied effect than had seemed true in previous decades. And it is almost a part of our received anthropological wisdom to assume that a shift in the way people speak about things is coupled with a shift in the way they organize their view of the world and their actions in it. One need not be either a Whorfian or an Aristotelian to accept some version of this possibility. Yet anthropologists have, at times, been too reluctant to consider whether language use may itself give off false signals, whether differences in speech—even when fairly extensive—may entail no significant shifts in cultural categories.

It is true that a feature of many revolutions—those of France and Russia perhaps most noticeably—is that they generated such a new vocabulary of relationships that a restructuring of concepts and associations quickly ensued.[24] But this sort of revolution has not, I suspect, occurred anywhere in the Arab world, and linguistic evidence alone does not betray a deeper change. For even if Arab usages are changing, even if the linguistic elements that constitute the logic of Arab lives are showing signs of new extension, the sheer availability of these terms is not enough to demonstrate that the pattern of connections is new or that such patterns do, indeed, differently inform the Arab's orientation towards others. We are still some way from being able to show that the logic of a conceptual order changes because some of its terms change or from fabricating a clear diagnostic to distinguish category shifts that affect worldview from those that sustain or merely reconfigure persistent patterns.

This problem of linguistic false positives may also be related to a second aspect of our view of culture. Throughout the past generation many anthropologists have, in their analyses of culture as systems of symbols, employed the idea of "shared symbols," as if the only problematic element in the proposition was the idea of the symbol. But we are becoming increasingly aware that the notion of the "shared" is no less problematic. The easy assumption that people must share symbols if they are members of the same culture is both circular as reasoning and insupportable as observable fact.

In the Moroccan case, as perhaps elsewhere in the Arab world, it is perfectly possible that ways of speaking about causality or likelihood are, even if widespread, not infused with the same implications for all who use them. It is not just that a math professor at the university in Rabat, employing a popular way of talking about probability, connotes other things than does an illiterate farmer. It is rather that they use the same symbols—even in speaking to one another—yet do not clearly integrate them differently than they would when speaking of opinion directly. And there is ample evidence to suggest that people do not need to share symbols very much at all in order to orient themselves towards one another for even those mutual contacts that carry overtones of the probable for each party. To capture a sense of continuity or of change we cannot, therefore, baldly assert that culture means shared symbols without at least inquiring, as anthropologists, about the very nature of the shared. What may be needed, if we are to grapple with gradual but fundamental conceptual change at the time of its occurrence, is to move away, in our general discussions of culture and society, from images of crystalline structures and catalogable logics to new and more suggestive images. Science often proceeds through changes of metaphor—from thinking of the eye as a beacon to thinking of the eye as a receptor, from the heart as a furnace to the heart as a pump, or from society as a clockwork mechanism to society as a living body.

Several new analogies for thinking about culture, society, and change may be worth considering. For example, scientists now know that many materials that were previously thought to be based on the regular latticework patterns associated with crystalline structures may instead be configured as irregular and disorderly arrays.[25] Whereas the atoms of a crystal are stacked quite regularly, those of what are called "amorphous solids" reach in different directions for different distances before being linked to their neighbors. The result is a far wider range of configurations and properties than was previously thought possible.

Societies, too, may be more like amorphous than crystalline structures in that small, even gradual, changes in concepts or relationships do not have the full systemic implications our residual functionalism suggests. Instead, they may create sets of connections far more malleable than we had imagined. Change and continuity then become not opposites or even the linked sides of a single coin but interchangeable facets of an amorphous entity whose very responsiveness turns on the irregularity of its constituent parts.[26] Indeed, although some anthropologists use the term "indeterminacy," no one has fully pursued its implications as an element of cultural change. But if in physics it is impossible to calculate rates of movement and direction simultaneously, then in studying human societies it may also be worthwhile to separate our observations of momentary pattern from ingrained process.

We might employ first the ideas of Donald Davidson and Richard Rorty, who suggest that those who share a common language and culture often have no more than a passing understanding of each other's orientation, but that is enough for a common order of references and relationships to be possible.[27] To see a culture not as a neat matching of persons, events, and ideas but as a moving system in which passing acquaintance of others is a characteristic feature may help establish a baseline along which conceptual absorption or alteration may be gauged. Anthropologists might recall something tuners of pianos know well, that the exact tuning of each unit actually yields increasing dissonance rather than what tuners call the "equal temperament" of inexact precision.[28] By moving back and forth between the imprecision of concepts and the inexactness of relationships, or, better yet, the particular sort of shared incoherences that appear as one looks at how people grapple with their world, we may be able to see what factors actually contribute to flexibility and inclusiveness in any given culture.

Indeed, the idea of indeterminacy may help us to see factors that might bring about fundamental change in a particular culture. Anthropologists usually avoid forward-looking and frankly speculative questions, but we should not be afraid to entertain them as useful thought exercises rather than as predictive devices. In this spirit I will offer just a few possibilities, all of which may, in fact, be already at work in some Arab countries as they have been in other forms in other times and places.

One thing that might precipitate broad-scale cultural change would be the entry into Arab thought of a serious concept of doubt. Reading the history of Islamic philosophy, the Western observer is constantly struck by the absence of doubt as an element in the discussion.[29] Franz Rosenthal, noting the elimination of doubt since early Islamic times, says:

> Doubt in whichever way indicated became the true pariah and outcast of Muslim civilization . . . a sufficient manifestation of ignorance . . . man's mortal enemy, depriving him of the certainty that his religion was intended and equipped to give him. . . . The common belief was that necessarily and simply, doubt in God was unbelief. . . . Doubting as an epistemological tool and, even more so, as a way of life was banned from Muslim society.[30]

To doubt God was to doubt reason, and to doubt reason was to doubt the orderliness of life that God had shown possible. Whereas some Christians came to test their faith through doubt, almost all Muslims affirmed theirs by excluding doubt. And because religion was not a separable aspect of the commonsensical, what was banished from one area of concern was effectively banished from any central conceptual role at all. Descartes could express a radical change in Western thought when, in turning the corner on doubt, he grounded his new certainty not on a direct belief in God but on man's own thought and hence existence. No comparable event has occurred in Arab thought, no separation of doubt from its immediate implications of unreason and unbelief. Yet one could imagine such a transformation taking place either as an unintended consequence of intensified religiosity or as a reaction to unaccountable events. One intriguing possibility is that given a language of intent that has deep roots in Islamic thought and practice, the elaboration of this language, in place of one based on the assessment of other persons, social connections, and characteristic local customs, might bestow upon it a heightened role with unforeseen implications. Just as Judaism and Christianity, at different times and with very different effects, developed languages of intent that transformed everything from the nature of responsibility to presumptions about human nature, so, too, in Islamic countries an emphasis on the rhetoric of intent could well turn attention to new means of deciphering that intent, and with them create new implications for those who engage in this search and benefit from its claims of success. If much of the strength of Arab culture has come from its ability to explain new things in its own conceptual terms, then ironically, too ardent a form of Islam—what Westerners call fundamentalism—could create so rigid a view of events that it would forge that sense of discrepancy within which the terms and implications of doubt could take root. Something like this might have been intimated, not in the Arab world proper, but in Iran, where state-backed fundamentalism and the medical profession have clashed directly and where confidence in the claim of religion as a total explanatory scheme could erode in the face of doubt about its accuracy in describing such matters as human ill-ness. What comes into doubt may matter less than that a vocabulary of doubt is engendered.

So far in the Arab world, direct signs of such a shift are not in evidence, in no small part because Arabo-Islamic culture continues, within what are re-garded as God's limits, to accept what the general populace does, to require few concrete beliefs of its adherents, and to avoid institutionalizing its religious leaders into a church hierarchy. If state-enforced doctrine falls too far out of line with the flexible mode of confronting new ideas that characterizes Arab culture, the implication for the way people think about things (rather than what they think) could be profound.

Another possibility concerns the role of professionalization. Earlier it was noted that knowledge is a key concept in Arab culture and that it has always been personalized. But as knowledge and social connections become sepa-rated—as one is less able to be confident of what a man knows because one does not know the man—knowledge could come to have greater value than its holder. Already a number of professions lay claim to authority because of the things they can affect. It is not inconceivable that others may lay claim to certain domains—the marketplace, the household, private life—for which expertise was once based on local attachment and knowledge rather than proffered technical skills. Again, neither the rhetoric nor the institutional sup-port appears to be in place yet for such a shift, and the tendency to assess per-sons and allow them scope as their attachments develop seems still to hold the upper hand.

Finally, the most fertile ground for conceptual change might be created by the fragmentation of traditional family forms. Certainly the history of the West points to the key role of families as the bastion of traditional modes of thought affecting many areas of life. Signs of possible change are manifest in Arab cul-ture. Nuclear family residence appears to be on the increase, single-person households are more evident, and migrant-worker absenteeism is readily doc-umented. If these shifts in family organization become entrenched, the terms by which emotional and sexual life are understood could shift as well. As we are now beginning to understand for history elsewhere, such changes are deeply intertwined with those of politics, art, and the overall shape of a people's speech.

Once again, however, I find myself urging the anthropologist's cultural conservatism. If anything, studies of Arab family history are suggesting that it is not so much fundamental change but a monolithic stereotype of Middle Eastern family structures that leads us to exaggerate perceived change. Ottoman records, medieval Jewish documents, and oral histories are suggesting more varied family forms than colonialist images ever provided, and the result may not be the elimination of any claims to change but a far more refined view of just exactly what the changes are and how they relate to their conceptual and emotional surround.

Indeed, in the case of Arab culture, what may also be needed to assess cultural change is a far more subtle appreciation of the concept and role of power in this part of the world. As we have already seen there is a deep ambivalence towards power in many parts of the Arab world that stands out sharply in a host of domains—sexual, religious, and political. In the Moroccan case, for example, we have seen that there are elements of wedding festivities that show men that power is not always where or what they think it is, patterns of relationship to saintly lineages that imply the dependence of the powerful on the powerless, and political attitudes that persistently undercut power formation. This open-ended approach to the very concept of power is one of the factors that makes it difficult for any one elite group to promote change or for any analysis of change—whether Marxian, Foucaultian, or economistic—to capture the absorptive dynamism of the Arab version of the Great Game. Fundamental cultural change in this environment may work, to the extent it does, only when the terms of discourse, which cannot easily be captured by one group, take so broad a hold on the imagination that they lose exclusive attachment to the very group that might have sought most urgently to purvey them.

Anthropology thus remains a long way from being able to grasp cultural change and identify it at the moment it is still in process. It should come as no surprise that the world is more disorderly than our theories about it, or that, given the unlikely prospect that the world will become vastly more orderly, it is our theories that will have to become more supple. But perhaps if we draw away from views of society as crystalline or organic, and from views of change as possessing a different logic for concepts than for relationships, and if we are also willing to hazard observations about how change might occur, we may be able to approach cultures like those of the Arabs—and issues like their vision of others' minds—knowing they are not indecipherable for being amorphous nor beyond our ability to calculate their course for embodying a logic of unique and irrefractable design.

PART THREE

Shifting Concepts, Discerning Change

Marriage Stories
Crossing the Boundaries of Nation, Gender, and Law

One goes to court with one lawsuit and comes home with two.
DANISH PROVERB

As Muslims move across national and cultural frontiers they bring the problems of their family lives with them. Whether accompanying the primary wage earner or remaining in the home country, the family unit is often placed under considerable strain. When the result is marital discord the problem then arises as to whose law shall apply, that of the home country (carried in personam into new territories) or the laws of a land so foreign in its views of the family, the individual, and the nature of property as to seriously undercut both the structure of ongoing relationships and the image the migrants may have of the order of the world and their place within it. These issues, broadly grouped under the jurisprudential heading of conflict of laws, is also a conflict of cultures. To trace the specific form these problems take in the lives of contemporary Muslims is to see the meaning of borders in the lives of the migrant—and the realities that attend on the theories applied by different jurisdictions.

Moreover, changes in the laws of the family that fail to take into account the realities of the relationships that take place in the shadow of the law may lead to distortions that legislators had not foreseen. Thus it is valuable, in tracing the actual course of disputes, to see how principles that have been adopted on paper play out in the actualities of family disputes. Here, too, borders are being crossed, even if only internal to a single country, for the categories that the statutes may address and the connections that disputants may fashion do not necessarily follow the same lines.

The case studies that follow are drawn from a long list of such instances that I have collected over the years. Those related here have been chosen both for the richness of their detail and the typicality of the problems they pose, even though no single instance can ever hope to serve for all. In the details of these marriage stories, however, both the practical problems of the legislator and the poignant problems of those caught up in the conflicts themselves come through with particular force—and with them an invitation to rethink with great care the laws applied to the lives that ordinary Muslims lead.[1]ᴼᴼᴼᴼᴼᴼᴼᴼ

A MIGRANT'S STORY

In the mid-1980s a Moroccan Muslim couple married and had a daughter. Soon after, they were divorced and the young child remained in the legal custody of her mother, Aziza. Aziza then remarried. The biological father made no claim to custody of the child and the new husband accepted responsibility for the child's support, placing its name in his own civil status (*état civil*) documents. In due course this marriage too ended in divorce, and not long after the mother went to study at a university in the United States, bringing the child with her. She then met and married an American, non-Muslim who formally adopted the child under American law. Problems, however, developed because of the mother's immigration situation, the status of the American marriage under Moroccan law, and the legal actions taken by Aziza's second husband back in Morocco.

Under United States law, individuals residing in the country on a student visa must, upon completion of their studies, return to their country of origin for a period of two years before being considered for re-admission to the United States. In the present case this provision would apply to the child as well as the mother since the former was born in Morocco and only later adopted by an American father. For mother and child to return to Morocco would, in this particular case, have posed more than ordinary difficulties. Both mother and child had developed serious illnesses for which they were receiving extensive medical care and for which they required careful, ongoing monitoring. For both to return to Morocco may have had significant implications for their overall health. Even if an exception were granted allowing the child to remain in the United States with her adoptive American father, the child would be separated for two years from her mother, the primary caretaker during the child's illness.

To compound matters, Aziza's second husband had gone into the courts in Morocco and obtained two orders. First, he obtained an order declaring that he had no further responsibility for the support of the child. In addition, he got an order stating that, under the terms of a 1993 law, the daughter was actually an abandoned child.[2] This claim was based on the proposition that the mother's marriage to a non-Muslim is not valid under Moroccan law and that, since neither he nor the American husband qualify as legal father to the girl, the child is indeed abandoned.[3] Were mother and child to return to Morocco several consequences might follow: Having been declared abandoned the child might be taken from the mother and placed with strangers. (Although there is no formal concept of adoption in Moroccan law—in the sense of full replacement of rights of inheritance and entitlement to use of an adoptive parent's family name—there is a form of agreement for support and upbringing [*kafala*], and another couple could be granted such rights by a Moroccan court.)[4] Alternatively, the second husband could move to have the abandonment order vacated and claim custody of the child himself. His claim would be based on grounds that have implications both for the custody of the child and the status of the mother.

Since Aziza's marriage to a non-Muslim is null and void under the traditional form of Islamic law codified in contemporary Moroccan statutes, Aziza has forsaken the right to custody of her child twice over—first, by re-marriage to any other man (which would allow custody of the child to revert to the "father"), and second, because her present marriage is, in any event, invalid and thus a form of illegal sexual intercourse which would disqualify her as a proper parent. Indeed, under Moroccan criminal law Aziza could actually be prosecuted for fornication, inasmuch as she is clearly involved in a sexual relation with a man who, whatever his status in America, is not a lawful husband in the eyes of Moroccan law.[5] For the mother to return to Morocco could thus result not only in loss of her child but imprisonment.

Of course, there would be ways of contravening some of these dire implications. The American father could convert to Islam, thus rendering his marriage to Aziza perfectly valid under Moroccan law: Marriage by a woman to a non-Muslim is regarded as a "temporary" impediment which can be rectified by subsequent conversion of the man.[6] But such conversion is, under Islamic and Moroccan law, irreversible, and any attempt to re-convert after a convenient period would have serious implications were Moroccan jurisdiction ever to be enforceable. It might also be possible to appeal the Moroccan court's judgment declaring the child abandoned on the grounds that the statute was intended not to deprive biological parents of the custody of their offspring where there is no demonstration of parental unfitness. To the contrary, it could be argued, the purpose of the statute was exactly the opposite, namely, to find a legal way (in the absence of a tradition of adoption) for the state to gain control of children who effectively lack any parents so that children in need of care can be assigned to parties who are willing to be responsible for their upbringing.[7] To return to Morocco to pursue the case would, however, expose Aziza to the sanctions already discussed.

Here, then, we can see how certain aspects of Moroccan law—whatever the values of Westerners—have consequences that go far beyond the normal when placed in a transnational context. Unlike some European countries, which allow the law of the parties' country of origin to govern certain aspects of their personal status, United States practice clearly gives priority to its own statutes and will permit recognition of foreign judgments only if they do not contravene the public policy of the state in which the parties are currently domiciled.[8] Thus were they to remain in the United States, mother and daughter would be in no legal danger. But because of federal immigration laws, they must now convince an immigration official or court that due to their medical condition, their vulnerability to legal processes in Morocco, or the overall impact on the family of their forcible separation, the consequences would be so antithetical to the principles of American law as to warrant either modification of their visa requirements or a grant of personal asylum. As indicated, it is also a serious question whether the Moroccan law itself was meant to cover this admittedly unusual circumstance, but so long as the Moroccan court decision and the law on which it rests remain in force, the risk to mother and child should they be required to return to Morocco is considerable.

A second set of problems relates to Moroccan use of the *état civil.* Moroccans themselves commonly, though mistakenly, believe that a woman cannot have an *état civil* document of her own—that she must be registered on that of some man, initially her father and later, in most instances, her husband. In fact, she can have her own document as well as being registered on that of a male. A child, however, is listed on its father's document and only on that of its mother if there is no legal father. Thus complicating matters is the need to get a child registered in such a way that whatever authority a woman has over her child is clearly and unambiguously indicated in the child's documentation. It might also be difficult, when a child has no legal father and the status of the mother is unclear, for the child to obtain a Moroccan passport even though he or she is regarded as a Moroccan citizen. Lack of clarity can result in lengthy and costly legal proceedings which tend to form the opportunity for additional tactical maneuvers.

Indeed, it is such maneuvers and their place in the larger realities of court proceedings in Morocco that would be vital to a full understanding of a case like the present one. It is not, for example, clear whether the former husband used the issue of abandonment in order to gain an advantage in his quest to be relieved of obligations of support under the earlier divorce decree: He is not the biological father of the child and there is nothing in the record to suggest that he has ever sought custody of the child. Thus we may really be faced with the sort of situation that is very common in Morocco, in which a husband pressures his wife to forgive him some debt if he is forthcoming on the question of child custody.

POWER, CORRUPTION, AND THE REALITIES OF LEGAL PROCESS

During his student years on the continent Ali married a European woman who returned with him to live in Morocco. After their children were grown they got divorced. Ali then married Tuda, a rural woman of limited education, and took her with him when he went back to Europe to work for a year. When the couple took up residence again in Morocco, however, things began to go badly. Tuda wanted children of her own but did not become pregnant; when the children from Ali's first marriage visited there was considerable tension. Finally, Tuda moved out, saying that Ali would have to deal with her father about their circumstances. Ali was reluctant to get divorced again but finally agreed to a *talaq khula'*, but rather than his wife giving up some financial claim in order to obtain the husband's divorce (the normal implication of this type of divorce), Ali actually agreed to make Tuda a gift of a sum of money.[9] A final divorce was accordingly registered. Ali, however, missed his wife so much that soon afterwards he offered Tuda, as a new bridewealth payment (*ṣdaq*), an apartment that she would own personally. She accepted and the couple were formally remarried.

Unfortunately, the same old problems recurred, and when Tuda fled to her father's house again she took many of the household items with her. The Code of Personal Status (Articles 115 and 35(1)) says that a man must support his wife, no consideration being given to any assets the wife may possess. It also says that there can be no theft as between spouses. Ali could simply have divorced Tuda again, but it would have cost him the apartment he gave her, the consolation gift (*muṭa'a*) required by the statute, and support (*nafaqa*) up to the time of divorce plus the waiting period of three months (*'adda*), during which any pregnancy on the part of the wife is attributed to the divorcing husband. Ali may have been willing to divorce his wife unilaterally, but his resolve to fight was strengthened when Tuda's father and brother broke into the apartment Ali had given his wife and took a number of Ali's personal and professional belongings. Ali reported the theft to the police and together they lay in wait to see if the thieves would return for the items they left behind. When they did, Ali joined his own suit for civil damages to the criminal charges brought against his wife's kinsmen.

Suit followed countersuit as the entire relationship devolved into a series of tangled proceedings running through several courts in different parts of the country. The tactic of Tuda and her family had, from Ali's perspective, been one of delay from the outset, as they sought to run up the support bill that would be owed by a man they regarded as highly educated and highly paid. By contrast, Ali's approach was based on his belief that the apartment he gave Tuda should be regarded not as a gift but as future compensation in the event of death or divorce, and that no further support—much less at the levels demanded by Tuda's father—should have to be paid. Pride and dependence, strategic maneuver and personal indignation at what each regarded as the other's legal advantage became indissolubly linked, particularly when both sides began, whether by compulsion or desire, to seek a more favorable stance in the courts by the offer of various "gifts" to relevant officials. These favors ranged from barely veiled solicitations from clerks and assistants for preferential listing on the court calendar to the production of true copies of documents that could otherwise have taken weeks to complete.[10] Tuda and her father sought delays in order, as Ali's lawyer said, "to keep the meter running" on the level of support that would ultimately have to be paid; Ali pursued the criminal conviction and monetary award against Tuda's kinsmen in order to force a more favorable settlement. Tuda was kept hidden by her father, so she could not be served with vital papers and the support clock would continue to run; Ali obtained court and police orders to seek her even though he knew that once found she would probably just hide somewhere else. A number of Moroccan women actually prefer to go to jail rather than be forced to return to their husbands. Commonly, in such instances, relatives and neighbors then pressure the husband to agree to a *khula'* divorce. In this case Tuda's desire for a divorce was either secondary to or submerged by her father's desire to gain a large support order against Ali and to retain the property given to Tuda.

Ali even got court permission to take a second wife, and when that marriage proved unsatisfactory he joked about taking a third or fourth wife so that no matter what happened Tuda and her father would get a diminishing share of his assets.[11] In turn, Tuda, whether on her own initiative or at her relatives' prompting, began to write letters to Ali's European friends urging them to intercede on her behalf and convince Ali to drop the charges against her relatives and stop contesting her right to the apartment. Tuda's sister was even conduced to claim that Tuda had made a gift of the apartment in question to her.

Ali lost his case for a reduction in the support order at the appellate level but won a substantial sum in the civil suit attached to the criminal action against Tuda's father and brother. He also won his case against Tuda's sister for conspiracy to deprive him of his belongings, even though the gift by Tuda to her sister of the apartment was recognized as valid. Both the father and sister were placed on suspended sentences, prompting Tuda to a new round of requests to Ali's friends to intervene on her behalf. Meanwhile the father began another lawsuit to get back the apartment and the sister began an appeal on her conviction for conspiracy. On his side, Ali geared up to appeal the support decision to the Supreme Court, retained the key to the apartment in an attempt to make Tuda appear for a hearing on being a recalcitrant wife, and initiated a separate suit against the father and brother for the return of his professional belongings. An ever-widening circle of courts, lawyers, relatives, and friends have been drawn into the drama, which is characteristic not only for the endless maneuvering but for the social and legal entanglements for which there is no clear end in sight.

WHEN INTRAFAMILIAL STRUGGLES GO INTERNATIONAL

In the early 1990s a woman named Mouna, the daughter of a well-to-do Moroccan family, became pregnant. Her parents tried to get her to have an abortion rather than bear the shame of conceiving a child out of wedlock, but Mouna refused and fled to Europe, where she gave birth to the child. When mother and child returned to Morocco, the maternal grandmother, in an attempt to spare the family the shame of such an event, told everyone that she was actually the child's biological mother. Indeed, the grandparents arranged for documents that certified them as the natural parents. The child's mother continued to live in the house with her parents and the child, but the child was never told who her true mother was.

A few years later Mouna moved to America, where she married a Muslim man. The grandparents said they would send the child to live with her, but they never did. Mouna then sought to get documents proving that she was the child's biological mother, including birth records from Europe and entries referring to the child in Mouna's passport. She succeeded in getting the child registered on her own civil status documents, but after filing a petition in the Moroccan court to force the grandparents to turn custody of the child over to her, the court case suddenly "disappeared" from the docket, raising suspicions that the grandparents had used their influence to get the case removed.

Over the course of the next year Mouna managed to win back her parents' favor enough for them to agree to let her see the child. Everything was arranged for a visit when events took a sudden turn: The grandfather of the child took ill and sought medical attention in the United States. The grandmother and grandchild accompanied him, and all lived together with Mouna and her husband while the grandfather was receiving treatment. Mouna and her husband, however, inquired of state officials as to their custodial rights, and, on the basis of the documents she produced and assertions to the effect that they were the legal parents so far as state law was concerned, Mouna and her husband took the child and moved to a hotel. The grandparents, in turn, contacted both state police and the FBI, accusing Mouna of kidnapping the child. The police located Mouna and the child and returned custody to the grandparents, who immediately left with the child for Morocco. Mouna was never under physical arrest but she did claim that she had been assured by the police that the child would remain under state protection until the custody issue could be sorted out. For a brief period she was actually charged with kidnapping, but these charges were soon dismissed: Indeed Mouna's lawyer argued that the police had filed a false report in which Mouna is said to have acknowledged that her parents had adopted the child.

Subsequently, Mouna filed suit against the state police. In a lengthy opinion the court rejected the defendants' motion to dismiss the case and stated that the release of the child to the grandparents violated Mouna's right to the integrity of her family.[12] The police had already begun to contact officials in Morocco in an attempt to make some sense of the whole custody issue, while Mouna's attorney was seeking to establish that there is no adoption under Moroccan law in any event. In the meantime Mouna had once again established contact with her parents and the child, but, her own husband having since died and her own finances being quite stretched, she did not have the wherewithal to return to Morocco to pursue the case there. She remained in a kind of legal limbo, her suit against the state police being her only hope for sufficient monetary and legal support to pursue custody of her child.

DISCUSSION

Notwithstanding their distinctive elements, a number of very important features of Moroccan social and legal procedure—and their cross-boundary aspects—are highlighted by the cases described, features that affect the legal circumstances of far less complex and dramatic cases.

When cases cross national frontiers it is especially important to understand the implications a foreign judgment may have back in the home country. The usual image of Muslim countries is that all of the legal power is in the hands of the men. This is far too simplistic. Though the range of variation across the Muslim world is considerable in this regard, the situation in Morocco is not altogether unusual. Delaying tactics may run up support charges, corruption can be used to tactical advantage, willful disappearance can be employed to a woman's benefit, and a wife may even be willing to go to jail rather than obey an order to return to her husband, thus drawing other relatives into the fray and restarting the support clock. These are tactics born to a considerable degree out of both statutory inequality and the possibilities inherent in the legal arrangements themselves.[13] But the question as to who has the greater power is not susceptible to a stereotypical Western answer. Women, for example, can demand a new place of residence away from the husband's relatives or call up at any time the remainder of any bridewealth payment that may have been outstanding from the inception of the marriage, both of which are powers of no small import. More recently, the 1993 amendments to the Code of Personal Status allowing a Moroccan woman to choose the jurisdiction where her case will be heard may have removed the advantage husbands had in forcing their wives to return from distant regions, but now wives and their kinsmen use control over the forum to run up the expenses of husbands who must often bring lawyers with them, pay bribes to avoid delay, and encounter increased costs of support.

As people move around notice becomes a very significant problem, one that is compounded by the quest for advantage. A man who works abroad may have an order entered against him on the basis of his European salary, or have his Moroccan resources attached without ever receiving notice, thus being unable to contest the Moroccan court order. Illiteracy exacerbates the problem, as does the absence of a common way in which Moroccans state their address. Where jurisdiction may lie either in the home country or a foreign court, widely different results may occur simply on the basis of who wins the race to the courthouse door. Reciprocal enforcement laws are insufficient when the underlying jurisdictional and notice requirements lack adequate uniformity. And since the Moroccan solution to many difficulties tends to be imprisonment for either recalcitrant wives or penurious husbands, the European image that deference to local law will actually lead to more legitimate and acceptable solutions to domestic relations problems often veils what actually occurs on the other side of the Mediterranean or Atlantic.[14]

Each of the parties in the cases we have been discussing is locked in legal battle, and the lives of each will only be rendered more complicated if Aziza must return to Morocco, if Ali once again seeks to spend a period of work abroad, or if Mouna cannot be fully reconciled with her parents. Each case exemplifies some of the implications presented by such matters for various international and binational accords. The American approach to conflict of laws, for example, is largely assimilationist and statist: "Private international law" is a term and concept that is absent from the American common law tradition. Familial arrangements entered into abroad will be recognized but only if they do not contravene the public policy of the state in which the parties are domiciled, there being no federal family law statute.[15] Anyone present in the United States is subject to the law of the state of his or her domicile, itself a function of residence and other attachments to the state. The result is a relatively high degree of clarity about one's legal status and a correlatively low, but by no means nonexistent, acceptance of non-mainstream familial arrangements. Proponents of jurisdictional absolutism may thus wish to weigh the implications of the present case against the solutions offered by European forms of private international law for the relative effects each produces both in their own legal regimes and in the process to which those residing in their midst may be subject if the laws of a foreign jurisdiction are to apply.

If, in addition, power is not always exactly what or where it seems to be in Moroccan marital life, any more than it is in other domains of Moroccan social and political life, it should at least be clear that just changing the gender of certain issues does not change all of the underlying difficulties. Nor does simply shifting the venue always yield an ideal result: The social problems that recur as people move across frontiers pose complications that classical conflict of laws theory can only address at the most formal level. Many of the applicable national approaches, and even many of the more recent bilateral accords, are either woefully out-of-date, were constructed in a very different context of familial and migrant problems, or have become deeply embedded in the politics of transnational migration. No one country can correct what it sees as the inequities in the laws of another nation, but far more attention to the human plight of people caught in between could lead to more appropriate and available forums for decision-making as well as more equal access by all to whatever process is applied. In order to fashion laws and procedures that are responsive to the realities of law as a system of living relationships, it may be necessary that all concerned move towards understandings that transcend borders.

Some of the implications of the cases described may, therefore, be summarized as follows:

- It is necessary to look at the process by which legal decisions unfold in a foreign jurisdiction and not simply concentrate on the statutes or treaty provisions. Neither the negotiation of international accords nor the decision of one's own courts should turn on uninformed or unrealistic views of the nature of proceedings in the foreign jurisdiction. This is not only a matter of comity or international politics: It is a matter of fundamental fairness.
- Toward this end consideration should be given to the purposes that underlie the law of a foreign jurisdiction to which one is prepared to defer. Thus it would be desirable that each accord give voice to the purposes intended by the substantive laws that will be allowed to govern those living in one's ambit but who will now be governed by the laws of another forum. For example, if a European country is to defer to a North African jurisdiction on matters of child custody, it should be clearly stated that nothing will be enforceable that is found to be inconsistent with the best interests of the child.
- A kind of legal limbo can exist as individuals, trapped in procedures that are unclear or internally contradictory, are left with no clear resolution to their problems. A woman who must choose between sustained contact with, much less legal custody of, her child or submission to the unequal powers of a husband—who may himself be supported in his position by transnational agreements—finds herself having to employ every tactic available to gain some leverage. A husband who faces jail for non-support when his wife's relatives are indeed trying to gouge him by their own tactics is drawn more easily into the petty corruption of daily life in North Africa for which he more often than not feels only contempt. In such circumstances both come to look at the law—foreign as well as domestic—as expressions of power far more than of protection, fairness, and legitimate authority. When those responsible for these laws and procedures fail to acknowledge the North Africans' concerns, the latter can hardly be faulted for losing confidence in the host country.
- It is important for foreign governments to appreciate that Islamic law is not a form of civil law adjudication but a variant of common law.[16] As a result, the role of case decisions is quite different, as is the relation of the law to the state. Failure to realize this most fundamental of differences may well lead to an overemphasis on statutes and insufficient attention to the course of legal cases. And it is equally important for civil as well as common law jurisdictions to realize that their own systems of law are themselves the product of highly pluralistic experiences, and that a place now needs to be made to accommodate those who are new to its exigencies.

In sum, understanding the impact of an international accord requires understanding of its context and its operation in the country to which one is prepared to defer. In stories of actual marital disputes one can see the implications of the transnational problems engendered by family migration; in the legal realities one can see the effects that international accords have on the way ordinary people must work out their relationships. A high degree of realism and care for the consequences is thus indispensable to both the legitimacy of the institutions involved and the hope for legal approaches that are as mobile as the people affected.

∽ 9 ∽

Euro-Islam

Sociocultural change is always reciprocal. Whatever the differential of power when cultures encounter one another, both are, to some degree, inescapably affected by the experience. The changes come in innumerable and unexpected ways. In "civilizing" the other one may adopt many of the counter's art forms; in adapting to the other, one's own manners or style of speech may yield to change. Even the slavemaster finds that, over the course of time, he has absorbed some of the music, the cuisine, and the costume—to say nothing of the genes and the ideas—of those over whom he imagines his power to be exclusionary and absolute. And when the immigrant arrives in a new land, he may find himself changed in ways that belie his own attempts at separation and transparency.

Muslims have been in contact with Europe since the earliest years of Islam, and the reciprocal influences have been immense. Muslims have also lived in Europe for centuries,[1] but it was not until the latter part of the twentieth century that a migratory influx of unprecedented size and complexity took place. Whether it was Algerians seeking employment or safety in the face of their own nation's convulsions, or "guest workers" from Turkey or Morocco whose families have followed them and established homes for more than a generation, the mutual impact of these huge movements of population have been crucial to the recent history and politics of the regions affected. Yet as much as the economic, political, and social aspects of this Muslim presence have received scholarly attention, remarkably little has been said about the possible ways in which the various forms of Islam practiced by these migrants from North Africa and the Middle East may have been affected by the experience of life among the Europeans. It is to this issue—the potential formation of one or more kinds of "Euro-Islam," with significant implications for the development of Islam in the migrants' countries of origin as well as in their lives in Europe—that the present essay is addressed.[2]⟨⟨⟨⟨⟨⟨⟨⟨⟨⟨⟨⟨⟨⟨⟨⟨⟨⟨⟨⟨⟨⟨

The numbers themselves tell a large part of the story. Although understandably approximate—since many of the migrants live in European countries illegally and some of these countries (e.g., France, Belgium) forbid the collection of religious data by government agencies—there are probably upwards of seven million Muslim immigrants living in Western Europe.[3] While this represents only two percent of the total population of these countries the numbers, proportion, and impact vary considerably. Over three million Muslims may now live in France (roughly 6 percent of the total population of the country), but probably a quarter of the 800,000 people living in Marseilles come from North Africa;[4] one-third of those living in the city of Birmingham, in the United Kingdom, are Muslims; more than a quarter of a million Muslim immigrants live in Belgium, but with low birth rates among the native Belgians the proportion of those living in Brussels under the age of twenty who come from Muslim backgrounds exceeds 23 percent;[5] and even with more than two million Muslim immigrants to Germany, most of whom are from Turkey, the non-Muslim birthrate is so low that without further immigration the total population of the country could fall from the current level of some 82 million to as little as 60 million by 2050.[6] In some countries, such as those of Scandinavia, a relatively homogenous society has had to cope, both intellectually and organizationally, with the new experience of Muslim immigrants; for others, such as Italy, France, and Spain, the immigrants, as residents of former colonial territories, have "come home" in ways that recall an inescapable history. Indeed, for all the commonality of the immigrants' experience in Europe, the timing and context of their arrival has had a profound effect on the social and religious lives of all concerned.

The major influx of migrants from North Africa to France came in the wake of the Algerian war and the acquisition of independence by the former colonies in the period from the mid-1950s to the early 1960s. The experience of the so-called *harki*s, the individuals and their descendants who fought with the French forces in Algeria, has been no less alienating than that of many of the *beur*s, the children of North African immigrant workers, even though the former moved more expeditiously to French nationality. In Germany, bilateral agreements that first brought 6,700 Turkish "guest workers" in 1961 soon yielded 429,000 in 1970, over a million in 1976, and 1.67 million by 1990.[7] As in

France, this means that we are well into the "second generation" (as the Germans call them) of Muslim migrants. Indeed, as different parts of Europe developed economically in successive stages, and as declining birth rates among the Europeans themselves have resulted in increased need for immigrant workers, a rolling wave of migrants has washed over different parts of the continent. For the Belgians the 30,000 in the mid-1960s grew to 100,000 in 1973 and 240,00 by 1985; for the Italians the great burst came in the 1980s, when other European countries were beginning to close down on immigration.[8] The most recent major target for migrants is Spain, which had only 14,885 Moroccan immigrants in 1989 but in 1999 alone expelled 17,000 mostly North African migrants compared to an annual influx of over 50,000.[9]

Consonant with these waves of migration has come a variety of political responses to the presence of what seemed at first to many to be a temporary influx of workers who would eventually retire to their home countries but soon became a far more permanent presence in the European countries as families joined the early arrivals. The philosophy of national inclusion, no less than the theory of social welfare, was tested in each country, and the results have been quite varied.

The French, for example, might almost be said to have become victims of their own theory of assimilation: On the one hand their adherence to a policy of excluding religious distinctiveness from public institutions (in line with the anticlericalism and egalitarian philosophy that flowed, in quite different ways, from both the Revolutionary and Napoleonic reforms) has come up against the theory that all colonials could become cultural Frenchmen (when in fact only a tiny elite could do so, and then not without considerable angst).[10] The result has been the unintended testing of the French approach over such issues as the wearing of headscarves by Muslim girls in public schools and the acknowledgment of Muslim holidays for immigrant workers.[11] At the same time the French have tried to limit the number of organizations to be recognized for certain religious purposes. Thus in 2000 a French court upheld the government's refusal to recognize an ultra-Orthodox Jewish group's claim to ritual slaughtering because there was already one recognized Jewish association for this purpose. The case was appealed to the European Commission on Human Rights, which reversed the French decision, but France ultimately prevailed on appeal to the European Court of Human Rights.[12] However, when the French government awarded a major contract for the slaughter of animals to the Paris mosque, the protest by rival groups resulted in the withdrawal of the contract.[13] Thus both the contradictions of internal policies and the larger question of who shall speak for any religious grouping remains very much an open question.

By contrast, the Germans, fearful of religious and ethnic minorities being reified and localized, allow more diversity in the public sphere than does France even as they accord official recognition to only a handful of community organizations. The result is the recognition of some and not other religious entities—as, for example, in granting permission to offer religious courses in the state schools—an approach that seeks a high degree of conformity within the context of a paternalistic state.[14] The British, though possessing an established church (and thus reading their own blasphemy law as protecting Christianity but no other faith), have tended to accommodate themselves to large numbers of South Asian immigrants by recognizing a wide range of Muslim (and Hindu) practices with the unevenness one might expect from a common law system operating in the absence of a written constitution.[15] Sweden only began to give way on its "One nation, One people, One religion" ideology with the adoption of the Freedom of Religion Act of 1951 and has had to redefine its social welfare system to find room for increasing numbers of immigrants, while Italy, despite a number of local agreements, has yet to enter into a formal agreement (*intessa*) with Muslims (as they have with other religious minorities), such that the Islamic Cultural Center of Rome, for example, is recognized as a "moral body" but not as a "church" much less a "religion."[16]

Each of these policy approaches, embedded as it is in a given nation's history and culture, necessarily affects, and is affected by, crosscurrents of racial and religious animosity. As the sheer size of the Muslim populations grew in many European countries in the 1970s and 1980s, the private forms of racism began to take on national political implications. The rise of politicians like Le Pen in France or neo-Fascist groups in Austria, Germany, and Italy cannot be understood except in terms of the backlash to the sudden challenge posed by large numbers of Muslim immigrants. Incidents broke out in numerous countries, ranging from the verbal harassment of workers and their children in Britain and Germany to the outright murder of North Africans in France in the early 1980s and in Spain in the late 1990s.[17] To some extent anti-Muslim sentiment was "legitimated" by political parties that used immigration issues as a vehicle for political advantage, while in other situations immigration stimulated greater concern by national governments for the treatment of their resident minorities. In every case the repercussions moved in both directions, particularly as they affected the development of Muslim voluntary associations and the respective governments' dealings with them.

One of the key organizations through which reciprocal contact has occurred is that of the mosque and its attendant institutions. For the most part Muslim immigrants initially established mosques in less visible structures normally devoted to other purposes, but by the 1970s, as families joined workers and greater permanency was evident, distinctive buildings with their attendant schools and social facilities became more common. Arab governments, particularly the Saudis, funded large mosques in major European capitals, but it was still the nationally distinct, locally dominant mosque that characterized most Muslim institutions. Where, as in Belgium and Germany, government policy favored recognition of certain religious organizations over others, the differences among diverse groupings in the Muslim community were exacerbated; where, as in France, mosques were carefully watched by the immigrants' home governments for fundamentalist and political leanings, these institutions incorporated both national attachment and national caution.[18] With over 3,000 mosques in European countries at the start of the twenty-first century, and quite different modes of official recognition, these gathering places have become a microcosm of the internal divisions within the Muslim communities and a flashpoint for both public and governmental contact: In Germany, for example, the city of Hanover has repeatedly turned down applications for new mosques, while in at least one instance in France a referendum, later held to be illegal, blocked the construction of a mosque to replace one destroyed by protesters.[19]

The rise of the mosques also correlates with the Muslim communities' assertion of their concerns about very specific public policies, particularly those relating to education, work, ritual practices, and matters of family law. In education, for example, the approaches of the European countries range from the French insistence on secularism—with the attendant furor that resulted in banning Muslim girls from wearing headscarves—to the British requirement that religious education in Local Education Authority schools be "of a broadly Christian character" from which individuals may be exempt. Moreover, recognition of Muslim schools eligible for state funding has not been as forthcoming as that accorded a few Jewish schools.[20] In Belgium, perhaps because Catholic schools receive state subsidy yet are accorded great autonomy, local schools have been given power to decide such matters as appropriate attire. Belgium also allows religious education to be conducted by figures chosen by the religious authorities who then receive state pay.[21] The Dutch, like many Europeans, have been concerned about the training of Muslim religious leaders and educators, finding that many who come from abroad constitute barriers to assimilation and perhaps ought not to receive government recognition and funding. Thus, in a 1998 document the government proposed training programs that would call for local recruitment and education of imams, a policy opposed by many of the Muslim groups resident in the Netherlands.[22]

Workplace rules have also occasioned a forum for both diverse approaches and reciprocal influences. After a slow start most countries have accommodated the religious holidays of Muslim workers, and many have made provisions for prayer periods and even spaces.[23] Employment discrimination laws still require a demonstration that there is no valid work reason to preclude the wearing of clothes required for a particular job or that the group in question is in fact a protected category. Proving these facts is as difficult for Muslims as for any other group. The Dutch have altered their employment laws to allow a weekly day of rest without specifying the exact day.[24] The 1992 pact between the Spanish government and the Islamic Commission of Spain provides time off for compulsory prayers and allows Muslims to finish their jobs one hour early during Ramadan, even though many of the terms contained in the pact actually appear more vague and potentially restrictive than those of the Constitution itself.[25] For the most part, however, statutes fail to address many issues with specificity: Does the Belgian law allow a whole day for Muslim weekly rituals or only a few hours? Is a Muslim prayer leader in Germany entitled to the same confidential relation with his co-religionists as other clergy? Is the category "Muslims" too varied to qualify as a "racial group" for purposes of the British Race Relations Act of 1976? What makes all these instances—particularly when they fall within the sphere of employment—so intriguing for reciprocal change is that the alterations are, to an increasing degree, coming about as a result of agreements between the two communities: The very fact of employment focuses the attention of both parties on revising laws, organizing representative groups, and utilizing mechanisms already applied to other minorities.

Similar issues arise in the organization of various ritual activities. Most European countries now recognize that ritually clean meat (*halal*), with its attendant Islamic slaughtering methods, is as acceptable as the practices of Orthodox Jews.[26] The German Constitutional Court, for example, overruled a 1995 decision that barred the slaughter of animals by cutting their throats and allowing them to bleed to death, arguing that such a ban effectively precluded Muslim ritual slaughter in the name of animal protection.[27] In Britain, changes came about in large part when the leaders of the London mosque formed an alliance with the Orthodox rabbinate. In France local authorities have turned a blind eye to the sacrifice of sheep on the occasion of the festival of Eid el Kebir,[28] while in other instances it is local officials who present the most difficulties, as, for example, when they bar the burial of non-national Muslims in local cemeteries.[29] In the realm of criminal law, a number of countries have specifically banned female genital mutilation, though attempts at enforcement have proven difficult. And some consideration has been given to the practices of Muslim immigrants' cultural backgrounds in such diverse situations as the corporal punishment of children and provocation for acts of assault.[30]

Perhaps no area has created more difficulty, however, than that of family law. As in many other domains countries have usually followed policies that favor either assimilation or cultural diversity, but as they have probed both the limits of diversity and the reactions of their national populations some European countries have backtracked from their multicultural approach. Moreover, as attempts to limit immigration took hold in the 1970s and 1980s, bilateral agreements with the immigrants' countries of origin began to be signed. These agreements were, in turn, complicated by international accords that sometimes contradicted the bilateral agreements and by the broad proposition that deference to Islamic practices must still not contravene the public policy of the European state. Thus Muslim countries who signed human rights conventions with the proviso that Islamic law not be violated have come up against European ideas of equal rights for men and women. To avoid public policy conflicts there has been an increase in the use of private agreements, often mediated by local Islamic officials. The overall result has been uneven, uncertain, and unstable—but it has meant that negotiations, within and between both religious and national communities, have had profound effects on all concerned.

Take, for example, some of the problems that arise in marriage and divorce. Most European countries now have bilateral agreements that recognize a wide range of marriages and divorces in Europe that were contracted in the Muslim home country. Though polygamy and child unions are not recognized at all, many other issues raise serious problems of jurisdiction and the conflict of laws.[31] Most of the female Moroccan clients of Dutch lawyers, for example, insist on their marriages being validated back in their home country: Even though few couples return to Morocco to live, the women consistently believe that a Dutch civil union is not a "real" marriage. But when, under similar circumstances arising from a bilateral accord between France and Morocco, there is a dispute about alimony arising from a revocable divorce entered in Morocco, it is the European judge who may be making up Islamic law. And if a Muslim woman must spend three months in virtual seclusion while her Islamic divorce becomes final, shall the European court recognize this practice, and grant her employee benefits during the period, or, by failing to recognize this period at all, subject her to the much longer period most European countries require for a divorce to become final?

One result of these difficulties has been the argument by some Muslims that they should simply have a set of laws that apply to them quite separately, a position that has been rejected in every instance.[32] But mediation and informal agreements have been encouraged by these conflicts such that Islamic officials often encourage the use of contractual clauses relating to education, property, and conditions for possible separation that are consistent with both Islamic practice and European laws. Though no Muslim adjudicative body operating in Europe can enter a judgment that is binding on that European country, the immigrant situation has stimulated the Muslim officials' role as mediators, though sometimes their reach is far more restrained than the resident migrants imagine or desire it to be.[33] Private agreements themselves may have their limitations: In Great Britain, for example, an attempt by a Muslim organization to provide a form will that would be consistent with both Islamic and British law failed to garner any support from the Muslim community. The same organization has also formulated a model marriage contract that, consistent with some schools of Islamic law, allows a woman the same power of divorce as her husband possesses and grants her the right to an uncontested divorce if the husband takes a second wife back in the county of origin.

In all of these instances, whether they involve such public matters as education and employment or relatively private arrangements such as marital property and contract, the effects on the millions of Muslims living in Europe have been profound. The question thus presents itself whether these reciprocal effects are actually leading to new, distinctive forms of Islam that are not only developing in the context of European migration but are producing various new forms of religious configuration that might broadly be thought of as forms of Euro-Islam. In addition, the question arises whether any such changes are not only affecting the lives of the Muslims living in Europe but have effects back home on the Islam practiced in the countries from which they derive and upon whose economies they have a tremendous impact. To the extent that such alterations may be underway, they appear to be occurring in several significant domains—in the range of choice available through the eclecticism and amalgamation of divergent schools of Islamic thought, in the formation of new institutions and alliances, in the differential effects that social change produces on family organization, and in the subtle effects produced through changes in belief and practice on conceptions of the self.

There are four classic schools of Islamic law—the Hanafi, the Shāfiʿī, the Hanbali, and the Maliki—which regulate everything from marital relations to styles of prayer. Though predominantly correlated with various regions of the Islamic world, a certain degree of admixture has been common throughout Islamic history. A number of Muslim immigrants to Europe have played on this possibility to further blur the lines among these schools of thought and to increase the range of choices available to fit both individual preference and adaptation to the constraints of the particular European host nation. Thus in the United Kingdom, for example, the Shariah Council, which seeks to mediate matters among Muslims of quite diverse backgrounds, will use the school of law of the disputants' place of origin but also shows them the range of choices available from other schools and allows them to choose the approach they prefer. Some people also speak of a developing "Anglo-Shariah," by which they mean that the British courts are sometimes called upon to determine Islamic law on a given matter and reconcile it with British public policy.[34] A wide range of issues arise: should the disfigurement of a Muslim girl's hand be valued in terms of her marriageability;[35] should the assertion that a Muslim girl is not a virgin be considered more slanderous because of the value placed upon virginity in the Muslim community;[36] should a Kenyan Muslim woman who was caught smuggling drugs be less culpable because she is expected to blindly believe and obey her deceased husband's brother who gave her the drugs to carry?[37] When called upon to address such issues it may be that forms of Islamic law are developing that affect both the Muslim community's perceptions of acceptable Islamic practice and the larger British common law. Other terms are also being heard elsewhere in Europe that reflect this eclecticism. *Takhyir,* a word formed from the root meaning "to choose," and *talfiq,* which stems from a root meaning "to invent, devise, fabricate, or piece together," are terms now coming into common usage to characterize this phenomenon. It remains to be seen, however, whether this process will yield either greater unity among Muslims of different backgrounds or new assimilative practices.

Orthodox Islam precludes the use of interest on loans. With the rise of fundamentalism one response has been the formation of Islamic banks, which give depositors a share in the profits rather than interest on their accounts, and which make use of various techniques, some involving forms of sale and resale that Western Orientalists categorize, like many Western practices, as legal fictions. A number of religious opinions (*fatwas*) have been issued that find mortgage interest permissible if some minimum housing is truly necessary or if, in the absence of a mortgage, genuine hardship would result.[38] The analogy is sometimes made to eating pork to forestall starvation. Given the acute housing shortage experienced not only by migrants in many parts of Europe but back in the Middle East, particularly in Cairo, the easing of restrictions on interest mortgages may be one of those adaptations that is paralleled in both Europe and parts of the Muslim home countries.

Indeed, the development of any form of Euro-Islam is deeply intertwined both with the changing structure of social ties within Muslim families in Europe and the reactions to the migrants' experience back in their countries of origin. As is true for immigrants generally, the experiences of the first generation of migrants are often very different from those of their children, many of whom have been born and raised in Europe. The parental generation often consists of men who grew up under colonial regimes and traveled to Europe—with limited literacy, skills, and welcome—and women who were poorly educated and dependent on their children to learn about the country in which they had been set down. The resulting generation gap is often quite wide. According to an official of the Paris mosque, fathers often eat and socialize separately from family members while their sons regard their fathers either as victims of the system or the perfect exemplification of the Arab saying that men resemble their times more than they do their fathers. Illiterate mothers, this mosque official told me, realize their ambitions in their daughters, while the daughters, in turn, liberate the mothers. Though commonly very distant from their parents in their social attitudes, he concludes, children frequently feel the desire to avenge their parents for the slights the parents have had to endure.[39]

These experiences yield rather different responses. In a series of Gallup poll surveys taken in the late 1980s, one sees that among the *beurs*, the French-born children of North African immigrants, 71 percent of those aged 18 to 30 say they feel closer to the way of life of France than to that of their parents, and 93 percent think it is possible to be integrated into French life and still practice Islam in private.[40] Studies also show that girls, who often act as mediators between the family and the bureaucracy while their fathers work and their mothers remain illiterate, are more receptive to change in social values and political involvement than the boys, many of whom seek to reassert control over their sisters as the young men attempt, perhaps, to redeem their discredited parents.[41]

Indeed, many of the second-generation children find themselves caught between two worlds. On the one hand, they have limited knowledge of their home countries and language; on the other, they are greatly limited in their opportunities in the host countries of Europe. As many of them say: "We are homesick everywhere."[42] When they visit their relatives, say, in Morocco, they encounter various derogatory terms: They are generally seen as a deviation, "another people," not a generator of change. This contrasts quite markedly with the experience of other Muslim migrants: Those from Turkey are said to have considerable impact on attitudes in the home country, even though the second-generation children remain deeply conflicted over their role in Germany.[43] Certainly the impact of the migrants on the economies of the home nations is enormous: Remittances to Morocco alone total two billion dollars a year, the second highest source of hard currency for the country.[44] But whereas in the past many migrants to Europe not only sent money home to build houses and commercial facilities but chose to retire there as well, in the absence of social welfare benefits most now plan not to retire to their home countries but to remain, with their families, in Europe. Thus the impact is at once—and quite variably—both centrifugal and centripetal: The Muslim communities in Europe become increasingly molded by their experience in Europe, and the effects they have on their home countries range from negligible to substantial. Regardless of the range, however, the signs of distinctively Euro-Islamic alterations are clearly visible.

These effects are also clear, if highly subtle, in the ways in which, religiously and socially, Muslims in Europe may be reconstructing their images of themselves. Olivier Roy has signaled this point in the following terms:

> What we see is that Muslims do adapt, not by changing Islam, but by adjusting their way of thinking about themselves as believers. . . . The real processes at work among the Muslims are that of individualization and reconstruction of identities along different patterns, all phenomena that undermine the very idea of "one" Muslim community in Europe. There is no Western Islam, there are Western Muslims.[45]

In what ways may this emphasis on individuation be manifest? For many it is expressed in a variation on ritual forms: Keeping only the first and last days of the fast of Ramadan, regarding Friday as a European-style Sabbath/weekend, avoiding regular prayers but intensifying the sense of identity through other cultural practices, and expressing a clear belief that no one should tell another how to be a good Muslim. Others, as we have seen, find the reinvigoration of national identity or attachment to strict orthodoxy more attractive, perhaps, as one leading fundamentalist has said, because it is the very fragmentation of the self—the violation of that divine sense of unity (*tawḥīd*) in which personhood and religious practice replicate the Qur'anic order of the cosmos, a fragmentation which was so vital to the Protestant experience—that is so antithetical to some immigrants' sense of well-being.[46] Yet even for this latter group the subtle effects on the sense of the self born of the European experience may be unavoidable: legal eclecticism, variant styles of family authority, estrangement from their home countries when they return claiming truer adherence to the faith. One writer has tried to characterize the styles of migrant adaptation by a typology that includes "silent agnosticism," "culturalist," "home-bound devotionalism," and "reinterpretation of founding principles."[47] The common denominator of many such responses may, however, be the changing relationship between the state and the individual as it is developing in the European Muslim experience.

Western commentators have, on various occasions, asked whether there is an equivalent in the Muslim experience to the rise of Protestantism in sixteenth-century Europe. The analogy is sometimes prompted by the hypothesis that as people move around more freely and kin-based associations count for less, the challenge to religious authority is matched by the challenge of a free-market economy. In other cases, the analogy is suggested by the possible reconfiguration of the state and with it the reimagination of how each self-fashioned person will construct the relation of community to self. Each of these analogies takes on distinctive forms when posed to the world of contemporary Islam, whether in the Islamic countries themselves or in the European hegira.

Obviously no strict analogy between present-day Islam and the Protestant Reformation is tenable. But there is an ironic aspect of the development of Islam among migrants to Europe that is worth considering. It has been argued that for the Puritans and other early Protestants the attraction of Protestantism came, in no small part, from the believers' view that they were, to a considerable extent, in conflict with the authority structure of the state and must, therefore, strengthen their communitarian ties, while at the same time others were attracted to the same beliefs precisely because it appeared to free them from the cloying bonds of both hierarchical authority and any other reading of the sacred than their own. Moreover, many were attracted to some alteration in orthodox belief and practice not because they were economically deprived but precisely because they could attribute whatever success they might have to their own efforts rather than those of "the system." Similarly, Muslims in Europe may find some attraction to increased fundamentalism or increased individualism/secularism as a result of the same forces—the desire to reconfigure their vision of authority and their need to assert their own place within the world.[48] Diametrically opposed as they may be in many respects, these two solutions may arise out of common experiences and share many more features in common than their adherents would readily acknowledge.[49]

Clearly no single new form of Islam is developing among the migrants to Europe, but a variety of new possibilities may well be in flux, and with them repercussions that could be significant beyond Europe to the Muslim countries from which these migrants have stemmed. If new ways of reconceiving oneself and one's relation to state, family, and ritual forms are occurring, if challenges to authority by fundamentalist and secularist alike belie a changing vision of choice and individuality, and if, perhaps most significantly, new institutions are developing through which these changing views are given political and cultural expression, it may yet be through the development of variant forms of Euro-Islam that the transformation of the religious lives of Muslims in many parts of the world and their relations with the West will transpire in the years to come.

Never in Doubt
Salman Rushdie's Deeper Challenge to Islam

No hinge nor loop
To hang a doubt on
Othello, 3.3.366–67

၈ၐ

The relation of faith to doubt is one of the most vexing problems facing any believer, and, at any given moment, each religion may come to some general resolution of the issues it entails. In moments of transition or situations of cultural contact, however, the issue of doubt and belief may well become the pivot
around which an entire religious and cultural orientation may turn. Shall the
findings or methods of science undermine faith or reinforce it? Shall the
calamities attendant upon loss to a superior force undercut or revivify confidence in the ancient gods? Shall the requirements of living among the heathen
permit amalgamations that raise questions about which among the articles of
faith or ritual practices are really essential to one's religious attachment? Like
nature, if doubt is cast out the door it has a tendency to come flying back in
through the window, and its dangers, no less than its possibilities, have been a
source of constant fascination to religious and irreligious alike.

Salman Rushdie will be forever remembered for the tribulations set in motion by his publication of *The Satanic Verses.* But if the questions of blasphemy
and politics, of death threats and public book-burning can be set to the side
and an effort made to return to the novel itself, some rather fundamental questions can be asked about the way in which the author has tried to cope with the
question of doubt as it is posed to those who have crossed borders of nation,
cultural context, and belief. Indeed, the issue of doubt can be seen to lie at the
heart of his novel just as, in many respects, it lies at the heart of any cross-
border experience. For as Rushdie says, in his explicit celebration of the hybridized, it is only through the commingling of the unitary that the full ambi-

guities and possibilities of human life and thought can be realized. Perhaps, as Hesse said, true suffering begins when cultures conflict. But Rushdie makes no such assumption, starting instead at the earlier point where the foundational question of how shall doubt itself be handled takes precedence over all other questions. Perhaps, in a sense, he feels that if this issue can be resolved in a way that allows degrees and variations of faith, then the conflict so worrisome to Hesse may itself be averted. Whatever Rushdie's success or failure in allowing the problem of doubt to become the central focus of his work, it may be valuable to peel away the politics of the book's publication just far enough to ask how the author himself approaches the problem—and then, by placing this issue back in the context of the dispute itself, to see how deeply challenging Rushdie's approach to doubt is for many Muslims today.∽∾∽∾∽∾∽∾∽∾∽∾

Neither the scandal occasioned by the publication of Salman Rushdie's *The Satanic Verses* nor the apparent end of the Iranian regime's decade-long support for its author's assassination should obscure the central theme of the book or the challenge, far deeper than any allegedly blasphemous passages, that the work as a whole poses to Islam.[1] It is not inaccurate to argue that "Rushdie has written a deeply Islamic book . . . a work of meticulous attentiveness to religion."[2] But it is also a book that seeks to insert among established orientations an unaccustomed style of thought and representation that goes well beyond unorthodox portrayals of the actions and intentions of the Prophet Muhammad. Put simply, *The Satanic Verses* attempts to introduce a concept of doubt into a religion that since its earliest days has equated doubt about fundamentals with unbelief. Moreover, it does so through a style of presentation—the creation of an entire epistemology pored forth in such profusion as to relativize its own believability—that trenches on the style of the central artifact of Islam itself, the Holy Qur'an. In doing so, Rushdie's novel merges the implications of a Western literary form associated with the questioning of basic beliefs with the foundational claims of Islamic legitimacy, a tactic that seeks to force a conversation many are unwilling to entertain.

The contrast between the role of doubt in the religious thought of the West and in the history of Islamic religious ideology could not be more striking. As Franz Rosenthal has put it:

> Doubt in whichever way indicated became the true pariah and outcast of Muslim civilization . . . a sufficient manifestation of ignorance . . . man's mortal enemy, depriving him of the certainty that his religion was intended and equipped

to give him. . . . The common belief was that necessarily and simply, doubt in God was unbelief. . . . Doubting as an epistemological tool and, even more so, as a way of life was banned from Muslim society.[3]

By contrast, for various Jewish and Christian thinkers, doubt became a critical test of faith. St. Augustine could put it at the center of his own quest for belief by saying "If I doubt, I exist" (*Si fallor, sum*), while the benefits of doubt have been variously commended, from Shakespeare ("Modest doubt is cal'd the Beacon of the wise"), Tennyson ("There lives more faith in honest doubt, believe me, than in half the creeds"), and Holmes ("To have doubted one's own first principles is the mark of a civilized man"), to popular sayings ("He that never doubted, scarce ever well believed").[4] This is not to say that there is no tradition of skepticism, both philosophical and mystical, in Islam. There is, however, a crucial difference between "intellectual skepticism and a religious core of protected immaculate belief" which, once transgressed, risks leaving the doubter not strengthened in his convictions but devoid of them altogether.[5] "He who believes, believes," says the Islamic Tradition; "he who cannot believe, disbelieves." To orthodox Muslims the image is thus much like that to which Wittgenstein alludes when, in distinguishing questions from doubts, he says that "some propositions are exempt from doubt, are as it were like hinges. . . . If I want the door to turn, the hinges must stay put. . . . The reasonable man does not have certain doubts."[6] Since the Qur'an is regarded as the direct and unaltered word of God delivered through His illiterate Prophet, to doubt its fundamental assertions is to become an unbeliever and thus to risk that the basis for a whole community of believers will become unhinged.[7]

In *The Satanic Verses* Rushdie explores, both explicitly and implicitly, the possibility of legitimate doubt within the framework of Islam. He does so through a series of complex interconnected "stories" that may be roughly summarized in the following way:[8]

Two figures, Gibreel and Chamcha, fall to earth from an airplane, their miraculous survival in Margaret Thatcher's corrupt and racist Britain paralleling their namesakes' careers in the days of the Prophet Muhammad. Gibreel, named for the angel Gabriel through whom the revelation of God's word was given to the Prophet, is the cowardly, demented Indian film star who betrays his wife, distrusts every friend, and is ultimately driven to murder and suicide. He is also embodied in the poet Baal, whose profanation of the new moral order during Muhammad's lifetime eventually leads the Prophet to kill him. Gibreel's companion, Chamcha, is transformed in Britain from an agreeable flunky doing voice-over advertisements for the Indian media into an exaggerated stereotype of the dark-skinned, oversexed immigrant who, like his analogue from the earlier time, Salman the Persian, survives his own self-hatred to return home bereft of any feelings or deep-seated attachments.

Each of these (and related) pairs of characters clash in different ways within and across their moments in time. Most crucial is the incident of the Satanic Verses itself, an occurrence contained in the Qur'an (Sura 53:20ff) and commented upon by a number of early Islamic scholars.[9] After hearing a voice he takes to be that of the angel Gibreel, Muhammad—whom Gibreel refers to by the medieval Christian sobriquet "Mahound"—recites phrases suggesting recognition of several pagan gods favored by the ruler of Jahilia, the city of sand where the Prophet conducts business (also the term for the pre-Islamic "Age of Ignorance"). The next day, as Muhammad wrestles Gibreel with homoerotic intensity to get at the truth of the previous day's "revelation," Gibreel finds the Prophet forcing words into his mouth that the Prophet in turn takes as divine utterances passed through the angel. Muhammad now claims the earlier verses urging recognition of the pagan deities to have been the work of the devil. As he dictates his revelations of God's word to his clerk, Salman, the latter begins to make alterations which the Prophet fails to correct as they are read back to him. After a number of increasingly bold alterations, Salman ultimately loses his courage and flees the inevitable confrontation when it would be "his Word against mine."

In the course of the novel Rushdie's protagonists call into question a wide range of Islamic precepts and traditions. Whether it is in the appropriation by the prostitutes who give protection to the poet Baal of the names of the Prophet's wives—and the consequent explosion in their attractiveness to their clientele—or in the portrayal of the Prophet's own quest for business advantage and worldly power, whether it is in the twinned tale of Ayesha, the modern Indic prophetess whose followers drown in the sea as they pursue her pilgrimage to Mecca, or in the Khomeini-like imam who can brook no views that go beyond accepted doctrine, Rushdie employs the full force of his Indian-English voice to question fundamental doctrines and explore the situations of those who live in the light and shadows cast by the Muslim faith and its progenitors.

Rushdie's narrative has been seen by some as a series of structural oppositions which, by the multiplicity of their temporal and emotional promptings, suggest that even the Prophet saw the singular truth he inscribed as entwined with "a promiscuity of sources."[10] Others have viewed the novel as a phantasmagoric account that challenges basic beliefs by the sheer profusion of its possible worlds,[11] or as an attempt "to reclaim language, to repossess the wells poisoned by the discourse of power, to invent a discourse for those underneath."[12] In any case it is difficult to understand how doubt enters the structure of the novel without appreciating the distinctively Arab-Islamic concepts of time and person against which such doubt is itself cast.[13]

Whereas Western stories traditionally begin with the invocation "Once upon a time," traditional Islamic stories begin "It was and it was not so, . . . it happened and it never did."[14] In the West time reveals the truth of persons, but in the Muslim world, particularly the Arabic-speaking world, it is not chronological unfolding but seeing people in a variety of contexts that shows what is most true about them.[15] Like the traditional story opening, Rushdie builds on the incapacity of time to reveal absolute truth, focusing instead on the sets of relationships his characters use in their various time frames, turning each, like a gem in the light, to reveal their multifarious qualities.[16] Whether it is in his constant pairing of opposites or his shifts from the modern confrontation with fundamentalism to the axial clash between the Days of Ignorance and the revelatory Days of the Prophet, the stage is set for recognizing that things are simultaneously so and not so, that simultaneous belief in a unitary truth and its counter is—at least in the optimistic outset of a story—both possible and desirable.

One of the few extended passages in which doubt enters *The Satanic Verses* explicitly occurs in the author's retelling of the moment when the angels themselves question Allah's choice of humanity as the central figure of His concern. Rushdie writes:[17]

> Question: What is the opposite of faith?
> Not disbelief. Too final, certain, closed. Itself a kind of belief.
> Doubt.
> The human condition, but what of the angelic? Halfway between Allahgod and homosap, did they ever doubt? They did: challenging God's will one day they hid muttering beneath the Throne, daring to ask forbidden things: antiquestions. Is it right that. Could it not be argued. Freedom, the old antiquest. He calmed them down, naturally, employing management skills à la god. Flattered them: you will be the instruments of my will on earth, of the salvationdamnation of man, all the usual etcetera. And hey presto, end of protest, on with the haloes, back to work. Angels are easily pacified; turn them into instruments and they'll play your harpy tune. Human beings are tougher nuts, can doubt anything, even the evidence of their own eyes. Of behind-their-own eyes. Of what, as they sink heavy-lidded, transpires behind closed peepers . . . angels, they don't have much in the way of a will. To will is to disagree; not to submit; to dissent.
> I know; devil talk. Shaitan interrupting Gibreel.
> Me?

Here Rushdie uses the example of the angels to contrast faith and doubt without equating doubt to unbelief. In doing so he must contend with a series of cultural and linguistic barriers. The primary word for doubt in Arabic (and in the Qur'an) is _shakk_, the root of which means "to pierce," "transfix," or "impale." The implication is that to doubt is to become immobilized, unable to move, incapable of expressing one's will through action in the world. Arab culture, by contrast, emphasizes that humans must constantly maneuver within the world, using their God-endowed reason to fabricate advantageous attachments within the confines of Qur'anic prescription and ordinary morality.[18] Belief in the truth of the Qur'an simultaneously attaches a man and gives him the ability to move through domains that might otherwise have been denied him: As one Arab told me, it is like an animal that has been shod and thus carries an additional weight, but one that allows him to traverse otherwise inaccessible terrain. Only at prayer, in that ritual reversal when force of personality is submerged in anonymizing uniformity, when constant movement is momentarily transfixed by the focus of worship, when submission (the meaning of the word _islam_) trumps mundane competition, is the immobilized person made to conform to a higher sphere of organizing movement.

Doubt, as an immobilizing force, and certainty, as a condition of a deeper reality, are posed against one another in various ethical and semantic ranges in the Islamic worldview. Thought, as conjecture, and knowledge, as certainty, are sharply contrasted in the Qur'an. Inductive thought—the level of evidence required to gain sufficient certainty to accept as valid a legal or theological claim—has long been the subject of intensive analysis among Islamic scholars.[19] But whereas knowledge (_'ilm_) is seen to be "established unshakably on the basis of reality,"[20] the mental process of thinking (_zann_) is equated with "surmise," "supposition," "uncertainty," and "doubt."[21] This distinction appears in the Qur'an, in the so-called Satanic Verses themselves, where those who disbelieve in the afterlife or accept the pagan gods as something more than "empty names and mere products of conjecture"[22] are said to "have not any knowledge thereof; they follow only surmise, and surmise avails naught against truth."[23] The "association" or "admixture" (_shirk_) of any powers with those of Allah is tantamount to idolatry and hence, throughout much of Islamic history, innovation has been seen as a threat to the faith. In general, wherever thought is opposed to knowledge the former is equated with supposition and conjecture. Thinking is thus deeply relativized, knowledge never is: The believability of the former lies in the credibility of its utterer, itself a function of those worldly consequent ties in which one is embedded, a diminishing but never absolute regress of public opinion and public consequence. "Man is man through men," says the Algerian proverb: "God alone is God through Himself."

To be in doubt is thus not a mental state that can be separated from its impact in the social and moral community of believers. To be in doubt is to go astray (*ḍalāl*), to commit excesses (*isrāf*)—attributes which, as Toshihiko Izutsu puts it, display "grave doubts concerning God's revelations, vain disputes about God, hearts too proud and insolent to believe in Him."[24] One Egyptian told me that when, as a teenager, he expressed doubts about his Islamic faith to a Qurʾanic teacher, the latter told him he must never give voice to such doubts since there was a great risk that he would never prise himself loose to be able to function in the world.[25] Certain domains of Islamic thought have traditionally been marked off as domains of uncertainty, but because foundational beliefs are not at issue they are not commonly subject to doubt. Most schools of thought thus reject the possibility of unequivocal answers to legal questions, the traditional absence of an appellate structure being only one demonstration of the incapacity of human judgment to claim absolute finality. Since assessment of believability depends on the degree of support that can be garnered for one's position—and working against the background of the Prophetic Tradition that says "my community will not agree in error"—the choice among alternatives to any issue is less a confession of doubt than an assertion of the need for social support of a proffered choice.[26] Rushdie must, therefore, address these background concerns when he seeks to put a wedge between doubt and unbelief since otherwise he not only risks immobilizing himself in a world of action by wandering off in the excessive pursuit of his own guidance but risks failing to garner the support necessary to legitimize doubt across the conceptual barrier separating certainty and surmise.

Rushdie is intensely aware, in this regard, of the place that language occupies in fabricating or undermining an individual's proper role in the world. In the world envisioned by the Qurʾan (as well as in contemporary Arab ideals), language is used to fashion ties of interdependence, ties that render each actor a credible witness to and creator of the social world. The world that Rushdie creates also depends on language: "Language is courage: the ability to conceive a thought, to speak it, and by doing so to make it true."[27] Ironically, as one pushes the limits of language one pushes the limits of truth. This is not, however, the same as lying. For if relationships can be forged through a revised vision of what is so—if one can conceive of an issue involving a rich man and a poor man as turning instead on the equal obligations of neighbors, or if a distant cousin can be conceptualized as like a cousin of much greater proximity and interdependence—then the resulting relationship validates the claim, renders it true because its consequences in the world are real. To lie is to over-step an utterance validated by relationship, oath, or reliant action; to profess an unvalidated counterfactual is like mentioning a price in the marketplace, an utterance that has no truth value unless it is accepted. "The best poet is the best liar," says a popular Arab proverb—but only because the poet pushes the lim-its of relationships which, if accepted, are indeed true.[28] The Qur'an, however, is careful to distinguish the Prophet from a poet: "Or do they say 'He is a poet for whom we await Fate's uncertainty'? Say: 'Await! I shall be awaiting with you.'" Since proof of the Qur'an's message rests not on miracles performed by the Prophet or his pushing the limits of the true in order to create the true, he is not to be equated with poets. But Rushdie and his characters are: They forge a whole new cosmology which if it sticks has the power of creating a world in much the way the Qur'an itself has done so. If, as Shelley said, "poets are the unacknowledged (but true) legislators of the world," then Rushdie and his characters challenge the Qur'anic paradigm of the poet with a view of social re-ality that is neither subservient to nor merged within the authoritative reading of holy text alone.[29]

To couple language with doubt, to create a unitary world out of uncer-tainty is, therefore, to challenge the very foundations of Islam. "Why do I fear Mahound?" reflects one of Rushdie's characters; "For that one one one, his ter-rifying singularity. Whereas I am always divided, always two or three or fif-teen."[30] Doubt, in Rushdie's account, arises when Salman notes how conve-niently an angelic revelation eradicates the disputing utterances of the faithful,[31] and most crucially when Salman makes alterations in the dictated Qur'an without the Prophet noticing. Thus Rushdie seeks to create, through his fantastical, dreamlike world, an affirmation of the contradictory nature of essential beliefs and hence the inability of any one person or group to claim ex-clusive power to arbitrate such beliefs.[32] Such "principled irresolution," a com-mon feature of the tradition of Western literature in which it is unclear who is the hero and who the villain, is a position that no orthodoxy can readily leave unresolved.[33] In order to forge a place for doubt within a system that has granted it no legitimate stance, Rushdie must, however, face two main issues: From what position can the author create his legitimate doubts, and in what form can his doubts be expressed?

Rushdie's position, in his own life as well as in his narrator's stance, is that of the immigrant, the man who has crossed cultures, spanned categories, the exile, the person who challenges each proposition by his interstitial circumstance. On the first anniversary of the Iranian death order, Rushdie wrote:

> *The Satanic Verses* celebrates hybridity, impurity, intermingling, the transformation that comes of new and unexpected combinations of human beings, cultures, ideas. . . . It rejoices in mongrelisation and fears the absolutism of the Pure. Melange, hotch-potch, a bit of this and a bit of that is how newness enters the world. It is the great possibility that mass migration gives the world. . . . *The Satanic Verses* is for change-by-fusion, change-by-conjoining. It is a love-song to our mongrel selves.[34]

Such boundary crossing also produces doubt. In a review of a book by Günter Grass, Rushdie could as well be speaking of himself when he says: "What Grass learned on his journey across the frontiers of history was Doubt. . . . [H]e suspects all total explanations, all systems of thought which purport to be complete."[35] Moreover, there is for Rushdie an implied progression associated with such doubt. Wendy Steiner specifies this connection as moving "[f]rom migration, to the constructedness of reality, to doubt, to democracy."[36] Modernity, with all its promise and foreboding, is itself linked to hybridity, says Rushdie: "Is not mélange, adulteration, impurity, pick'nmix at the heart of the idea of the modern, and hasn't it been that way for most of this all-shook-up century?"[37] There is thus a crucial threat contained in Rushdie's work for those in the Muslim world who claim an exclusive and authoritative voice, namely that distinctly European forms of Islam may develop around the millions of migrants now living abroad and that the forms of Islam they develop, hybridized and Westernized as they will be, would grant a role to multiple voices, to recasting fundamentals, to entertaining doubt in a way that seriously undermines existing authorities' claims to legitimate power.

Privileging the stance of the immigrant in the discussion of Islam would not, however, be enough to constitute a profound challenge to Islam. Rushdie has also had to face the problem of choosing a form in which such doubt could be expressed. And it is here, perhaps, that his even deeper challenge to Islam arises. It is, of course, very significant that Rushdie employs the form of a novel: As Bakhtin has said, in a novel voices compete, but with no single voice being authoritative.[38] And many who are offended by *The Satanic Verses* find, as Homi Bhabha has phrased it, that "[i]t is the medium Rushdie uses to reinterpret the Koran that constitutes the crime."[39] This reaction arises, however, not simply from the ironic tone, the admixture of categories, the scatological scenes referring to the Prophet or his wives, or even the fictionalized account of the Prophet's brief consideration of several pagan idols. Nor is it due only to

Rushdie's use of vivid word-pictures that challenge the traditional Islamic ban on representation or the use of humor which makes the word of God seem like a thing of play.[40] Nor is it even due to Rushdie "asserting—in earnest—that the Muslims' most basic beliefs were also fiction"[41] or, as Rushdie himself has said, to his own attachment to those exemplars of the novel "which attempt radical reformulations of language, form and ideas, those that attempt to do what the word *novel* seems to insist upon: to see the world anew."[42] Rather the challenge posed by his choice of literary form comes, I believe, from Rushdie's creation of a place for doubt through a medium that mimics the basis on which the Qur'an itself lays claims to its own legitimacy. To understand the serious nature of such an approach, one must understand something of the nature and style of this most central artifact of Islam.

The Qur'an is the centerpiece of the Islamic faith—far more important than the Prophet, the Traditions surrounding his words and deeds, or the actions of the community of believers. Over and over the Qur'an asks: What is the proof that this revelation is true? The answer lies not in miracles performed by the Prophet or wondrous powers that adhere to those who accept the faith. Rather, the words themselves are the sign of the Qur'an's veracity. If anyone should question this, says the Qur'an (52:34), "Then let them bring a discourse like it" (see also 2:21 and 17:90). Indeed, there is a field of scholarship in Islam, called *i'jaz*, whose purpose is to show that no human being could possibly construct verses like those of which the Qur'an is composed.[43] Significantly, the word *i'jaz*, which also translates as "miraculous," comes from a root that means "impotence" or "powerlessness," not in a sexual sense but in the sense that humans do not have the power to create such verses, and they are therefore miraculous because no other being could replicate them.[44]

Rushdie challenges this paradigm of truth by replicating it. He uses words to construct his world, he lays claim to whatever truth his story contains not by its protagonists' deeds or their effects but by his own inimitable prose, and he seeks the legitimacy of his own interpretation through the uniqueness of his own voice. By competing for control of the story of Islam, so jealously guarded by the very idea of *i'jaz*, he risks the danger noted in the Qur'an (34:18), which says of unbelievers: "We made them as but tales, and We tore them utterly to pieces."[45] In Arabic "The Satanic Verses" can be translated as "The Satanic Qur'an,"[46] and by his claim that out of words alone one man may create a world of truth other than the precise truth conveyed in the Qur'an, Rushdie lays claim to a part of the very legitimacy of the Qur'an itself.

But the author's challenge goes still farther. For the way in which Rushdie claims possible veracity for his own views imitates the repetitive, replicative, copious, cornucopian style in which the Qur'an itself is constructed. The Qur'an, in proving itself as a sign of its own truth, pours forth in a profusion of words, words that are to be chanted and memorized for all their textual foundation. Situations tumble forth without reference to chronology because truth is demonstrated by seeing the aspects of things in multiple lights until the fullest range of their truth is revealed by the fullest range of contexts in which they are placed. Rushdie seeks a similar basis for his own created world. He is working in the tradition of what Terence Cave has called "the cornucopian text."[47] As in the works of such writers as Rabelais, Ronsard, and Montaigne, the writer "give[s] reign to the liberties of writing"[48] and through the sheer abundance of his speech simultaneously grasps the world and invents it. Since, as Cave points out, "the deviations of the text undo meaning as fast as it is produced," the role of the critic is "to ironize his own analysis in order to exhibit the plurality of the discourse it questions."[49] By disguising its own artistry as similar to the profusion of the natural world, "[t]he figure of the writer asserts itself as the guarantor of a text which might otherwise appear as wholly anonymous."[50] The liberties of writing are limited, like nature, as prose proliferates without simple repetition, thus "endlessly deferring the realization of sense."[51] The French Renaissance texts, "written in the shadow of an impossible ideal," embraced this cornucopian style, thus partaking of "a centrifugal movement, a constantly renewed erasure of their origins."[52] And just as in the sixteenth century in the West, characterized by "the displacement of theological problems into imaginative literature,"[53] so, too, Salman Rushdie embraces the open texture that authoritative reading of sacred text rejects, at once giving centrality to his own "intuitive recognition" and demonstrating that "the proliferation of materials is affirmed by virtue of the unity of the hidden source from which they are presumed to spring."[54] Where, very importantly, he ultimately diverges from the program of most cornucopian texts, as we shall see, is in his acceptance of possible resolution.

Here, then, we can see why Rushdie's choice of style is so challenging. For *The Satanic Verses*, like the Qur'an, justifies itself by the creations of its own language; it claims authority by conducing the community of readers to ratify the believability of its author. Simultaneously, it professes to bespeak a unitary voice that comes from an invisible source while, by the very structure of its "linguistic plenitude"—its never-before-done-like-that, boy-no-one-but-Salman-could-write-like-that profusion of fanciful instance and multiple meanings—the book lays claim to its own self-justifying cosmology even as its deviations challenge all that came before. What Rushdie has done, in a sense, is to take the Qur'an, which is itself a cornucopian text, and appropriate its license as his own, its cosmology-formation as his own, and, until almost the very end, to combine it with the incoherence that the Western tradition imputes to all such texts, thus rendering a universal source subject to his critical ideals. It is an astonishing act of replication and denial, "blasphemy" and poignant imitation, deep-seated doubt and fundamental approbation from which no singular result can ease the believer's sense of derogation.[55]

Indeed Rushdie is very explicit in part of his challenge. At several crucial points in his book he asks of Islam, as of any faith, two basic questions: First, when it is new and politically weak, one asks: What kind of idea are you? And later: Having won, how are you going to conduct yourself?[56] What Rushdie apparently wants as an answer is for Islam to be the sort of idea that is like a person relying on his or her reason to maneuver in a world of considerable uncertainty and, having won, to be open to its own revision—to become, as he later says, an "unafraid Islam."[57] To accomplish this goal several very distinct orientations in Islam would have to be revised.

Islam has no tradition of the individual trying to create a moral realm of his own making: That order is given by Allah and the community of believers, and the Western notion that one can fashion oneself, not just as an actor in the world but as a moral entity, is quite foreign to Islam. This does not mean that one is not responsible for developing one's reason and learning how to conform to the precepts of the faith and ordinary cultural morality. But it does mean that the person is not the center of moral self-construction in the way that is meant in the West. Christians may imagine themselves conforming to the highest ideals by acting "Christ-like," but Muslims would not imagine themselves in an analogous role however much they may try to fashion their behavior, in part, along the lines of the *hadith,* the Traditions of the Prophet's utterances and actions.[58] If one were to try to become some sort of Muslim Descartes, it would still be necessary to establish a sense of resultant forms of belief and action. Would all boundaries, of the Qur'an and of the sacred law, be open to revision? Would one who raised doubts about fundamentals still be regarded as likely to be rendered immobile? In the chain of connections so much would be affected by such doubt that some plan for its boundaries or goals would be called for, not merely relativizing for its own sake.

Another issue goes to the role occupied by intent in Muslim thought. "There is no fault in you if you make mistakes, but only in what your hearts premeditate," says the Qur'an (33:6); "All acts are in their intention," says a Prophetic Tradition. A number of Muslims have couched their criticism of Rushdie precisely in these terms: He knew what he was doing, they say, by writing this book; he knew how offensive he was being.[59] Rushdie has responded to this criticism by writing: "He did it on purpose is one of the strangest accusations ever leveled at a writer. Of course I did it on purpose. The question is, and it is what I have tried to answer: what is the 'it' that I did?"[60] The "it," as I have argued, is the introduction of doubt into a system that equates such doubt with unbelief. But the point here is that the Muslim emphasis on intent cuts both ways. In the West, particularly in the novel (and even more so in the cornucopian novel), authorial intent has largely been displaced, while for Muslims it remains a central feature of assessing believability. As a result, both the form of the novel and its content are likely to be read very differently than in the West. For Rushdie to open a place for doubt, he must also contend with the issue of intent, and the very different meaning that it conveys to the believing Muslim than for his non-Muslim English-language readers.

A number of Western scholars have suggested that doubt is an inherent aspect of virtually every religion. Jack Goody suggests that skepticism is "intrinsic to the nature of religious belief itself," sometimes because of the failure of the divinity to deliver on its promises, sometimes (as in many monotheistic religions) because the scope allotted the exercise of human powers raises questions about whether God really possesses the powers to which He lays claim.[61] To Geddes MacGregor, one can universalize the Western concept of doubt as a kind of double-mindedness: "Doubt, therefore, is not to be equated with unbelief or disbelief but rather with a vacillation between the two opposites: unbelief and belief. . . . To the extent that religious people deprecate doubt, what they are deprecating must be indecision rather than unbelief, and what skeptics find praiseworthy in it must be not unbelief but a willingness to recognize two sides to a question."[62] And Jean Pouillon remarks on the double-edged meaning of the verb "to believe" (*croire*), which by implying both uncertainty and acknowledgment, constitutes a process in which believers "take aim within uncertainty."[63]

Doubt in Islam may share in some of these features, but not all. The vacillation of which MacGregor speaks is, for Muslims, a fear of the consequences of doubt: Doubt yields immobility, which leads to disaffection from the community and to the social chaos (*fitna*) such disaffection implies.[64] Belief is indeed a kind of direct knowing, but the uncertainty associated with this concept in the West is substantially ameliorated in the Muslim cultural paradigm by the inclusion of a wide range of local practice as not merely acceptable within Islam but *as* Islam.[65] Wendy Steiner, who is one of the few to note Rushdie's emphasis on doubt, says: "The difficulty with embracing doubt . . . is that it requires tremendous energy. Nothing stays in place; the reality one constructs so laboriously out of scraps and pieces constantly falls apart and needs to be re-constituted."[66] For Rushdie there is actually a twin problem: Within standard Islamic thought the instability of doubt is a threat to actual social order, as well as to the felt sense of the world as an orderly place. To genuinely doubt that world's foundational precepts is to call all order into question. Thus it is not merely a matter of the energy involved in doubt but its consequences, its dissolution of points of attachment without supplying any alternative, and the fundamental change in the rules of human engagement that introducing doubt would set in motion.

Rushdie appears to be aware that his challenge may devolve into *fitna* or be dismissed as directionless relativizing. But, as one writer has noted, "Rushdie's aim is not to expose the utter meaninglessness of an absurd world."[67] Rather, to borrow another's phrasing, "Rushdie's furious organizing energy seems to mark him as an angel of coherence."[68] For whereas in each of his previous nov-els Rushdie has concluded with an overall sense of fragmentation, uncertainty, and insuperable ambiguity, *The Satanic Verses* draws its antipathies together and closes with a generalized, if slightly forced, sense of an orderly world.[69] *The Satanic Verses* thus ultimately departs from cornucopian texts in that it does not lead to irresolution. This is, in a sense, one of those instances in which op-posites meet to confirm one another. The Qur'an is nothing if not resolved and unambiguous as to what is required of the believer and what will happen to him if he fails to meet his obligations. Rushdie, too, gives final resolution to his otherwise cornucopian text, thus confirming that self-validating texts (like his novel and the Qur'an) can raise fundamental questions and undo even their own prior assumptions without ultimately yielding to irresolution. And by this turn Rushdie confirms the moral tone of his work, distances it from its West-ern progenitors, and demonstrates its attachment to Islamic sources. Given the reaction it engendered it is, therefore, all the more ironic that, in its actual con-struction and attention to Islamic values, the novel should ultimately turn aside from its structural predecessors in order to avoid being self-indulgent and perpetually subversive.

At the same time, Rushdie, as immigrant, may be too far separated from the deeper currents of cultural change that may be occurring in many parts of the Muslim (especially the Arabic-speaking) world to appreciate that the ground-work for a new kind of skepticism and a new kind of pluralistic synthesis may, in fact, be coming into existence. For the first time, as we have seen, an inde-pendent concept of probability is showing itself, as people are less sure of the predictability of others' actions now that they are not as deeply embedded in negotiated ties as they once were. Causation is now often put not in terms of tracing events to the individual who engendered them but to a variety of forces and circumstances.[70] The line between acceptable interpretation in the holy law (*shariʿa*) and the Qurʾan proper has never been securely defined, and instances like the proper amount that women should inherit or whether custody should depend on "the best interests of the child" rather than the gender of the parent or child pose real challenges to practical thought. Rushdie may have pressed his challenge to authority before the groundwork for certain aspects of its revision have been set in place by these far deeper cultural currents.

Indeed, either through lack of knowledge or artistic decision, Rushdie has chosen to ignore the approach of the vast majority of Muslims, whose tolerance of individual uncertainty informs their daily lives and who find that voice submerged beneath the author's own attack on religious fanaticism. It may well be, as Akbar Ahmed has said, that "fundamentalism is a reaction to how to live in a world of radical doubt."[71] Indeed, by subscribing to the Western "theology of doubt," Rushdie can reconfigure the traditionalists' categories to conceptualize as a true Age of Ignorance (*jahilia*) one in which ignorance and religious certainty are combined.[72] It may even be that the ayatollahs—and critics of Rushdie's work generally—see in *The Satanic Verses* the possible reform of Islam occurring among those migrants to Europe who lie beyond the ambit of their complete influence. But by failing to give a place in his constructed epistemology to those who already embody the very traits he seems to commend, and by posing his attack on the extreme without fully representing the forbearance at the center, Rushdie is condemned to a kind of living death, a voice unable to have effect in the world, a doubt immobilized for all time, its intellectual challenge transmuted, transfixed, silenced.

In the end Rushdie has posed a far more significant test for Islam than whether the Prophet treated his wives well or wavered over some acknowledgment of two pagan gods. Whether Rushdie's book will endure as an example of unforgivable insult or as a satire that must be judged not by its fairness but by its intellectual honesty;[73] whether it is seen as the displaced migrant's voice of self-hatred or as "a gesture of wrenching loyalty"[74] by a writer who, having engaged in "some kind of contest with Revelation,"[75] has used literature to fill the "God-shaped hole"[76] within him; or whether Rushdie's book will be remembered because it fails to give any voice to the tolerant Muslim majority, it is clear that Rushdie's challenge to Islam cannot be reduced to the mere denigration of a great religion. Rather, the author has tried to consider how doubts about fundamentals could exist without fear that such doubts would destroy the faith. It remains to be seen whether, by his choice of the medium through which to explore that issue—by his very utilization of a style that ironically weds elements that the Qur'an and the cornucopian novel share—the challenges he poses may be lost to view, the author's deeper concerns never afforded the benefit of the doubt—even as far more subtle forces of change may be at work than he, for one, has succeeded in assisting with his artistic voice.

Notes

INTRODUCTION

1. John Ruskin, *Modern Painters,* vol. 3, *Of Many Things* (New York: Wiley and Halsted, 1857), ch. 17, p. 313.

CHAPTER ONE

1. Ward [1888] 1987.

2. See the essay entitled "Islamic Law as a Common Law System" in Rosen 2000. On the use of chain stories in the common law style of legal reasoning, see Dworkin 1986, 28, and White 1996, 586–87.

3. Dayan 1993, 35.

4. See, in this regard, Rosen 1972a and chapter six below.

5. Munson 1991, 334.

6. Reprinted in Pryce-Jones 1989, 96. Michael Gilsenan relates the following story that bears on the question of "corruption": "'Free giving' takes varied culturally appropriate forms, of course, and may require considerable virtuoso performative capacity to be taken as such. During my research in north Lebanon in 1971–2, I took a trip with friends to visit people in a large, high mountain village. The village was known for the military toughness and experience of its shepherd fighting men, and for its two major families of religious specialists, themselves central to the fighting force and to local politics. One sheikh came into the reception room, his arms crammed full of packets of tobacco and cartons of 200 (relatively expensive, prestige-brand) cigarettes. In what looked like an entirely random manner, he literally hurled the cartons at us with great force as we sat on the floor cushions around the walls. His arms empty, he exited as abruptly as he had entered, without a word. Everyone knew this was a disbursement made possible by sums he received from a powerful political figure in Beirut who had local electoral interests and used the sheikh as his agent. Everyone also behaved 'as if' it was a possibility created by grace alone, since there was an immediate tacit understanding that we treat the showering of benefits (a local *sparsio* so to speak, like the Roman emperors hurling gold coins to the crowds) as having no contaminating personal motivation or interest, precisely *not* a gift from the politician to us, and therefore having no other entailments of reciprocity or obligation" (Gilsenan 2000, 614 n. 7; italics in original). I have wit-

nessed similar events in Morocco—as, for example, when a patron divides up the meat and hands it around from the platter presented to guests in a client's own home—as if the patron were (which in a dramatically demonstrated way he really is) the source of nurturance in that home. In Gilsenan's case, as in those I have observed, however, it may be as reasonable to interpret these displays not as demonstrations of gift-giving but as proof that the patron is not corrupt, i.e., that he shares the largesse that has come his way with others. Indeed, his may be seen as precisely an act of reciprocity for the choice made by his clients to depend on him rather than some other "big man." For additional stories of "corruption" in the Moroccan context, see McMurray 1993.

7. Hammoudi 1997.

8. Transparency International (www.transparency.org), in their 1998 annual ranking, placed Morocco 50th out of 85 countries (with a Corruption Perception Index of 3.7 out of a perfectly uncorrupt 10), just below Brazil and Jamaica but well ahead of China, Turkey, Mexico, and Egypt. By 1999 Morocco had risen to 45th out of 99 countries, with a CPI of 4.1, just ahead of South Korea and behind Poland and Uruguay. In the 2000 survey, the latest in which it was included, Morocco ranked 37th out of 90 countries (with a CPI of 4.7), just behind Greece and Malaysia and just ahead of Italy and Jordan. This increase in ranking may reflect the efforts against corruption made by the new King Muhammad VI, who made an anti-corruption campaign a policy priority following his accession to the throne upon the death of his father Hassan II in 1998. On corruption generally, see Rose-Ackerman 1999, Noonan 1984, and Waterbury 1976. Though useful on the subject of bureaucratization, there is oddly no discussion of corruption in Herzfeld 1992.

9. See chapter seven below.

10. Gittes 1983.

11. See, e.g., the title and argument of Pryce-Jones 1989.

CHAPTER TWO

1. Cited in Berque and Charnay 1967, 15.

2. The phrasing varies. For example in northwestern Morocco: "The groom's legal right to his bride is expressed in the challenging cry of his relatives to her family, relatives and neighbours: 'Hâdi hiya diyalna, mashi dielkum' ('This one (woman) is ours, not yours')" (Evers-Rosander 1993, 118).

3. Merton 1976.

4. Merton 1976, 8. Merton writes: "The sociological theory of ambivalence . . . refers to the social structure, not to the personality. *In its most extended sense,* sociological ambivalence refers to incompatible normative expectations of attitudes, beliefs, and behavior assigned to a status (i.e., a social position) or to a set of statuses in a society. *In its most restricted sense,* sociological ambivalence refers to incompatible normative expectations incorporated in a *single* role of a *single* social status (for example, the therapist role of the physician as distinct from other roles of his or her status as researcher, administrator, professional colleague, participant in the professional association, etc.). In both cases, in the most extended and the most restricted sense, the ambivalence is located in the social definition of roles and statuses, not in the feeling-state of one or another type of personality" (ibid., 6–7; original italics).

5. Merton 1976, 17. For Merton's specific case studies, see ch. 2 ("The Ambivalence of Scientists"), ch. 4 ("The Ambivalence of Physicians"), and ch. 5 ("The Ambivalence of Organizational Leaders").

6. Merton 1976, 19. This sentence is italicized in the original.

7. Merton 1976, 24–26.

8. Mills 1983, 281.

9. Mills 1983, 283 and 285.

10. Merton 1976, 26.

11. Connolly 1987, 20.

12. Connolly 1987, 24.

13. Sennett 1980.

14. "'Power' (*Macht*) is the probability that one actor within a social relationship will be in a position to carry out his own will despite resistance, regardless of the basis on which this probability rests" (Weber 1964).

15. Parsons 1986.

16. Lukes 1974, "Introduction"; Lukes 1986, 1–18.

17. Galbraith 1983.

18. Foucault 1980.

19. Walzer 1974. The issue is addressed as well by Jack Goody when he notes that he had to undergo a ritual among the African tribe with whom he worked because of his own "dirty hands": "Indeed, as an ex-soldier, I had to undergo this ritual [cleansing], for even those who had killed honourably had to go through the same acts as a murderer. Blood was on their hands and it had to be removed; killing humans was dangerous in itself, regardless of motive or context" (Goody 1997, 260).

20. Levine 1985.

21. Even so materialist an anthropologist as Marvin Harris noted that ethnographers do not always see that "in human cultural repertoires there may actually be more domains which derive their salient semantic order from ambiguity and variation than there are domains whose orderliness reflects consensus and uniformity" (Harris 1968, 582).

22. Connolly quotes Stanley Diamond: "The principle of ambivalence is incorporated into myths and rituals of primitive peoples to an extraordinary degree . . . And this laughing at oneself means accepting the ambivalence of the human condition, for which civilization gives us little instruction or structured opportunity" (Connolly 1987, 23). Vanessa Maher, who also uses the term "rituals of ambivalence," quotes Richards (1956, 169): "Single explanations of ritual behaviour, however satisfying to the observer, seem to me to deny the nature of symbolism itself and its use in society to express the accepted and approved as well as the hidden and denied, the rules of society and the occasional revolt against them, the common interests of the community and the conflicting interests of parts of it" (Maher 1984, 117).

23. The quotes from William James, *Principles of Psychology,* vol. 2 (New York: Henry Holt, 1890), 429, and the internal quote from Campbell (1965, 306) are cited in Boehm's argument about human nature (Boehm 1989).

24. Goody writes: "Cognitive contradictions exist in those situations where an understanding of the world could go in two or more directions because of the very nature of that cognition. Those situations are necessarily unstable in the long run. That is to say, if a group chooses one line of thinking, the other remains a potential contradiction (an actual one at the analytic level) and at the individual level we have ambivalence. When such contradictions become explicit (as they are more likely to do when the formulations take a written form), but sometimes even when they remain implicit, they may lead to a shift from one alternative to another" (Goody 1997, 254). Goody does not believe such contradictions are "hard-wired" into human beings. See also Goody 1996.

25. Hammoudi 1997, 3. Hammoudi's reference to "attitudes" also signals the implicit social psychology associated with his thesis. In his extension of Foucault's approach, he argues that relationships of power involve constant "microdefeats of conceptualization," instances in which the ability of those with apparent power to control fully the terms of relationship are themselves undermined by "emotional inconsistencies generated by symbolic violence, a phenomenon comparable to motor disorders, verging on paralysis, that some particularly radical experience of fear can engender" (ibid., ix). In the section marked by ellipses in the text quoted, he says: "It seems that every individual has two coexisting personalities with features and comportments in one-to-one opposition and, most important, that the domineering personality is temporarily repressed and

hidden by the display of submission while in fact preparing for its own sudden emergence" (ibid., 3).

26. Hammoudi 1997, 5. Hammoudi writes: "So mystical initiation . . . converges with sacrifice and masquerade (which can still be observed today) in some crucial respects: both entail ambivalence, the disciple's seeking access to the saint's masterhood through a period of inversion, the son's conquest of the father's position after a lifetime of submission. There lies the cultural diagram of access to authority which informs all precedence relations and particularly the relation to the chief" (ibid., 146).

27. At some moments Hammoudi seems to give priority to the Sufi master/disciple relationship; at others to the relation of saint to follower: "If the royal institution and its legitimacy function in and through the hegemony of sainthood . . . *it seems logical to consider the master-disciple relationship in Sufi initiations as the decisive schema for the construction of power relations*" (Hammoudi 1997, 85; emphasis added); "As a cultural reference, the master-disciple relationship, as manifested in the initiation and discourse of sainthood, is by no means the sole space where a relationship of domination is played out. We have already remarked on the importance of the father-son relationship and the configuration of power in the family and in the work sphere. *The discourses of sainthood provide the symbolic anchor for all these relationships*" (ibid., 157; emphasis added). Of course, the two domains—of Sufism and saint veneration—are very closely related, but since rather few people belong to Sufi orders and far more acknowledge particular saints, whether there is a preeminent foundational schema or different ones for different individuals in different situations remains an important analytic distinction to keep in mind.

28. An example of ritual inversions of power is described by Hammoudi himself in Hammoudi 1993. The tradition of a student at the mosque-university of al-Qarawiyyin in Fez being made king-for-a-day was brought to an end some years ago by King Hassan II who was offended by a student who commanded the King to perform what was seen as a political, rather than the more traditional charitable, act.

29. Hammoudi 1997, 35. On the "ethics of closeness," see p. 50.

30. Hammoudi 1997, 78.

31. Hammoudi 1997, 43

32. Hammoudi 1997, 153.

33. Hammoudi 1997, 134: On colonialism and stasis, see p. 125.

34. For other views of patriarchy in North Africa and the Middle East, see Saaf 1989 and Sharabi 1988.

35. Caton 1987.

36. Berque and Charnay 1967.

37. Rosenthal 1997, 42. For additional examples of ambivalent concepts and their role in relation to power, see chapter six below.

38. Berque and Charnay 1967, 452–61. See, generally, Berque 1978.

39. Such red and black dyes are usually painted on the hands, feet, and sometimes faces of women in both rural and urban areas (Westermarck 1914, 102, 110, and 117). Berber women also used to go out on the field of battle and throw henna on any of the men who they thought were not fighting with sufficient courage. As one seventeenth-century traveler wrote: "The *Brebers* or *Mountainiers* likewise maintains this fewde, who are most shot and Swoord men, uppon the day of bataile their women follow hard behind them, with a colour in their hands called *Hanna:* And if they see any of their side offer to run away, or retyre, presently they will throwe some of this *Hanna* uppon their clothes, which will stayne, and the party ever after is held for a coward and a dishonoured Jew. For feare of this infamy few forsake the field, but either conquer their enemies, or dye like men, who are presently stripped and buried by these women which follow them" (Sherley 1609, facing page K3).

Henna may also be applied to the feet of boys during their circumcision ceremony. Maher says of the symbolism of henna in this context: "It is as if the dangers of the contact between male and female spheres, which occurs both during the marriage rites and when the child leaves the female world to join the male community, must be neutralized by this sign of female concern and blessing" (Maher 1984, 121). See also the re-study of Westermarck by Evers-Rosander (1993). By contrast, I see this less as a ritual of disjunction between gendered domains than as a blurring of gender lines, another example of that inversion of sexuality and gender that underscores the inherent ambivalence of roles and hence their manipulability for the construction of person-centered networks of dependence.

Hammoudi also suggests that one can distinguish between ambivalence and ambiguity insofar as the former carries more of a psychological and the latter more of a cognitive charge (personal communication). It could be argued, then, that in the case of Moroccan (and perhaps more generally Arab) culture cognitive ambiguity may be "handled" or "resolved" through mechanisms of cultural ambivalence.

40. Westermarck 1914, 25. While Westermarck is careful to note (p. 110) that the garment involved is a white *haik*—a large cloth women wrap around their bodies, an edge of which may be held across the lower face as a veil—others have, I believe mistakenly, described the same garment as a "blanket" (Combs-Schilling 1991, 667). Combs-Schilling not only sees the use of the "blanket" as part of the groom's rite of passage but as the transformation into manhood by replication of the pattern of monarchical attributes. The biological and cognitive theories on which her analysis are based are not only internally inconsistent and unfalsifiable but dependent on several metaphors that she has taken literally. See Combs-Schilling 1989. See also Maher 1984, 121–22 (describing the covering of babies at their circumcision with "large white blankets," later described as "veil/blanket[s]"). However, to describe these as "blankets" is like describing the headcovering of an Arabian as a tablecloth or dishtowel: The purpose defines the meaning of the cloth, which Westermarck was almost certainly right to characterize as a female garment and not a bed covering. Sometimes, too, a transvestite is brought in to dance at the beginning of the wedding festivities, which Hammoudi sees as an inversion that sanctions the rite of passage, and which, again, I would emphasize as a demonstration of the elusiveness of power rather than the transition from one prescribed role to another that is implied in the concept of rites of passage (Hammoudi 1997, 142).

41. Westermarck 1914, 27 and 152.

42. Westermarck 1914, 110. Westermarck says this is called *r-rbeṭ*—an extremely important Moroccan concept incorporating not only tying-up but creating a point of attachment, like those formed to a Sufi sheikh—but he offers no explanation for its occurrence. The image of the groom's immobilization is also represented by the chants he says were sung as the procession made its way back to the groom's home: "When they walk along the streets the boys of the bridegroom's party sing: He (that is, the bridegroom) took her, he took her, and God did not leave her behind. The boys of the bride's party sing: She took him, she took him, she wrapped him up in his *ksa* [the white cloth wrapped around a man's turban or body]" (Westermarck 1914, 166). Westermarck notes (p. 111) that the backs of the groom's slippers are also pulled up, thus further capturing him. The groom is also subjected to a ritual beating "inflicted on him by his bachelor friends because he is deserting their class" (p. 120)—or, as I would suggest, as a ritual demonstration of the uncertainties of power.

43. Westermarck 1914, 220. Correlatively, there may be fear that the bridegroom will fail to appear. Thus in her re-study of Westermarck's work, Evers-Rosander says: "However, when dealing with the buja [the ceremonial conveyance of the bride in a cage-like structure] there are other fears and worries and other threats at stake for the bride and her family. Will the bridegroom really appear in the buja or will he change his mind in the last minute and withdraw from the wedding? Will the envy of other people win and the bride be left with the shame of being abandoned, because the bridegroom has been exposed to a spell? The cage, which is a central space for evil magical powers, is often used for male manipulations, offering both conscious and

unconscious justifications for breaking up marriage promises and contracts" (Evers-Rosander 1993, 118–19).

44. Westermarck 1914, 315.

45. Westermarck 1914, 355.

46. Hammoudi 1997, 148.

47. I have explored this notion in numerous writings, most extensively in Rosen 1984.

48. Gellner 1988, 148 (original italics). While I disagree both with Gellner's analysis of segmentary tribal organization and with his assertions about trust and specialization—there were, for example, lineages of Berber law specialists in the Middle Atlas who were neither separated from their fellow tribesmen nor frowned upon—Gellner's recognition of such ambivalence should be taken as additional support for its prevalence. On the question of trust, see my essay, "The Problem of Trust in Arab Society and Law," in Rosen 2000, 133–50.

49. Westermarck 1914, 119.

50. Westermarck 1914, 339

51. That many Moroccans regard saints as still alive in their tombs does not contradict this interpretation. Supplicants use many of the same means—ritual sacrifice, gift-giving, etc.—to conduce the saint as they would a living person to respond to their requests. Being dead there is the added advantage that the saint makes neither counteroffer nor counter-demand, hence their being "better" than living saints. On ambivalence to dead saints in a Sudanese community, see Ibrahim 1994, 78.

52. Lewis 1988, 99.

53. On the failure of the *shari'a* to act as a limitation on power, see Lewis 1988, 113; on the *bay'a* in Morocco, see Hammoudi 1997, 24–25.

54. For an excellent example of the way in which the terms *jihad* and *fasād* failed to achieve resolution as sultan and "rebel" each sought to establish legitimacy by capturing the terms applicable to the other, see Bennison 2002. The point about tribal chiefs being dependent on recognition by their enemies is made in Brett and Fentress 1996, 65.

55. On the metaphor of games and power in Arab culture, see Khuri 1990.

56. Gellner 1988, 153.

57. It is worth quoting Foucault's argument about the relation of power to the concept of the individual at some length: "[P]ower . . . is not that which makes the difference between those who exclusively possess and retain it, and those who do not have it and submit to it. Power must be analysed as something which circulates, or rather as something which only functions in the form of a chain. It is never localised here or there, never in anybody's hands, never appropriated as a commodity or piece of wealth. Power is employed and exercised through a net-like organisation. And not only do individuals circulate between its threads; they are always in the position of simultaneously undergoing and exercising this power. They are not its inert or consenting target; they are always also the elements of its articulation. In other words, individuals are the vehicles of power, not its points of application. . . . The individual, that is, is not the *vis-à-vis* of power; it is, I believe, one of its prime effects. The individual is an effect of power, and at the same time, or precisely to the extent to which it is that effect, it is the element of its articulation. The individual which power has constituted is at the same time its vehicle" (Foucault 1980, 98). Amelie Rorty puts the matter more concisely: "Of course, if we focus on the action of individuals—whether individual persons, classes, subcultures, or institutions—*power* fragments and disperses. To understand power, we need to consider the ways that structures constrain and direct individuals, the ways that political and economic structures define interactions among individuals and groups. That is why power is often invisible; it is not lodged in any person or institutions" (Rorty 1992, 10).

58. Galbraith 1983, 75.

59. In a footnote, Galbraith characterizes Islam as a system in which there is a lot of conditioned power, along with a certain amount of condign punishment. He does not see it as an ex-

ception to his general rule that power leads to resistance, which in turn leads to submission (Galbraith 1983, 175).

60. For an example of how the social scientist may fail to capture the diversity of power attributions in a society, see Sertel 1972.

61. See text accompanying note 23 above.

62. "[T]he ambiguities of life are systematically underrepresented, when they are not ignored altogether, by methodologies oriented to constructing facts through strictly univocal modes of representation. . . . For the truth of the matter is that people have mixed feelings and confused opinions, and are subject to contradictory expectations and outcomes, in every sphere of experience" (Levine 1985, 8–9).

CHAPTER THREE

1. See Landau 1991, quoting each writer, for Darwin's argument that cooperative instincts may develop in a tribal context but moral sense depends on the "praise and blame of our fellow-men" (p. 54), as compared to the later view of Sir Arthur Keith: "Tribal organization provides the machinery of isolation or segregation which is necessary if physiological processes are to work towards a new racial type" (p. 84).

2. On the image of the closed circle, see Pryce-Jones 1989: "It is as though the Arabs have trapped themselves inside a closed circle from which they sense that they must break out for their own good, but within which identity and its supportive values paralyze endeavors of rescue" (p. 403). On the view that Arab states are just puffed-up tribes, see Glass 1990; for an example of an influential political analyst who, after lengthy description of Lebanese politics, concludes—with no definition or explanation—that Near Eastern politics is all just tribal, see Friedman 1989. See also Friedman 2002: "[A] few U.S.-educated Saudis . . . , when alone with me, confided what I think is the truth. One put it like this: 'The tribal mentality here is very strong, and in the desert, when the tribe is attacked, you'd better stick together or you're dead.'"

3. *Indian Claims Commission Act,* 25 U.S.C. § 70a (1946). See, generally, Danforth 1973. On the role of anthropologists in the proceedings of the commission, see the discussion and references in Rosen 1977.

4. Most introductory anthropology textbooks still use this paradigm even though only a few cultural anthropologists—but most archaeologists—continue to accept its utility. Among those cultural anthropologists who rely on evolutionary models, see, e.g., Johnson and Earle 2000 and Earle 1997.

5. Royal 1951, 66. See also the definition and references in Barfield 1997, 475–76.

6. Lewis 1968.

7. A great deal of writing has, of course, been done over the years on the structure of tribes in the early Islamic period. For two examples that are germane to the thrust of this essay, see Landau-Tasseron 2000 and Wolf 1951.

8. Evans-Pritchard 1949 and Evans-Pritchard 1940; Montagne 1930. For a partial English translation, see Montagne 1973.

9. See, generally, Evans-Pritchard 1940, especially those instances, for example, where he says of intra-tribal disputes: "These combinations [of tribal sections] were not always as regular and simple as they were explained to me and as I have stated them" (Evans-Pritchard 1940, 144). On the relation of Evans-Pritchard's theories to his style of presentation, see Geertz 1988, 49–72. In the case of Morocco, it is actually the early French anthropologists, like E. Doutté, who understood that tribes did not follow rigid segmentary principles (Doutté 1914).

10. Gellner 1959, especially 264–65. On Gellner's position in British philosophy, particularly after the publication of *Words and Things,* see Mehta 1962. On Gellner's intellectual biography, see the essays in Hall and Jarvie 1996.

11. Indeed, Adam Kuper entitled his obituary of Gellner "The Last of the Central Europeans" (Kuper 1996).

12. Throughout his life Gellner was drawn to the mountains, and it is not irrelevant that, whether in the High Atlas of Morocco, the Alps, or the Himalayas of Nepal—places that in the West have always been associated with images of political independence and resistance—he should have been intellectually attracted to mountain communities. See, in this regard, his account—both descriptive and metaphorical—of having once been lost in the mountains (Gellner 1974, 10–13). On the influence of Evans-Pritchard's study of the Nuer on Gellner, Kraus states: "According to Paul Stirling, his one-time supervisor, at first Gellner was not at all aware of the relevance of Evans-Pritchard's seminal Nuer study [Evans-Pritchard 1940] to his data" (personal communication, 19 May 1996). That would not necessarily be surprising, however, since Gellner came to these issues in terms of the nature of anarchy, and Evans-Pritchard, from questions of political structure and descent theory.

13. Gellner 1974, 4 (original emphasis). Gellner quotes William James's *Pragmatism:* ". . . if you know whether a man is a decided monist or a decided pluralist, you perhaps know more about the rest of his opinions than if you give him any other name ending in *ist*" (pp. 1–2). There is some irony in Gellner citing an American pragmatist, from whom he is intellectually so distant and from whom Gellner's rival, Clifford Geertz, derives a significant part of his own intellectual heritage. See Geertz 2000.

14. Gellner 1974, 14

15. Gellner's antipathy to pluralism and Wittgenstein coalesce in his attack on the latter's idea of "forms of life": "Forms of life and cultures are precisely what thought does not and need not automatically accept. Cultures must not be judges in their own case, as the claim that they 'have to be accepted' would have it. They often fail to be viable and collapse through sheer internal incoherence. . . . The seemingly modest abstention from transcendence, in fact here amounts to the immodest, dogmatic, and *carte blanche* endorsement of all and any 'form of life'" (Gellner 1974, 20).

16. One can see this in such instances as the legal cases involving the Indian Claims Commission, referred to above, or the case involving the definition of "tribe" and its applicability at different moments in the history of the Mashpee Indians. See Clifford 1988.

17. See Hoebel 1978.

18. Emyrs Peters was the archetype of one who kept finding fault with his own previous structural account but then always opted for yet another structural explanation. If at first it was family organization that was key but he found exceptions there, he asserted that it was ties to maternal kin that was crucial; and when that produced only more anomalies he substituted an explanation based on some other structural constant. See Peters 1990. This pattern led a commentator on a paper Peters once delivered to suggest that he had no idea what was wrong with the account Peters had just presented but he was quite sure that the author would explain what was wrong with it in his next paper.

19. Fried 1966. For an application of this argument in the context of the Barbarians of Western Europe, see Wells 1999.

20. See Wells 1999.

21. The point has been made by Kenneth Brown. Similarly, in a number of Native American tribes the chief of one group essentially had to be acknowledged by rival groups for his own people to recognize him as their leader.

22. Glain 2000: "At least three-quarters of the Iraqi people are members of one of the nation's 150 tribes . . . A big problem with the U.S. approach, according to a senior diplomat in the region, is that it tends to focus on cultural, ethnic and religious differences—instead of the family ties that bind tribes and offer the most fertile sources of opposition when they unravel."

23. "The most enduring example of the gentle authoritarian tradition was that of the Ottoman Turks. . . . The more popular support the Ottoman rulers garnered through the ages, the

more they sought to sustain their authoritarianism without resort to force, but instead by building bridges to key sectors of the societies they ruled, by allowing others to share in the spoils and *by never totally vanquishing their opponents,* but instead leaving them a way out so that they might one day be turned into friends" (Friedman 1989, 92; italics added). In the war in Afghanistan that followed the terrorist attacks of September 11, 2001, many of the Taliban fighters only agreed to surrender if it was to a particular Northern Alliance soldier, who often then embraced the defeated man (Pratt 2001).

24. See, generally, Roy 1990 and Roy 2000b.

25. Geertz et al. 1979, 35–47, and Rosen 1984. For more detail, see below at p. 100 For an example of how this point may be insufficiently appreciated, see the discussion of tribes in Hourani 1991, 104–8.

26. For an example of a regional dispute involving just such shifting claims of affiliation, see Geertz et al. 1979, 53–57.

27. *Mashpee Tribe v. New Seabury Corp., Federal Reporter,* 2nd ser., vol. 592 (1st Circuit 1979), pp. 575ff. See also Clifford 1988, 277–346, and Getches et al. 1998, 352–58

28. On the relation of Islamic law to custom, see Rosen 2000, 85–98. See also Layish and Shmueli 1979.

29. On the role of women in the religious associations to which their sons may be tied, see Dwyer 1978.

30. Dresch 1990, 255.

31. Boon 1982, 102.

32. Edouard Doutté especially comes to mind in this regard, but it was true for a number of *affaires indigènes* officers and scholars in the period surrounding the establishment of the French Protectorate of Morocco in 1912.

33. On forms of alliance, see Geertz et al. 1979, 43–45, and Rosen 1984, 105–6.

34. Diamond 1997, 272–73.

35. Diamond 1997, 283.

36. Diamond 1997, 286.

37. Diamond 1997, 288–89.

38. Clastres 1974, 35.

39. Clastres 1974, 181. Clastres romanticizes tribes when he says: "Primitive societies, like Western societies, are perfectly capable of handling the possibility of difference within identity, of otherness in homogeneity; and in their rejection of the mechanistic can be read the sign of their creativity" (p. 47), as well as with his claim that chiefs never succeed in placing their own interests ahead of the tribe: "If it 'worked' [that chiefs could do so], then we would have found the birthplace of political power, as force and violence; we would have the first incarnation, the minimal form of the State. But it never works" (p. 177). He fails too to see that speech, far from being mere palaver, is crucial in many tribes to the acquisition of *temporary* authority, which may be quite extensive, as well as to the mechanisms through which it can be withdrawn, terminated, or rotated. See, for example, Meeker 1979.

40. Munson 1989, Dupree 1984.

41. Kraus 1998, 16

42. Kraus concludes: "Even if its formal simplicity may not be apparent in social action, only a naïve empiricism should deceive us into overlooking the more than just subtle ways in which segmentation structures and restructures society, demarcates rights and obligations, and posits persons ready for action" (Kraus 1998, 19). This, of course, fails to specify what is meant by "posits persons ready for action" or why this is not precisely a call for the sort of interpretive approach Gellner, as an anti-pluralist, could not credit. Kraus does not cite the detailed studies (such as Rosen 1984) that demonstrate an alternative paradigm and provides no specificity as to how people can "clearly hold a model" that re-orders social relations only occasionally (p. 16).

43. Lindholm 1995, 818 (italics added). Lindholm says: "The contradiction between the inter-pretivists' own credo which gives priority to local knowledge as the basis for understanding cul-ture and their simultaneous depreciation of the importance of pervasive local dogmas of social organization seemed to bother almost no one. This new concern with 'negotiated realities' was preadapted to accommodate itself to Said's attack on all forms of cultural constraint, since it was a small logical step from arguing that the traditional anthropological-native categories were a disguise for the reality of maximizing individuals manipulating for advantage within culturally-constructed webs of meaning to arguing that all categories whatsoever were merely reflections in the colonizing eye of the Western onlooker" (Lindholm 1995, 807). The internal contradictions, the illogical connections, the implications of "preadapted" bias, the absence of any substantive ar-gument, and the inability to distinguish among authors in this passage are characteristic of the ar-ticle as a whole.

Lindholm also relies on Edward Said's critique of Orientalist scholarship for his attack on Geertz, but he does not bother to note that Said himself specifically exempts Geertz from his own critique: "Thus interesting work is most likely to be produced by scholars whose allegiance is to a discipline defined intellectually and not to a 'field' like Orientalism. An excellent recent instance is the anthropology of Clifford Geertz, whose interest in Islam is discrete and concrete enough to be animated by the specific societies and problems he studies and not by the rituals, preconceptions, and doctrines of Orientalism" (Said 1978, 326).

44. "So in the end, whilst the model is propounded in part because any model is better than none, this modesty, or hedging of bets, if you wish, is a good deal less than total" (Gellner 1981, 85). It is as if one had tried to import into scholarship the argument of Ibn al-Furat, a tenth-century vizier of the caliphs of Baghdad, who said, "It is better to keep the affairs of government moving on the wrong path than to stand still on the right one" (quoted in Lewis 2000, 223). David Hart, who struggled for decades to make segmentarity work for North African tribes, seems to make the same suggestion when he asks, rather rhetorically: "[I]s a segmentary model, or a segmentary lin-eage model, no matter how inappropriate or inept, really no better than no model at all, as Gell-ner has suggested?" (Hart 1993, 233). After asserting, quite erroneously, that "certainly no *other* model of comparable validity has been put forward," he says of segmentary theory that "its inad-equacy is nonetheless patent and profound," that "in almost all concrete cases, the fit is at best fuzzy and at worst procrustean," and that "not to mince words about the matter, it is not really present at all" (Hart 1993, 233; original italics). Similar ignorance of the literature and hostility to a more cultural approach is evident in Roberts 2002. As with others cited here, this dismissiveness and failure to join issue speaks to both scholarly temperament, the dead weight of "ordinary sci-ence" at its worst, and the utter impoverishment of the whole segmentary debate.

45. Caton 1987.

46. Thus Dresch, without specification, writes: "A noticeable theme in recent writing, how-ever, has been to sever oneself from anthropology's past. The result, if one may tread on this deli-cate ground, is often that the generalized passive observer of the functionalist period is replaced by as generalized and as suspect a figure, though eminently modern, the figure of an interpreter who purports to speak from only God knows where" (Dresch 1988, 61). And in a reference to the work of myself and others, he says, without clarity or support: "Certain of the formulations which then resulted put one more in mind of Radcliffe-Browns' immediate students than of the writers' own contemporaries, suggesting very strongly the loss of tempo that can result from a particular read-ing of the subject's past" (Dresch 1988, 63, note 11). Leaving aside whatever is meant by "loss of tempo," the implication that one has not considered the history of an issue just because a separate essay on the subject has not been written, or that no thought has been given to the criteria for in-terpretations, is simply to ignore the works of those one is criticizing.

47. Quoted in Khaldun 1967, 292, or Khaldun 1987, 107–8.

1. This passage from Frankfurter's decisive vote in the 5–4 decision will be found in *Louisiana v. Resweber,* 329 U.S. 459, 470–71 (1946). Blackmun's decision is from *Furman v. Georgia,* 408 U.S. 238, 405–6, 414 (1972). In February 1994 Blackmun finally said that he could no longer support the death penalty because there was no way to insure its fair application: "I feel morally and intellectually obligated simply to concede that the death penalty experiment has failed."

2. On this style of questioning as a way of engaging the other in the validation of utterances that otherwise have no inherent truth value, see Rosen 1984.

3. Bohannon 1966. It is also only in Morocco that I have ever heard anyone ask, apropos the impeachment of President Clinton, whether it isn't obvious that the Republicans sent Monica Lewinsky to the president in order to entrap him in an embarrassing situation.

4. For the medieval period, see Morris 1972. For a brief account of the sources for that period and how they compare to the Arab context, see Rosen 1991.

5. As one writer has put it: "The individual was encouraged to perform, to the best of his ability, the duties assigned to him by his religion or by custom, rather than to forge a subjective world for himself, based on his individual perceptions and needs" (Sandler 1976, 137). For an elaboration of the concept of the person in Arab society, see Rosen 1984. On the more theological and philosophical aspects of personhood in Islam, see Lahbabi 1964.

6. Goitein 1977, 5–6.

7. Goitein 1977, 7 (original italics). Rosenthal also speaks of "the Muslim view . . . that all matters human have a positive as well as a negative side" (Rosenthal 1997, 42).

8. Gilsenan 1976, 198.

9. Thus, we learn, chess became the theologically correct game in the early years of Islam, rather than games of chance, because it demonstrates how humans must use their God-given reason to overcome their passions and further the well-being of themselves and their dependents. See Rosenthal 1975. The Qur'an itself refers to life as a diversion and a sport (57:19). For an extended exploration of the metaphor of games in understanding Arab social and political culture, see Khuri 1990.

10. Rosenthal 1974. On Islamic biographies, see also Hourani 1991, 165–66.

11. See Rosen 1989a.

12. See Geertz 1979.

13. Geertz et al. 1979, 315–91; Rosen 1984.

14. See Rosen 1984, 165–79.

15. For discussion of some of these points, see Hammoudi 1994. On the biographies of saints, see Katz 1992.

16. Referred to in Sandler 1976, 145.

17. This may also be an example of what Rorty means when he suggests that in some instances it may be one's emotions that are assembled in an orderly fashion rather than one's ideas.

18. Kerr 1963, 11.

19. Dresch 1990, 256 and 281.

20. On the personalistic nature of the surrender of some Taliban soldiers, see note 23 to chapter three, above.

21. Lewis 1988, 107.

22. See, e.g., Meeker 1979.

23. "The notion of the ruler as the father of his country or people, common in the West and expressed in such terms as the Latin 'paternal' or the Greek 'patriarchal,' is absent in Islam. . . ." (Lewis 1988, 17). See, generally, Sartorius 1983.

24. See Lewis 1988, 35–37. See, generally, Arkoun 1989.

25. Geertz 1973, 247. Geertz elaborates: "In Morocco, the main obstacle to defining an integral

national self has not been cultural heterogeneity, which in comparative terms has not been so very great, but social particularism, which in comparative terms has been extreme. Traditional Morocco consisted of an enormous, ill-organized field of rapidly forming and rapidly dissolving political constellations on every level from the court to the camp, every basis from the mystical to the occupational, and every scale from the grand to the microscopic. The continuity of the social order lay less in any durability of the arrangements composing it or the groups embodying it, for the sturdiest of them were fugitive, than in the constancy of the processes by which, incessantly reworking those arrangements and redefining those groups, it formed, reformed, and re-reformed itself" (Geertz 1973, 246).

26. Pipes 1983 as cited in Muñoz 1999, 15.

27. I therefore disagree with those who, like Thomas Friedman of the New York Times, assert that all Arab governments are "illegitimate." For even though Friedman does not define the term, neither control through elections nor some unspecified level of satisfaction with its operations renders a government illegitimate to its people. Indeed, to suggest that these governments are illegitimate in the eyes of their fellow countrymen is, for purposes of developing policies towards them, dangerously misleading. The issue of legitimacy must, I believe, be addressed at the more specific cultural level this essay seeks to exemplify.

28. "... Islam has so miserably failed to create democracy and tolerate human rights. . . . Perhaps it is the absence of the 'legal person' the West inherited from Roman law—local governments, colleges, societies, corporations that run their affairs and can be held responsible, subject to suit" (Rosenthal 1999).

29. See Toledano 1981, Rosen 1989a, and Rosen 1989b (reprinted in Rosen 2000).

30. See Rosen 2000, 38–68.

31. On the role of customary law in colonial South Africa, see Mamdani 1999. Although Mamdani has many insightful arguments for the African context and for certain kinds of tribal situations, his argument cannot be generalized to the Arab world, where the emphasis on customary law was simply a response to Western colonialism, where ethnicity plays less of a role in legal localism, and where, it may be argued, the problem Mamdani sees for the future—joining representation in the central state with participation in the local sphere—may actually have been settled in much of the Near East by the combination of Islamic law as customary law and the dispersion of power through personalistically constructed networks.

32. Frisch 1997, 347.

33. On Pharaoh in political imagery and sayings, see Goldberg 1991, 17–18. See also Douglas and Malti-Douglas 1994.

34. Elster has written: "If in ancient societies the rulers could get away with overt discrimination, it was only because they had superior force at their disposal, but also because their behaviour could no more be assumed to be just and rational than one would expect a hurricane to be, and hence did not create resentment among the subjects." This would not apply to Arab leaders, whether of the classical period or the present, inasmuch as they are, far from natural phenomena, quintessentially the product of their social systems and are, in the eyes of those over whom they may for a time hold sway, themselves dependent on the very system that has cast them up, as it has, to some degree, most everyone else. On political legitimacy in the Arab world more generally, see Sonn 1990 and Ayubi 1995.

35. "Seuil de tolérance" 1999. On Hassan's style, particularly in the years leading up to his death in 2000, see Denoeux and Maghraoui 1998.

36. A survey by Freedom House in 2001 showed that of 47 predominantly Muslim countries, only 11 (or 23 percent) could be classified as democratic (Croisette 2001). None of the Arab countries of the Middle East is generally classified as a democracy. On violence, see, e.g., Patai 1981; on romantic fantasies of the past, see Fouad Ajami as quoted in Croisette 1998. Some political scientists assert that the repression of any alternative to authoritarianism—itself bolstered by the ab-

sence of civil society, state monopoly of the economy, social inequality, distance from democratic neighbors, and Islam itself—explains the absence of democracy in the Middle East. But neither this claim, nor the claim that such repression would fade in the presence of fiscal health, international support networks, or population mobilization, accounts for the quite forceful reassertion of authoritarianism through its connection to personalism. It is this level of specificity, not some generalized "cultural explanation," that is required. On democracy in the Arab world, see Cotran and Sherif 1999, Luciani 1990, Mernissi 2002, and Vatikiotis 1987; for Indonesia, see Hefner 2000. For additional historical and regional comparisons, see Anderson 1974, Anderson 1995, and Potter et al. 1999; on authoritarianism in various Middle Eastern contexts, see Abou El Fadl 2001, Al-Azmeh 1997, and Heydeman 1999.

37. For the contrasting view, see Pandolfo 2000, 138ff. For the contrast to the West, where it is assumed that the self is divisible and that many mental health problems must be understood against this "natural" fact, compare Lifton 1993.

38. On the role of masking in certain Moroccan rituals, see Hammoudi 1993. On Moroccan youth fluctuating between hedonistic and fundamentalistic identities, see Bennani-Chraibi 1994.

39. For the contrary view that class trumps personalism, see Hammoudi 1997, 25.

40. See Rosen 1984, 172–77.

41. Waterbury 1970, 259. Waterbury also says: "What is striking about the tribes of the Central High Atlas is that their political system was so structured as to defy all attempts at routinization" (idem). Notwithstanding Waterbury's (and my own) criticisms of Gellner's *Saints of the Atlas,* I believe Waterbury's point has great currency for both North Africa and Middle Eastern political culture generally.

42. Another example would be the use of taped sermons by the Ayatollah Khomeni in the years of exile leading up to his triumphal return to head the new Islamic Republic of Iran.

43. Meital 1997. See, generally, Danielson 1997.

CHAPTER FIVE

1. In book 12 of the *Metamorphoses,* Ovid speaks eloquently of the place of rumor:

> There is a place in the middle of the world, 'twixt land and sea and sky, the meeting place of the three-fold universe. From this place, whatever is, however far away, is seen, and every word penetrates to these hollow ears. Rumour dwells here, having chosen her house upon a high mountain-top; and she gave the house countless entrances, a thousand apertures, but with no doors to close them. Night and day the house stands open. It is built all of echoing brass. The whole place resounds with confused noises, repeats all words and doubles what it hears. There is no quiet, no silence anywhere within. And yet there is no loud clamour, but only the subdued murmur of voices, like the murmur of the waves of the sea if you listen afar off, or like the last rumblings of thunder when Jove has made the dark clouds crash together. Crowds fill the hall, shifting throngs come and go, and everywhere wander thousands of rumours, falsehoods mingled with the truth, and confused reports flit about. Some of these fill their idle ears with talk, and others go and tell elsewhere what they have heard; while the story grows in size, and each new teller makes contribution to what he has heard. Here is Credulity, here is heedless Error, Unfounded Joy and panic Fear; here sudden Sedition, and unauthentic Whisperings. Rumour herself beholds all that is done in heaven, on sea and land, and searches throughout the world for news. (vol. 2, Frank Justus Miller, trans. [Cambridge: Harvard University Press, 1921], 183–85)

2. See Voinot 1948, Zafrani 1998, and Deshen 1989.

3. King Hassan II died in July 1999. His eldest son ascended to the throne under the name of King Mohammed VI.

4. The King's speech was delivered on January 14, 1986, to a representative group of architects selected by the Ministry of the Interior (Alami 2001). On this moment in Sefrou's architectural/ political history, see, generally, Geertz 1989. In May 2000 the new king, Mohammed VI, visited Sefrou as part of a tour of drought-affected regions. No mention was made publicly of his father's criticism of the town's appearance. Indeed, since Sefrou was raised to the level of a province in the 1990s, the newly installed governor, working with the city council, has made a considerable effort to improve the city's overall appearance.

5. See especially chapters 4–6 of Westermarck 1926.

6. See, in this regard, Waterbury 1972.

7. See Berque 1958 and Geertz 1968.

8. This story is told more fully in Rosen 1972b and Rosen 1984.

9. On the role of the Jews in Sefrou and Morocco see chapter one above, as well as Rosen 1968, Rosen 1972a, and Rosen 1984. For another interpretation see Stillman 1977 and Stillman 1991. On ambivalence in Moroccan culture, see chapter two in this volume.

10. It is also interesting to note that the history of annual celebrations (sing., *musem*) did *not* figure in any of the accounts. Briefly, there had been such events until the early years of the French Protectorate. Unlike *musem*s in some other parts of Morocco, however, it was not the French who stopped these celebrations in Sefrou but several important families of the city who were not themselves descendants of the saint and who convinced officials that the celebrations were costly, disruptive, and of little benefit to the town as a whole. Many years later a related event, also not mentioned in this connection, took place. As reported by Chtatou: "In the early 1970s, the inhabitants of the city of Sefrou decided to celebrate their patron saint Sidi 'Ali Busserghine by holding a *musem* in his honour. The celebrations were underway when a terrible hailstorm hit the city; this was interpreted as the displeasure of the saint with the way the *musem* was conducted, especially that there were many people consuming alcoholic beverages in the vicinity of the *hurm* [sacred precincts]. Many people argued quite strongly that the saint, unhappy with the turn the celebrations had taken, withdrew his *baraka* from the function and as a result, the storm occurred. Since then, no *musem* has been organised" (Chtatou 1996, 68).

11. See the discussion and literature cited in Marcus 1985, 456, and Geertz 1968.

12. By contrast, the saints honored by Jews are said by their adherents neither to be in competition with one another nor are their wonders evident until after their deaths. See Stillman 1982, 495 and 499.

13. Marcus 1985, 464. Marcus may overstate the case somewhat: Local saints can still constitute the focal point for legitimacy of groups who exercise economic or political power, and in moments of crisis they may constitute "points of attachment" through which people secure allies against uncertainty. Nevertheless, by comparison with other moments in Moroccan history Marcus's assertion is quite supportable.

14. During the 1990s about 2,000 Israelis came to Morocco on such tours each year. See Levy 1997.

15. Levy 1997, 14, writes: "The emphasis on the reversal of relations between the tourists and the Muslims helped the travelers hide the fear they felt in the course of their journey. As long as they were within the shelter of the bus, their fear was not concealed as there was no need to do so. But when the tourists were exposed to direct contact with the Muslims in the touristic frame—in the *suq*, the cafes, and in the souvenir shops—the tourists employed the tactics of 'reversal of relations,' emphasizing elements that would present a façade of superiority and wealth." One way in which this was made manifest, says Levy, was in the Israeli tourists' use of local prostitutes, who in the past would have been regarded as off limits to Jews. On the tour, however, one could demon-

strate self-confidence vis-à-vis the Muslims and consort in public with a Muslim whore. "The symbolic reversal in power relation inherent in the use of whores was clear to the tourists who consorted with the whores, and they tended to defiantly emphasize this in the presence of Muslims" (idem).

16. The individual in question, himself also named Haim Pinto, is said to have reburied the remains at Kiryat Malachai, near Ashkelon, Israel—not far from the site of several revered Moroccan Jewish saints whose tombs are the subject of major celebratory visitations. See, generally, Weingrod 1990.

CHAPTER SIX

1. Douglas 1995.

2. Among the works I have found most stimulating are Boyarin 1994, Crane 1997, Connerton 1989, Fentress and Wickham 1992, Geary 1994, Hutton 1993, Irwin-Zarecka 1994, Kammen 1995, Kuchler and Melion 1991, Le Goff 1992, Nora 1989, O'Brien and Roseberry 1991, Group 1982, Roth 1995, Valensi 1992, Valensi and Wachtel 1991, and Yerushalmi 1988. The modern starting point for studies of collective memory is Halbwachs 1925. For works that specifically deal with memory in Morocco, see Brown 1976, Burke 1976, Eickelman 1985, Munson 1984, and Waterbury 1972.

3. The absence of such studies by anthropologists is particularly noteworthy. Although many anthropologists speak with informants about their memories during the course of initial fieldwork and return to speak to the same people over the course of many years, I have been unable to find a single study in which an anthropologist, over the course of decades, has considered the ways in which the categories through which past events are constructed may have changed. A study that does discuss the different ways men and women view their own history in the light of European contact is Sturzenhofecker 1998. Macfarlane (1978) also shows how changes in the idea of responsibility contributed to the termination of the European witch craze. Anthropologists' own memories sometimes capture conceptual shifts, as in Read 1986. Other ethnographers have considered the reshaping of present memories in their ethnographies, as for example Rosaldo 1980, Schieffelin and Crittenden 1991, Teski and Climo 1995, and Rappaport 1990. But this is not the same as asking whether the structuring of memory itself is one of those domains in which whatever cultural changes may have occurred can be detected. By comparison, Geary (1994) is concerned with the structures through which the past is preserved, reorganized, and recalled. However, his study is almost entirely limited to the use of written records in this process. Other examples along these lines include Baker 1985, Smoller 1998, Thelan 1989, and Zonabend 1984.

It should be noted that studying reconstructions of history and studying the changing structures through which memory operates are, for all their analytic distinction, complementary rather than contradictory endeavors. Starting from the former endeavor Nathan Wachtel captures the relation of the two when he writes: "[T]he aim of the historian has changed: he is less interested in the content (the factual data) of the recollection than in its developmental process, less in its reliability than in the work of the memory. Thereafter the recollection is no longer treated as a more or less accurate reflection of the past, but as a representation that is part of present reality. And since every memory has a history, is it not possible to construct a history of the memory?" (Wachtel 1986, 210–11).

4. Some of these possible shifts are explored in chapter seven of this volume.

5. This is the traditional opening for stories, rather similar to the English "Once upon a time." The Arabic phrasing quoted is translated in a variety of ways, including "There was, there was not / In the oldness of time"; it also appears in other variations, such as *Kan ma kan / La han wa la han* ("There was, there was not / Not here, not there"). See Bushnaq 1986, 65. Salman Rushdie uses the version "Once upon a time—*It was and it was not so,* as the old stories used to say, *it happened and it never did*" to highlight inherent antitheses (Rushdie 1988, 35).

6. See Scelles-Millie and Khelifa 1966.

7. For a full-length elucidation of this argument, see Rosen 1984. For an application of this argument in the legal domain, see Rosen 1989a.

8. For a striking discussion of relationships in Arab social life that build on the actual metaphor of game-playing, see Khuri 1990.

9. The quoted saying appears in many classical and modern sources. See, e.g., Rosenthal 1983, 39. Whether "the times" or the persons who constituted them were responsible for events was a topic of some debate in medieval Islam (ibid., 43).

10. See Rosen 1984, 172–77. Time may also be viewed, therefore, as discontinuous, the "point" of the story being the qualities of the characters or their exemplification of unalterable moral principles. This is seen as well in the Arab world in the way popular history is sometimes told. Referring to modern comic strips that have political import, it has been said that in the work of certain artists "history is sundered from temporal continuities and considered in an essentially synchronic manner. This distant past is a field peopled with exemplary characters whose actions are considered almost uniquely from an ethical perspective. Morality flattens out history into a collection of good and bad actions, a very old form of historical conceptualization" (Douglas and Malti-Douglas 1994, 94).

11. See generally, Rosenthal 1995 and Eickelman 1977. For an interesting study of the ways in which concepts of time may change, see Miller 1991. See also Florescano 1994.

12. On *niya,* see Rosen 1984, 47–56, Rosen 1989a, 51–53, and Rosen 1995a, 187–88. Kapchan sees references to people having *niya* in the past as examples of nostalgia but at the same time shows that people place it in the category of *bekri* rather than *zaman.* She relates this to the rise of a middle class based in the marketplace: "The emergent middle class seeks to remove itself from the chaos and dirt associated with the suq [marketplace] in order to constitute itself as a class apart. One consequence of this stratification is nostalgia for a time (*bekri,* "in the early days") when there was still *niya,* a word that may mean trust, good intention, belief, or naiveté, depending on its context. . . . [N]arratives portray niya as a quality of the past that is inappropriate and ineffectual in the marketplace where one must be perpetually on guard. The coincidence of social nostalgia for niya with the development of the middle class in Beni Mellal is no accident. The fetishization of a conceptual past, a time when there was order and trust, is an attempt to be situated in relation to rapidly changing social practices and their accompanying values. Against this ethic of niya stands the diversity of danger of the marketplace" (Kapchan 1996, 43 and 45).

13. For additional examples, see chapter seven.

14. Thus the phrase *mwalin z-zaman* in colloquial Moroccan Arabic refers to well-to-do people, masters of (literally those who characterize and are characterized by) a period of time, hence the ones whose resources have shown them to be both worldly and timely in their achievement of wealth.

15. For the historical backdrop to Arab nostalgia, see Crone and Moreh 2000.

16. A possible exception that suggests the transition is supplied by reference to the "year of the mosque," when King Hassan II coerced contributions to the building of the largest mosque in the world in Casablanca. Most people regarded the process of fund-raising as an act of hypocrisy since all contributions were supposed to be voluntary but were, in fact, taken out of one's pay. This was, however, less a moment marked for reconfiguring relationships as such than calling into question one aspect of the relation of citizen to monarch.

17. It has been argued that the idea of probability appears in the West as relationships become more complex, multiple, and uncertain. In Morocco, it may be argued, the contributing conditions have as much to do with the specific uncertainty associated with indicators of social background and connections and hence less ability to predict and constrain relationships through bonds of indebtedness. Compare Seligman 1997 with the chapter entitled "Whom Do You Trust? Structuring Confidence in Arab Law and Society," in Rosen 2000, 133–50.

18. For the argument that miraculous occurrences cut into the flow of time and validate it by interruption, see Gardet 1976, Gardet 1977, Hasnaoui 1977, and Rosenthal 1995. In a sense, characterizing what the French did as "wondrous" reaffirms that they too cut into time—albeit in a profane way—thus, by hindsight, placing their actions beyond the ordinary time that affects continuous relationships. Recall, too, the usage of this term in the story related in chapter one.

19. On the semantic construction of Arabic verb forms, see Rosen 1984, 21–23, and Izutsu 1966. The semantic and psychological reality of these multiple meanings will, of course, vary with the literacy, personal history, and sophistication of each of those who use and hear such proverbs—a fact that is undoubtedly true everywhere of such utterances. In the case of the second proverb, for example, I vividly recall expressing my uncertainty about the meaning of *tenz'a*, which the dictionaries say means "to take away," even though my elderly informant was clearly explaining the saying to me in terms of drawing near. When I asked exactly what he meant by the term he silently grabbed my forearm tightly and pulled it towards him, inclined towards me and looked me carefully in the eye while smiling slyly. The tug of his hand and the ambivalence of his silent gesture and regard remain deeply ingrained in my memory and govern my choice of the gloss "to hold on to" even though that is not the usual dictionary definition of the term.

20. Rosenthal is here referring specifically to the Muslim view of the stranger, a view "nourished by the adab literature" (Rosenthal 1997, 42). On the role of ambivalence in Arab culture and literature, with special reference to its place in Arab literary forms, see Charnay 1967.

21. On this quality of tribal organization see chapter three.

22. Brett and Fentress 1996, 65. The recognition *even* by an enemy may be an example of the argument by exaggerated inclusion that Bernard Lewis calls the trajetio ad absurdum. See note 38 below. Also present is the idea that, as the Arab saying goes, "it is better to have an intelligent enemy than a stupid friend"—a notion that reinforces both one's own intelligence and the need for the predictability, even restraint, that an intelligent enemy can appreciate. Finally, there is the idea contained in yet another common saying: "Where your enemy is, that is where your friend is." This implies not only that you should make useful friends among your enemies and that enemies at one moment are friends in another: It also fits with the idea that it is the regard accorded by a clever enemy that contributes to one's own well-being.

23. Each "native affairs" officer would draw up a *mémoire de stage,* incorporating a detailed branching list of all the tribal fractions in the area. Updated versions of these lists were still on the walls of local administrators' offices in the late 1960s—and probably in many to this day. In 1967, while interviewing a number of these administrators, it was not uncommon for them to want it believed that none of the people in their area had really resisted the French—when in fact they clearly had—as a way of asserting that they were loyal to any orderly government and hence to the present government which the administrator represents.

24. Hammoudi 2001. The situation Hammoudi describes may, however, have varied from one region to another. On the memories many Frenchmen have of their experiences in Morocco, see Knibiehler et al. 1992.

25. For an example of a dispute in which tribal fractions alter their genealogies to fit the circumstance, see Lawrence Rosen, "Social Identity and Points of Attachment: Approaches to Social Organization," in Geertz et al. 1979, 53–57.

26. Stefania Pandolfo writes: "The French *passé simple,* grammatically, is the tense of an impossible narration. Rarely used in the first person and almost untranslatable in English (*je fûs,* 'I have been,' but in a remote past, a past forever severed from myself), the *passé simple* conveys without mediation the uncanny temporality of the cut . . . [T]he tense called 'preterit,' or literary preterit, in English is in fact a literary and narrative tense, which does not convey the sense of separation and fracture of the French *passé simple.* The French 'simple past' is the tense of an impossible narration, and this is why it is never used in the first person. When in historical writing the 'je' intervenes, the grammatical tense switches to the *passé composé*" (Pandolfo 2000, 119 and 144).

27. Other alterations in the physical appearance of the city also occurred in response to local politics and the views of the King on what a traditional Arab city like Sefrou should look like. See Geertz 1989.

28. Our interviews and his account of what they reveal about Moroccan history has been written up by Burke 1993.

29. Space does not permit me to argue in what ways the King was symbolically important in the past. I can only assert that he was not, in my opinion, the omnipresent male figure in men's lives as argued in Combs-Schilling 1989. My argument here is that national history had taken the place of local history from about the late 1930s until the 1980s, when the past could be edited in a rather different way as the terms for comprehending it changed.

30. Compare this phenomenon to Lucette Valensi's description of the way a Jewish inform-ant linked the account of his own birth to the perduring traditions of Judaism: "[H]e drifts con-stantly from the preterite, which would indicate unique events that happened to him alone, to the use of the imperfect, marking actions which lasted and were repeated" (Valensi 1986, 296).

31. Among the most useful sources, for purposes of this essay, on the psychology of memory are Neisser 1982 and Neisser and Fivush 1994. For more popular studies of memory, see Johnson 1991 and Schachter 1996. For a fascinating example of how memory itself may be reconstructed in a particular historical context, see Hacking 1995.

32. This is not, I must emphasize, a simple substitution or wholesale alteration of categories. It is, instead, a shifting emphasis on various elements of the relational repertoire, a process I could document as having characterized Arab and Berber sociocultural organization for a very long time. There also appears to be less reworking of one's genealogy than there was in the past—by comparison, say, to the Tunisian groups studied by Dakhlia, of whom she writes: "In this type of lineage society, a group insures its legitimacy precisely by 'reworking' its origins" (Dakhlia 1993, 75). See also Dakhlia 1990.

33. "The present development of the government is in sharp contrast with the small number of institutions that characterized archaic power centers, as well as the relative simplicity of the or-ganization put in place during the period of direct imperialist domination" (Hammoudi 1997, 153). For suggestions about an alternative—that the state may be in the process of becoming more like a city-state than a nation—see Spruyt 1994.

34. Collective memory can, of course, cut both ways in these circumstances, reinforcing na-tionhood or reinforcing localism. As Ernest Renan said of the former possibility: "The essence of a nation is that its people have much in common and forgotten much" (quoted in Pfaff 1993, 58).

35. Williams 1970, 23.

36. See Rosen 1968 and Rosen 1972a. Elements of this form of Muslim-Jewish relations are still present in the reduced circumstances of the Jewish community of Morocco—which has declined from a quarter of a million in 1948 to less than five thousand in the early years of the twenty-first century. Thus André Levy describes how, in Casablanca, higher income Jews play cards at the beach with Muslims in an almost ritualized game of control and non-competition (Levy 2000).

37. One of these forms of wordplay common twenty years ago was called *mica*, from "formica," because it reflected back on its speaker all by itself, without implications of reciprocity, and with that degree of self-humor that made the jokes and inversions it expressed of no relational consequence.

38. "Here I may draw attention to a rhetorical device very common in classical Arabic us-age—an argument by the absurd. It is, however, very different from that device which we call the *reductio ad absurdum*. The purpose of the *reductio ad absurdum* is to demonstrate the falsity of an argument by stating it in its most extreme and therefore absurd form. The Arabic rhetorical device to which I refer has the opposite purpose—not to disprove but to emphasize and reaffirm; it is not thus a *reductio ad absurdum*, but rather a *trajetio ad absurdum* (if I may coin a rhetorical term). A principle is asserted and an extreme, even an absurd, example is given—but the purpose is to show

that the principle still applies even in this extreme and absurd formulation" (Lewis 1990, 34). A literary example is supplied by Mahfouz when liberals in a fictive prison say of the oppression of a foreign traveler by a corrupt government: "They heard my story and one of them commented on it with the words 'Even foreigners!'" (Mahfouz [1983] 1992, 69).

39. Significantly, the river, generally known as the Oued Aggai, was called the Oued el-Yahudi ("the Jewish river") after it passed the Jewish quarter (*mellah*) located in the center of the city of Sefrou. The anecdote about the French and the Jews is related in Geertz 1989. The comparison of Jewish experience in North Africa with that in Europe has been much debated: See, e.g., Cohen 1991 and the response by Stillman 1991.

40. See Deshen 1989, 26, and Stillman 1977.

41. There is a double irony in some of the Hebrew terms, for the phrase *nifqadim nokekhim*, or "present absentees," is also a phrase Israelis invented specifically to refer to Palestinians who left Israel in 1948, while the more general term *nifkad* suggests a presence even though the individual is absent. In Hebrew, as in Arabic, there is really no present tense: Things that "are" exist, in a sense, as aspects of a person or thing: Knowledge is instantiated in someone so that absent presence is an aspect of personhood more than a statement of independent existence. On the Jews' own memories of North Africa, see Goldberg 1988, Malka 1978, Deshen 1989, Bahloul 1996, Awret 1984, and Memmi 1971.

42. Fuentes 1985–86.

43. Lightman 1994, 188–89.

44. Bergson [1896] 1988.

45. On the idea of "memory holes" and their development by earlier scholars, see Douglas 1995, 18–19).

46. On the idea of a "community of memory," see Bellah et al. 1985, 153. On the relation of social institutions to forgetting, see Douglas 1986.

47. It has been argued that "[i]f collective identity of the preliberal sort is based, at least to an important extent, on the possession of common narratives, whatever undermines those narratives will inevitably tend to qualify, even if it does not destroy, one's sense of belonging to the collectivity whose past has been revised" (Knapp 1989, 144). Where accounts of the past emphasize common processes of relationship and maintain the memory of past figures only to the extent that they continue, in a sense, to interact with the living world—whether as saints who are said to be alive in their tombs or the dead who revisit the living on one of the last days of the fast of Ramadan—collective identity arises less out of a direct link to past values and beliefs, as Knapp suggests, than from the cultural construction of all kinds of persons—past, future, and impersonal—into types of consociates, figures who are remembered only to the extent that they affect the continuing play of the game. On the forging of various social categories into types of consociates, see Rosen 1984, 141–44, 176–79.

48. Osiel 1995, 569. The reference is to Borges 1993, 83–91. It might also be suggested that fundamentalism may, in part, be an attempt to create a sense of timeless relationships informed by faith when the sense of perduring processes no longer holds, when ordering rules of the game are replaced by "too much history." For a discussion of how language would play a role in such instances, see Shotter 1990.

49. Lequin and Mettral 1980.

50. See, generally, Hammoudi 1997.

51. One of the few national holidays that is not based on the Islamic calendar is the "Festival of the Throne," which marks the ascension of the first sultan of independent Morocco to the throne. Even the chosen date for this holiday, the third day of the third month (March 3), partakes of the mystical significance in Islam of the number three, ironically applying it to the Western calendar for a political purpose. Locally, too, there is no nostalgia for some golden age of the past. See Geertz 1989. The absence of such nostalgia among Moroccans contrasts markedly to parts of the

Middle East heartland, and its absence comes as quite a surprise to Arabs from the east first encountering Morocco. Factors contributing may, of course, be that Morocco was never colonized
by the Ottomans, that the French policy in Morocco was one of avoiding the kind of intense immigration of Frenchmen that occurred in Algeria, and the relatively brief colonial period, in which
many rural areas were not subdued until the early 1930s and independence was achieved by 1956.
On Arab nostalgia, see Lewis 1975.

52. The phrase "principled irresolution" is borrowed from Osiel 1995, 689.

53. On screen memories, see Freud [1899] 1989, 117–26.

54. Generational differences are neatly represented in the colloquy between an older warrior
and a younger one in the Tunisian playwright Al-Madani's re-telling of the revolt of the blacks
against the Abbasids from their base in southern Iraq in A.D. 879–883:

> 'Ali: Do you recall how we started our struggle? . . . With three dull
> swords, plenty of clubs, and a few arrows.
>
> Rafiq: So! You remember the history of our struggle as if it was a tale
> from *A Thousand and One Nights* . . .
>
> 'Ali: Those battles were fought between a strong force and a weak one;
> but our hearts were, and still are, full of faith. . . .
>
> Rafiq: But you're always living on memories that I've no way of recall-
> ing! (Al-Madani 1995, 165)

CHAPTER SEVEN

1. Hacking 1975.

2. Shapiro 1983.

3. See Foucault 1970, Krüger et al. 1987, Patey 1984, and Toulmin 1958.

4. Nor is any alteration attributable, in the Moroccan context, to the increase in literacy: The
rate of adult literacy in 1995 was 43.7 percent (females 31 percent , males 56.6 percent) (United Nations Development Program 1998, 129). Moreover, as various scholars have shown, literacy and
orality are complementary, rather than contradictory, phenomena: Any shift cannot be accounted
for by emphasizing the literacy side of the equation alone. See Ong 1982 and Goody 1987.

5. See, generally, Rosen 1984.

6. Marmura 1968.

7. Fakhry 1970 and Leaman 1985.

8. al-Laheidan 1980, 160. On the different religions' versions of the story of Potiphar's wife,
see Goldman 1995.

9. If the facts cannot be determined, an Islamic judge may allow the party who the court believes is most likely to know the truth about the matter to swear a holy oath. If the party takes the
oath, that act by itself decisively ends the matter in his or her favor. If the potential oath-taker
chooses, however, he or she may refuse the oath and refer it to the other party. If that person then
takes the oath, he or she is declared the winner. For further description and analysis of the decisory
oath, together with comparisons to its use in Western law, see Rosen 1989a, 33–35.

10. Rosenthal 1983, 36.

11. It is also said of a curer in Morocco that only the possession of the correct niya permits the
sale of certain curative herbs and that the curer's niya can heal a patient even if the packet of herbs
is itself of no value. Traders also use the phrase *dir niya*—"to put one's niya"—to refer to that moment in the bargaining process when the seller transfers the intent to the buyer such that the seller
is no longer responsible for the goods in question. See Kapchan 1996.

12. Cited in al-Laheidan 1976, 162.

13. See Strathern 1975.

14. As Max Black put it more generally, statements of probability do not actually have to rely

on the observation of repeated events, nor does the recognition that an outcome may be favored without being necessitated mean that one cannot still believe that some particular outcomes are themselves completely determined by events (Black 1967).

15. Lloyd-Bostock 1983, 150.

16. Toulmin 1958, 90–93.

17. Sambursky 1956. See also Kubler 1944.

18. Collingwood 1940, part 3c.

19. On the concept of chains of consocication in Arab culture, see Rosen 1984, 141–44.

20. On the European comparison, see Shapiro 1983, 81.

21. Gibb 1949.

22. I should note, however, that other scholars see radical change in Arab culture where I do not. One of the most thoughtful of these scholars, Ernest Gellner, argued, for example, that the introduction of state-sponsored universal free education has provided the vehicle by which high Arab culture has finally triumphed over the often contrary little traditions of the uneducated (Gellner 1983, 75–87). Yet it can be argued that great and little traditions were never as sharply divided in the Arabo-Islamic world as elsewhere because, notwithstanding objectively identifiable differences, local traditions are regarded by their practitioners as being what Islam is, not as something separate from it. Support for this belief exists in Islamic doctrine itself, with its stress on consensus and the rights of humankind. Hence, what to some outsiders (and indeed some Westernized Arabs) appear as conflicting traditions constitute for most ordinary believers not some schizoid double-mindedness but aspects of a single, inclusive realm.

Gellner also finds that Arabs now express forms of proper organization through the terminology of rule-like propositions. The state, through its bureaucracy, has not merely imposed rules on its people but created rule-mindedness among them, and Arabs now look to rule-like formulations when testing propositions for their legitimacy. By contrast, it may be argued that an emphasis on distinctive modes of reasoning in Arab culture, law, and history still possesses controlling force. The ways of assessing a person's background and involvements, of calculating consequences and of weighing evidence suggest not a radical change in the criteria of legitimacy but an insufficient appreciation by Western scholars of how central these modes of thought have been to the continuity of Arab culture and its capacity to confront change.

And where Gellner sees the pendulum that has swung back and forth in Arab history between the fundamentalism of the mystics and the orthodoxy of the central religious figures as now having become fully unhinged owing to the power of the state to support whatever orthodoxy controls its levers, it may be argued instead that such oscillation itself is nonexistent. A more complex image is needed if one is to represent a culture that does not see as contradictions what Westerners would regard as such. One such image might be that of levels of inclusion that create innumerable points of contrariety—like the arabesques that grace so much of Islamic art and architecture—and by this very contrariety reinforce existing styles of thought and action.

23. Rosenthal 1975, 167. It is noteworthy, too, that in various card games and in backgammon, contemporary Arab players do not engage in probabilistic calculation. The same was true even in ancient Greece, where players of dice did not develop ideas of probability even though much of the mathematical groundwork for such a step had already been laid (Sambursky 1956). On the metaphor of games for understanding Arab culture, see Khuri 1990.

24. Rorty 1986.

25. Edelson 1986, Glieck 1987, and Wright 1988.

26. For an elaboration of this argument, see Rosen 1991.

27. Davidson 1980 and Rorty 1986.

28. Sullivan 1985.

29. See below, chapter ten, on the issue of doubt in the work of Salman Rushdie.

30. Rosenthal 1970, 300, 301, 303, and 308.

CHAPTER EIGHT

1. A number of features that bear on the identities of the parties described in this essay have been altered in order to preserve their privacy. The alterations do not, however, affect the overall description and analysis of the social and legal points discussed. For additional examples, see Rosen 1970, Rosen 1989a, and other sources cited therein.

2. Article 1 of Royal Edict (*Dahir*) No. 1–93–165 of September 10, 1993, states that any child under eighteen may be declared abandoned if born of unknown parents and found deserted; orphaned and without support; lacking parents who, as a result of circumstances beyond their control, are unable to support the child; or whose divorced parents "do not assume their responsibility of protection and orientation in order to guide the child to the right path." Precisely how this applies in the present case was not indicated in the court opinion.

3. The record does not indicate it, but Moroccan attorneys with whom I have discussed the case suggest that the former husband would probably have had to ask for a court order requiring the mother to produce the child in Morocco, and—bearing in mind that he was not the child's biological father or (absent such a possibility in Moroccan law) the child's adoptive father—when the mother failed to appear, the former husband may have moved to set aside his support obligation under their divorce decree and sought the order of abandonment. It should also be noted that the American adoption of the child is not recognized by Moroccan law.

4. See Said 1994, 78–79. A similar contract can be made by a supportive parent with the state for the upbringing of an abandoned child. The basis for the Islamic prohibition on full adoption is said to be the passage in the Qur'an at Sura 33:4–5: "God has not assigned to any man two hearts within his breast . . . neither has He made your adopted sons your sons in fact. . . . Call them after their true fathers; that is more equitable in the sight of God. If you know not who their fathers were, then they are your brothers in religion, and your clients."

5. Article 490 of the Penal Code states: "All persons of different sex who, not being united by bonds of marriage, have sexual relations are punishable by imprisonment from one month to one year" (Ruolt 1996, 509). As Ruolt notes, this provision "poses a more delicate interpretation when the participants (*co-auteurs*) are adults and can be expected to be free to conduct themselves, notably when it is a question of foreigners whose own national legislation imposes no such restrictions" (Ruolt 1996, 509).

6. The marriage of a Muslim man to a non-Muslim woman is permitted under Moroccan law. The marriage of a Muslim woman to a non-Muslim man is forbidden but regarded as a temporary impediment that may be overcome by conversion of the man to Islam. Moroccan Code of Personal Status (*Mudawwana*), Article 29 (4). See, generally, R'chid 1991, 54.

7. For example, in 1997 in the city of Casablanca 364 babies were found abandoned. Without the 1993 legislation, and absent any form of legal adoption, such children could not be given into the legal custody of parent-figures and would have had to remain in state-run orphanages. *Jeune Afrique*, February 9–15, 1997, p. 30 (reprinting an article from the *New York Times*). Said (1994, 81) cites data from Mme. Bennis Sabah, "L'Abandon: Causes et Conséquences" (thesis for the doctorate in medicine, Rabat, 1982, p. 35) showing the number of abandoned children in one child-care center in Rabat as follows: 1974 (61), 1975 (95), 1976 (124), 1977 (173), 1978 (180), 1979 (193), 1980 (240). "Informal" adoption, however, is not uncommon in Morocco. See Bargach 2001.

8. See Foblets 1999, who also cites a number of the European statutes and treaties affecting jurisdiction and private international law affecting transnational Muslim marriages. For example, France has a specific accord allowing Moroccans residing in France to be governed by Moroccan personal status laws. See Deprez 1996, 63–64. By contrast, Belgium has three separate accords recognizing Moroccan custody and visitation orders. See Foblets 1996, 135.

9. Normally a *khula'* divorce is a way in which a woman, unable to divorce the man herself and having no grounds for a judicial divorce, "buys" her freedom by forgiving the husband a debt, such as the unpaid portion of her bridewealth or legally required support payments. She may also

be forced into such forgiveness of a debt as the price for the husband not contesting her claim to custody of a child who, under the statute, would otherwise go the husband or one of his kins-women. Whether Ali misunderstood the nature of *khula'* because of his years abroad or was try-ing desperately to get his wife to return to him, his should be understood as an unusual case in re-gards to his involvement with the practice of *khula'*.

10. For similar aspects of corruption in the courts, see the description in chapter one of this volume.

11. The 1993 revisions of the Code of Personal Status (Article 30) provide: "The first wife must be advised of the desire of her spouse to take a second wife in marriage." The statute does not, as even some educated Moroccan women mistakenly believe, require the consent of the first wife, only her notification. In Ali's case, notice was sent to Tuda four times, and when she failed to re-spond the court granted Ali permission to take a second wife.

12. *Mouna Kandy Suboh v. City of Revere,* Civil Action No. 00–10396-WGY, United States Dis-trict Court, District of Massachusetts, Memorandum and Order of March 30, 2001.

13. Where a portion of the bridewealth payment is due on demand or where a stipulation in a marital contract places limits on a man's legal powers, the opportunities for maneuver are in-creased. Thus it is not simply a gap between law and practice that is at issue but legal forms that embrace alternative goals and interests. For the Iranian situation in this regard, see Mir-Hosseini 1993 and Mir-Hosseini 1996.

14. The tactic of dragging one's feet through the courts, for example, is hardly limited to the Arabic-speaking parts of the Middle East. Ziba Mir-Hosseini (1996, 19) describes the Iranian situ-ation in the following terms: "The fact that more than 50 percent of all divorces registered in any given year in Tehran are of *khul'* type [where the wife 'forgives' the husband of some legal obliga-tion] suggests that, by forgoing their *mahr* [bridewealth], women often succeed in inducing their husbands to consent to divorce. . . . On the other hand, women who come to court to resist a di-vorce petitioned by the husband can count on the court's support, especially when the judge deems the man's decision to be based on caprice. In some cases the husband has left the marital home and has set up a new one with a second wife, who is now putting pressure on him to divorce the first. In others, the husband is cruel and mean to the wife and children. A woman's strategy in such a case is to delay a divorce as long as possible, and meanwhile to take as much as she can. She makes one petition for *nafaqa* [marital support], and another for *mahr* [payment of her bridewealth], and makes their waiver contingent upon getting custody of the children, a share of the marital home and a set maintenance payment for the children."

15. A number of family law matters have nevertheless been accorded federal constitutional protection. Thus state laws categorizing certain children as illegitimate or interracial marriages as impermissible miscegenation have been struck down for violation of the equal protection clause (whereas anti-polygamy laws have been sustained), while state laws banning the use of contracep-tives have been found to violate the so-called "right to privacy," itself regarded by the Supreme Court as an unenumerated but "penumbral" constitutional right.

16. See my essay "Islamic law as a Common Law System," in Rosen 2000, 38–68.

CHAPTER NINE

1. For the medieval period, see Watt 1972. For the Renaissance period in Britain, see Matar 1998. See, generally, Rodinson 1987, Lewis 1982, Lewis and Schnapper 1994, and Lewis 2000.

2. I am not concerned in this essay with changes that may be occurring in other Muslim mi-grant communities, such as the United States, Latin America, or the Persian Gulf States. In the United States, for example, the number of mosques increased by 25 percent (to 1,200) from 1995 to 2001 (Niebuhr 2001), though only a small proportion of American Muslims attend mosque ser-vices weekly (Goodstein 2001). A number of American companies have made accommodations

for workplace worship (Milicia 2001), and American Muslims may be leading the way on such issues as the acceptance of medical transplants as consistent with Islamic beliefs (Christian 2000). On Muslims in the United States, see Haddad and Smith 1994 and Moore 1995. Further studies of all these immigrant populations will be necessary to understand the multiple forms of Islam that may be developing in the wake of this historic movement.

    3. Vertovec and Peach 1997, 13. Around 1990, for example, it was estimated that there were about 60,000 Muslims in Denmark, Austria, and Sweden each, about 20,000 in Norway, and over a million in the United Kingdom (Vertovec and Peach 1997, 14). These numbers have undoubtedly risen significantly in the last decade: For example, the number in Sweden may now exceed 200,000 (Sander 1996, 276). Estimates for the mid-1990s place the Muslim population of Switzerland at about 200,000 (Haenni 2000), 628,000 for the Netherlands (Van Bijsterveld 2000, 125), 400,000–500,000 in Italy (Schmidt di Friedberg 1998; Allievi 1996, 317), and over 250,000 in Spain (Martinez-Torron 2000, 47). There are also some five million Muslims in those countries of eastern and southeastern Europe that were not part of the former Soviet Union and another twelve million in the European portions of the former Soviet Union. These figures do not include those who convert to Islam, a number estimated by one source at anywhere from 6,000 to 27,000 in Belgium alone. See, generally, Dassetto 1996.

    4. Tayler 2000, 58. Cited in Torfs 2000, 73.

    5. Nonneman et al. 1996, 191.

    6. Cohen 2001b. On July 4, 2001, a bipartisan commission in Germany recommended that fifty thousand skilled workers be imported each year to handle the country's labor deficit. It was the first formal acknowledgment that the country's "guest workers" would remain in Germany and that more permanent immigrants will be needed (Cohen 2001a).

    7. Vertovec and Peach 1997, 19. The bilateral agreement on migrant workers with Turkey was unilaterally revoked by the German government in November 1973, a "general enlistment stoppage" (Anwerbestop) that also affected migration from North Africa, the former Yugoslavia, and parts of southeastern Europe (Stoll 1998, 266–67).

    8. For example, there were about 5,000 Moroccans in Italy in 1981 and 75,000 by 1987. The numbers had grown by the end of the century to about 119,000 recognized Moroccan immigrants plus another 20,000 who had received some form of residency card. (Personal communication from Octavia Schmidt di Friedberg.)

    9. The earlier figures are given in Lopez-Garcia 1993, 32; the later ones, in Simons 2000a. In 1999 Spain had over 70,000 illegal workers, but because they are badly needed Spain does not penalize employers who used such illegals and, indeed, approved a law early in 2000 that would make illegals eligible for residence permits and allow them to be joined by family members. But already by 1999 over 3,000 people had died in attempts to get across the Straits of Gibraltar in small boats ("Morocco" 1999); in 2001 another 700 perished ("Gibraltar in Reverse?" 2002).

    10. The French have also added a proviso to their acceptance of the UN Convention on Economic and Political Rights in which they claim that in France there are no minorities hence no need to specifically protect their rights. For a brief comparison of the French, British, German, and Italian immigration policies, see Melotti 1997. See also the essays in Modood and Werbner 1997.

    11. In 1989 the Conseil d'État ruled that headscarves could not be banned outright: wearing them does not constitute proselytism or a form of oppressing others. Each case must now be decided on its particularities. For a brief analysis of the matter and the way different localities in France have treated the issue, see Basdevant-Gaudemet 2000, 109–10. See, generally, Dupret 2000–2001.

    12. *Cha-are Shalom Ve Tsedek v. France*, Application No. 27417/95, June 27, 2000.

    13. Viorst 1996, 93

    14. Schiffauer 1997, 159–60. In December 2001, following the terrorist attacks of September 11, 2001, in the United States, Germany banned the Caliphate State, a Turkish group of about 1,100

members, under newly passed regulations outlawing political parties that incite racial hatred or that develop their own tax and legal system ("Germany Bans Radical Organization" 2001). For a comparison of the French and German approaches, see Ewing 2000. See, generally, Kruger 2000–2001.

15. See, generally, Poulter 1989, Poulter 1998, and Vertovec 1996, 170–84. About 70 percent of the Muslims in Britain are also citizens of Great Britain, an unusually high proportion by European standards. In France nearly half of the North Africans are French citizens while nearly 60 percent have lived in the country for a decade or more (Leveau 1997, 148).

16. Allievi 1996, 323.

17. On the attack in El Eijedo, Spain, on North Africans in February 2000, see Cohen 2000 and Simons 2000b.

18. On the role of informers among the Muslim population of Europe, see the article by Bastenier in Gerholm and Lithman 1988, 139. McMurray's Moroccan informant tells of returning from Europe: "And look at the way the religiously militant migrants were greeted back home! The cops at the Moroccan customs bureau treated them like criminals. They knew who the troublemakers were because the government spied on the migrants in Europe. The consulates and the Moroccan migrants' associations were full of spies who kept track of everyone. When the migrants got to the Moroccan border, the customs agents went through all their possessions, looking for religious tracts. They even began confiscating the migrants' audio and video cassettes. Supposedly the militants smuggled the sermons of subversive preachers into the country on these tapes" (McMurray 1993, 389). Although most mosques appear to be organized by nation of origin this is not universally true, particularly where numbers of a nation's immigrants or of available mosques are few. In London, for example, the Moroccan community grew from 360 in 1962 to over 25,000 by 1998, but there is still no separate Moroccan mosque (personal communication from Mohammed ben Madani, editor and publisher of *The Maghreb Review*).

19. Vertovec and Peach 1997, 25. See, generally, Dassetto 2000. That some mosques and Islamic charities may have served as vehicles for the recruitment or financing of Al Qaeda terrorists involved in the events of September 11, 2001, has raised additional questions about the treatment of such institutions by European states.

20. Poulter 1989, 10–11. On such issues as sex education and worship in state schools, see Bradney 2000, 187–91.

21. Torfs 2000, 81–84. Muslim students may not, however, be exempt on religious grounds from physical education courses, a valid medical excuse being required (ibid., 84).

22. Landman 1999. See, generally, Abu-Haidar 1996.

23. But see Queens Bench 1978 (British school authority is not required to give Muslim time off on Fridays for weekly prayers), and *Ali v. Capri,* cited in Bradney 2000, 191 (1991 British case holding that employer did not engage in unfair dismissal when he afforded Muslim employee a place to pray but no separate time for Friday prayers than the same lunch hour afforded all other employees).

24. Van Bijsterveld 2000, 132–33

25. Vicén 1996, 310, and Martinez-Torron 2000, 48–52.

26. See Vertovec 1996, 170–71. See, generally, Poulter 1986, 278–84.

27. Homola 2002.

28. Some 60,000 sheep are slaughtered in the Île-de-France alone on that day. In the Val-d'Oise département public authorities provide a recognized site and professional Muslim slaughterers for the occasion (Vertovec and Peach 1997, 26).

29. Personal communication from Khelil Merroun. Basdevant-Gaudemet (2000, 108) explains that, consonant with the French emphasis on secularism, cemeteries, which are under local authorities, though religiously neutral, have been encouraged by the state since 1975 to designate group "religious areas," a practice specifically encouraged for non-French Muslims by a 1991 cir-

cular from the Ministry of the Interior. However, since the matter is very much under the control of local mayors their discretion to create such areas or not remains undiminished.

30. See, generally, Renteln 2002.

31. Such cases arise, for example, when a young woman is forced back to her home country for purposes of an arranged marriage, or where child custody involves transnational movement. For a notorious case involving the removal of a young Norwegian/Moroccan to her parents' house in Morocco, see Wikan 2000. For other such situations see the chapter eight in this book. See, generally, King 1993.

32. For the contrary argument, that the jurisdiction of domicile should have exclusive jurisdiction, see Foblets and Verhellen 2000.

33. See Shah-Kazemi 2001.

34. Another term used is "Angrezi Shariat." See, generally, Pearl 1986.

35. *Bakhtiari v. The Zoological Society of London, New Law Journal,* vol. 141 (1991), pp. 55ff., discussed in Poulter 1998, 64 (court awards larger sum than would be given to a white girl because of disproportionate effect on an Iranian girl's marriage prospects when disfigured).

36. *Seemi v. Seemi, New Law Journal,* vol. 140 (1990), pp. 747ff. Discussed in Poulter 1998, 64 (Muslim woman awarded £20 thousand for slander by former husband about her virginity, a factor of great importance in her community).

37. This was the situation in the British case of *R. v. Bibi* [1980] 1 W.L.R. 1193.

38. According to M. Manazir Ahsan of the Islamic Foundation, Leicester, UK (personal communication). When Islamic banks are used a loan invariably costs more than the rent would have cost. As a result, in parts of Great Britain some Muslims are using rotating cooperatives similar to those found in many areas of South and Southeast Asia to fund their housing requirements. Here, too, one sees forms of association that could have dramatic implications arising out of the European experience for the adaptation of Islamic ideas. The broader idea of necessity (*ḍarūra*), including the necessity when living under non-Muslim rule to adapt to local circumstances—including even the appointment of Islamic judges by the non-Muslim authorities—has a long and contentious history in Islamic thought. See Lewis 1988, 104–7, and Muslehuddin 1975. On mechanisms developed in the United States by Muslims to finance home loans without interest payments, see Sachs 2001. For a highly critical appraisal of the use of fatwas by religious authorities in Muslim India, see Shourie 1995.

39. Personal communication, Abdelhamid Chirane.

40. Cited in Leveau 1997.

41. Leveau 1997, 153. On the role of girls as mediators to the bureaucracy, I am grateful for the communication of Halimah Boumedienne.

42. Or, as one Senegalese woman told a reporter, "'When I visit Senegal,' she says, clenching her small fists, 'I feel European. But when I'm here, I feel black. I can't feel at home, even in Marseilles, the capital of Africa'" (Tayler 2000, 62). Those among the migrants who become more attached to Islam during their sojourn may return, only to encounter the derision of their countrymen. Writing of a Moroccan migrant, David McMurray notes: "Locals in Nador also complained of the way the bearded migrants came home and preached to them about the 'true' Islam. The locals viewed them as hicks from the countryside who had spent most of their adult lives in Christian Europe. Now they were coming back every vacation to Islamic Morocco and had the gall to preach to people who had never abandoned their country and its religion" (McMurray 1993, 389).

43. "The children of immigrant workers, the so-called "second generation," can no longer imagine returning to the land of their parents, despite their inner struggles with living in Germany" (Stoll 1998, 268).

44. ("Morocco" 1999).

45. Roy 2000a, 1 and 29. See, generally, Roy 1999. A similar argument is made for Muslim experience in Switzerland in Haenni 2000.

46. The thinker referred to here is Rachid al-Ghannouchi, the exiled head of the Renaissance Party of Tunisia who, though he describes himself as a "democratic Islamist," has no sympathy for a secular West that fractionates the self. See Armstrong 2000, 185. See also chapter four on personalism in this volume.

47. Dassetto and Nonneman 1996, 196. Estimates of migrants' attachment to Islam are quite varied and perhaps worthy of some skepticism. Several studies put the number of those who are "observant" at about 25 percent (Dassetto 2000, 36). What is clear is that the proportion who identify themselves more strongly with Islamic practices began to increase in the 1970s and has continued to increase over the past few decades.

48. Indeed the attraction of fundamentalism for many within the Muslim world itself may lie in part in its challenge to the claim by the religious establishment to be the sole authority on sacred text, whereas to the fundamentalists—like the Protestant reformers—each individual may be capable of an authoritative reading of the texts. As one scholar of fundamentalism, Mohamed Tozy, has put it: "Fundamentalists are urbanized, educated individuals who claim, beyond social and political reform, the right to grant themselves individually the role of interpreting the Qur'an and the Traditions of the Prophet. . . . It is this fundamental idea that makes credible the proposition, elsewhere so debated, of the 'modernity' of fundamentalists" (Barrada 1999, 10; translation by author; italics in original). See also Tozy 1998.

49. Goldberg 1991 has formulated many of these points, summarizing part of the paradox of the Western experience by arguing that "Puritanism can be the basis for resistance to one kind of state and for dogged acquiescence in another" (p. 32) See also the essay entitled "Flux and Reflux in the Faith of Men" in Gellner 1981 and Gellner 1997, 76–77 (in which he argues that Protestant-type religions radically diminish the distance between the laity and the transcendent, elevating the culture of ordinary people to that of the high culture).

CHAPTER TEN

1. Among the more useful sources on the Rushdie affair are Mozaffari 1995, Banville 1993, Slaughter 1993, Appignanesi and Maitland 1990, MacDonogh 1993, Ahsan 1991, Abdallah 1994, Cohn-Sherbok 1990, Equality 1990. Fischer and Abedi 1990, and Lewis 1991. On the history of blasphemy laws, see Levy 1993, Marsh 1998, and Lewis 1997. On the blasphemy laws in the United Kingdom, which only protect the Christian religion, see Unsworth 1995.

The text of the fatwa issued in the name of the Ayatollah Khomeini on February 14, 1989, which called for the death of Rushdie "as well as those publishers who were aware of [the novel's] contents," is reprinted in Appignanesi and Maitland 1990, 74–76. On Islamic law and the fatwa, see Yapp 1990 and Gandjieh 1994. It has also been suggested that the fatwa was issued, in part, to distract attention from the fact that Iran was not winning the war against Iraq, whose leader, Saddam Hussein, the Ayatollah Khomeini had declared a heretic. And indeed *The Satanic Verses* had been reviewed but ignored in Iran for some months until demonstrations in Pakistan and moderate opposition to Khomeini may have led the latter to see in Rushdie an opportunity to reject any cooperation with the West. See Sonn 1990.

Technically, under Iranian Shi'ite law, the order is a *hukm*, rather than a *fatwa*, the former being irrevocable whereas the latter has no force after the death of the person who issued it. Although the Iranian government claims that the fatwa is indeed irrevocable, they have also stated that the affair is now "completely finished" and that they will not support the efforts of the Islamic charity that has posted a reward for anyone who kills Rushdie ("Rushdie's Nightmare Is Over" 1998). A few days after the announced change, however, an Iranian Foreign Ministry spokesman said that Rushdie had increased the "hatred of the Muslims toward him" when, in an interview following the announcement, Rushdie expressed no regret for writing the book and stated that there was "not a chance in hell of the book being withdrawn" (*Times* [London], September 28, 1998, p. 13).

Subsequently, three senior religious figures in Iran announced that the fatwa has not been canceled, and they renewed the call for Rushdie's death (*International Herald Tribune,* September 29, 1998, p. 1). A majority of the members of the Iranian Parliament also signed a statement saying the fatwa was still in effect and should be carried out; and new rewards were offered for Rushdie's death by a conservative student organization and the charitable foundation that offered the original bounty (*Guardian* [London], October 12, 1998, p. 2). On the irrevocability of the fatwa, see Al-Azm 1994, 21–23.

Elsewhere, pressure has continued against other Muslim dissenters: Death threats have been renewed against novelist Taslima Nasrin (Popham 1998 and Weaver 1994). Forced divorce has been imposed on Egyptian scholars found guilty of heresy (Miller 1996, Balz 1997, Weaver 1998). And reformers have been tried and executed for apostasy (An-Naim 1986), condemned to death for blasphemy or stating known facts about the Prophet's life before the founding of Islam (Bearak 2001), or excommunicated and later assassinated (Haddad 1998). Additional examples are cited in Ibrahim 1994, 8–9, Pipes 1990, Taheri 1987, Warraq 1995, chs. 1 and 10, and Erickson 1998, 149. On the temptations to blasphemy and the way such utterances and writings have played out in Islamic thought, see Manna 1997 and Wilson 1988. Rushdie, who had been denied a visa by India, the place of his birth, was finally able to pay a visit to the country in April 2000. See Rushdie 2000 and Dugger 2000.

2. Suleri 1990, reprinted in Fletcher 1994, 222.

3. Rosenthal 1970, 300–308.

4. The Shakespeare quote comes from *Troilus and Cressida,* 2.2.16; Tennyson's is from "In Memoriam"; Holmes from Holmes 1915, 3; and the popular saying dates from mid-seventeenth-century England. The more interesting example to explore in the Islamic context would be that of the great Urdu poet Mirza Asadullah Khan Ghalib (1797–1869), whose subtly expressed doubts about fundamentals seldom figure in these discussions. The more stereotypical view is that expressed by T. E. Lawrence, who says of the Semites that they "were a dogmatic people, despising doubt, our modern crown of thorns. They did not understand our metaphysical difficulties, our introspective questionings. They knew only truth and untruth, belief and unbelief, without our hesitating retinue of finer shades . . ." (Lewis 2000, 17, quoting from Lawrence's *Seven Pillars of Wisdom* [1926]).

5. Fisher 1996, S72. This is not the sort of doubt Rushdie himself cites as having characterized some of the greatest Muslim thinkers when he says "Islam contains the doubts of Iqbal, Ghazali, Khayyam as well as the narrow certainties of Shabbir Akhtar of the Bradford Council of Mosques. . . ." (Rushdie, "In Good Faith," in Rushdie 1991, 393–414 at 409). On Ghazzali's doubt, see also Ormsby 1991. Note, too, that many writers cited as examples of Islamic doubters were regarded as heretics. Rushdie, of course, does not invite martyrdom as a heretic but the creation of a place in Islam for legitimate doubt about religious fundamentals.

After the issuance of the death order against him, Rushdie told an interviewer: "The thing I didn't understand—or underestimated the force of—was that whereas in the Judeo-Christian tradition it is accepted that one may at least dispute whether good and evil are external or internal to us—to ask, for instance, Do we need such beings as God and the Devil in order to understand good and evil?—the parts of my book that raised this question represented something that is still very hard to say publicly in the Islamic world; and to hear it said with all the paraphernalia of contemporary fiction was very upsetting for many people, to which I'm afraid my only answer is, That's tough—because this kind of thing needs to be said" (Banville 1993, 35). On the crucial difference it makes in Islamic practice to express such reservations publicly (where they are not tolerated) versus privately (where they may be), see Rosen 2000, 187–99.

Difference of opinion is also central to Islamic jurisprudence, where it is to be resolved, as in other domains of society, by coalescing opinion around one's own perspective. Historically, scholars differed as to what were central or marginal concerns, and the idea that any individual could grasp with certainty a precise answer to each issue was anathema to most legal scholars. Although Calder finds such choice to be "in effect a confession of doubt" by some scholars—which also enhanced their role in society—I see such examples not as doubt about fundamentals but as residing within that range of "the rights of Man" which God requires human reason to address. See Calder 1989 and Weiss 1985. On doubt in the Shi'a tradition of jurisprudence, see Gleve 2000. For more general discussions, see Henderson 1998 and Stroumsa 1999.

6. Wittgenstein 1972, p. 44, pars. 341 and 343, and p. 29, par. 220. Rushdie himself has vacillated about the novel's perspective and his own identity as a Muslim. He has written that "*The Satanic Verses* is a serious work, written from a non-believer's point of view" ("In Good Faith," quoted in Webster 1990, 102). Later, when he claimed to have converted to Islam, Rushdie told an interviewer: "[E]verything that is said in The Satanic Verses which is held to be hostile or offensive to Muslim sanctities, is material that I personally do not agree with, and the ideas expressed in those passages, the hostile ideas expressed in those passages, are ideas I absolutely, as a person and as a writer, reject. I feel that had I been a Muslim at the time that I wrote the book I would have written it differently, clearly, and I want to make that point, and let there be no argument about it" (Ahmed 1991, 21). Afterwards, when he recanted his apology and his conversion, Rushdie said: "It was a peacekeeping gesture, an attempt at compromise. I said words that were not true. I said I had discovered religion, and I am not a religious person. I let myself down, and I regret it" (Grove 1998, 7). On Rushdie's background, see Kenneth Cragg, "Salman Rushdie: The One it's all about . . . absent as ever while we suffer in His name," in Cragg 1994, 147–65.

7. The challenge doubt poses to the inspiration that moves us to give effect to our beliefs is highlighted by the Nobel-laureate physicist Richard P. Feynman when he says: "[T]he strong feeling that you are doing right is weakened when the slightest amount of doubt is expressed as to the existence of God. . . . So I do not think it is possible to not get into a conflict if you require an absolute faith in metaphysical aspects, and at the same time I don't understand how to maintain the real value of religion for inspiration if we have some doubt as to that. That's a serious problem" (Feynman 1998, 46–47). Compare both Rushdie's and Feynman's approach to that of Kierkegaard, who wrote: "Belief and doubt are not two forms of knowledge, determinable in continuity with one another, for neither of them is a cognitive act; they are opposite passions" (Kierkegaard 1971, 105).

8. I am indebted here to the summaries/interpretations of Rushdie's book found in Craige 1992, 62–64; Pipes 1990, 53–68; Werbner 1996, S60–S64; and Rushdie's own summary in his essay "In Good Faith," in Rushdie 1991, 397–403.

9. On the role played by the verses in early Islam, see Ahmed 1999.

10. Werbner 1996, S64.

11. Al-Azm 1991.

12. Erickson 1998, 132.

13. "Doubt, it seems to me, is the central condition of a human being in the 20th century. One of the things that has happened to us in the 20th century as a human race is to learn how certainty crumbles in your hand. We cannot any longer have a fixed certain view of anything—the table that we're sitting next to, the ground beneath our feet, the laws of science, are full of doubt now. Everything we know is pervaded by doubt and not by certainty. And that is the basis of the great artistic movement known as Modernism. Now the fact that the orthodox figures in the Muslim world have declared a jihad against Modernism is not my fault. It doesn't validate an entire way of looking at the world which is, to my mind, the most important new contribution of the 20th century to the way in which the human race discusses itself. If they're trying to say that this whole process has gone out of the window—that you can't do that, all you have is the old certainties—then, yes, I do argue" (Rushdie, interview of January 27, 1989, reprinted in Appignanesi and Maitland 1990, 24–25). In the brief period during which Rushdie apologized for his book and claimed really to be a Muslim, he still insisted on the role of doubt when he told Akbar Ahmed: "Now, clearly we live in

an age in which there is an enormous tension between, on the one hand the needs of believing and faith, and on the other the needs of disbelieving and doubt. That tension objectively exists in the world, probably internally exists to a greater or lesser extent inside each one of us and it becomes a function of the writer to reflect that and to portray that and to try to understand it" (Ahmed 1991, 22).

14. This phrase and translation are used in *The Satanic Verses* at p. 35. However, at p. 143 the author uses "*Kan ma kan / Fi qadim azzaman . . .* It was so, it was not, in a time long forgot." I would translate this phrase, more awkwardly but with more of an eye to the differentiations of concepts of time, as "It was and it was not / In a packet of time set long ago." Other variations include "There was, there was not / In the oldness of time," and "There was, there was not / Not here, not there" (Kan wa ma kan / La han wa la han).

15. See Rosen 1984.

16. Erickson 1998, 136, argues that "for Rushdie, ever mindful of the parts as well as of the whole, the phrase takes on a special importance for his narrative, for it suggests an antinomical narrative in which opposites, mutually contradictory propositions, are not only possible but consciously invoked." On the relation of this point to the way the novel ends, see the text and references accompanying note 69 below.

17. Rushdie 1988, 92–93.

18. On the nature of energetic activity as an attribute of the admirable in Arab thought, see Bravmann 1972 (ch. 2: "Heroic Motives in Early Arabic Literature," pp. 39–63). Islamic attributes vary a good deal by local context. In Java, for example, immobility may be an indication of holiness, whereas in Arab cultures the antithesis may apply. See Geertz 1968. The concern in the Arabo-Islamic world thus appears to focus on the relation of action to identity rather than on the inherent attributes of human nature alone, the latter being a crucial issue in the West, such that Alexander Pope could write of humankind: "He hangs between; in doubt to act or rest; In doubt to deem himself a god or beast."

19. See Hallaq 1990.

20. Izutsu 1966, 132.

21. The translation of *zann* as "surmise" is taken from Arberry 1964. The other terms for *zann* are from Wehr 1994.

22. Izutsu 1966, 133

23. Qur'an 53:29. The same phrase is repeated many times, e.g., at Qur'an 10:37.

24. Izutsu 1966, 176. See also his discussion of the moral dichotomy that accompanies belief and unbelief at pp. 105–8.

25. See also the account of his own youthful doubts in Al-Azm 1991, 44–45. As a young North African told one investigator in France: "A Muslim who begins to pose questions is no longer a Muslim" (Gonzalez-Quijano 1987, 820). A Muslim would, therefore, find unimaginable the American poet's suggestion that "Apostasy is such, if you doubt on, / You return by the road you set on" (Ammons 1990, 156). On the crucial implications of making certain statements in public or in private, see Rosen 2000, 187–99.

26. On choice as a confession of doubt, see Calder 1989. On the role of the listener in validating the utterances of another, see Rosen 1984, 120–33, and Seminck 1993, 28–29.

27. Rushdie 1988, 281. It is curious in this regard that Rushdie did not explore doubt through those elements of Arabic grammar and language use by which the same terms simultaneously mean one thing and its opposite. "To be just/unjust," "to express doubt/certainty," "to be a friend who speaks with certainty/with a sense of futility," are only a few of the ways Arabic embraces inherent contrariety. Such antinomies do not, of course, go directly to fundamentals of the faith, but perhaps Rushdie's lack of knowledge of the language and his own Indic background precluded his grasp of this more subtle way of expressing doubt in Arabic. On these ambivalent concepts, see Berque and Charnay 1967.

28. The Qur'an does not generally speak well of poets: "And the poets—the perverse follow them; hast thou not seen how they wander in every valley and how they say that which they do not?" (Qur'an 26:224–25). See, generally, Shahid 1983. Yet popular approaches may be closer to the idea, as expressed by John Ciardi: "The poet lies his way to the truth." For the Islamic equivalent— that "the best poetry is the most deceptive one"—see Burgel 1970–71 and Burgel 1979.

29. Shelley 1904.

30. Rushdie 1988, 102.

31. Rushdie 1988, 364.

32. On the role of dreams as they bear on Rushdie's work, see Asad 1993, 274.

33. See the discussion and citations in Osiel 1995, 689–90.

34. "In Good Faith," in Rushdie 1991, 393–414, quoted in Steiner 1995, 114 (italics in original). Homi Bhabha writes: "[T]he book is written in the spirit of questioning, doubt, interrogation and puzzlement which articulates the dilemma of the migrant, the émigré, the minority" ("Down among the Women," *New Statesman and Society,* July 28, 1989, quoted in Asad 1993, 275). Pnina Werbner adds: "Rushdie has attempted to create a true hybrid, an integral unity of Islamic and Western myths, a new organic whole. Most Muslims, however, do not see this as a valid project: they wish to retain their traditions in their compartmentalized purity. Hybridism, the response to change, novelty, and other cultures, and fundamentalism, a return to a past complete, whole, and unchangeable, stand in implacable opposition" (Werbner 1996, S65). On the relation of *The Satanic Verses* to the problems of Muslim migrants to Europe, see King 1989.

35. Rushdie adds: "To experience any form of migration is to get a lesson in the importance of tolerating others' points of view. One might almost say that migration ought to be essential training for all would-be democrats" Salman Rushdie, "Günter Grass," in Rushdie 1991, 280, quoted in Steiner 1995, 116.

36. Steiner 1995, 116. On the political context of Rushdie's work, particularly as it relates to the Muslim migrant, see, generally, Fischer and Abedi 1990.

37. Rushdie 1999.

38. Morris 1994.

39. Bhabha 1994, 226. Sadik J. Al-Azm, who strongly supports Rushdie's freedom of speech and has himself been charged with blasphemy, notes the power of Rushdie's chosen form of discourse when he writes: "Rushdie's enemies are right in seeing *The Satanic Verses* as an all-out polemical assault on their fortresses and a vicious attempt to discredit the mindless certitudes of their positions through biting satire, skeptical iconoclasm and ribald irreverence" (Al-Azm 1991, 48).

40. Jack Goody suggests it is physical representations that often heighten the sense of doubt about the things represented, and it is thus an open question whether the traditional ban on representational art in Islam diminishes or is consonant with the elimination of permissible doubt about that which might be portrayed (Goody 1997). As for humor, the Qur'an (49:10–12) admonishes believers not to make fun of one another. Citing Goffman, Bergson, and others, Ibrahim says: "Koranic attitudes toward humor put severe limits on playfulness, defined [by Goffman] as the license to transform a primary text into a secondary text. In fact, we may go so far as to say that Islam grants no license for joking at all. Secondary texts are unacceptable as long as the primary text is Allah's text and, as such, perfect and meaningful in every detail. Joking makes its object look like a thing or a temporary plaything. Making a toy of any of God's creatures . . . is blasphemous" (Ibrahim 1994, 130–31).

41. Craige 1992, 70.

42. "In Good Faith," in Rushdie 1991, 393 (italics in the original), quoted in Craige 1992, 135–36, n. 10.

43. The miraculous nature of the Qur'an may not have been equally central to Islamic thought from the outset: "It was the contribution of the 10th century to insist on the formal or

rhetorical uniqueness of the Koran to such an extent that it become part and parcel of the theological argument for the Book's supernatural character" (Grunebaum 1974, xvii). See also Grunebaum 1986, Boullata 1987, and Boullata 1988. Any challenge to the miraculous nature of the Qur'an's revelation is regarded very seriously by both Sunni and Shi'ite Muslims. The modern Iranian writer Ali Dashti had noted that certain early Muslim scholars, "before bigotry and hyperbole prevailed, openly acknowledged that the arrangement and syntax of the Koran are not miraculous and that work of equal or greater value could be produced by other God-fearing persons" (Dashti 1985, 48). After Dashti's 1937 book was republished in Iran following the Islamic revolution he was arrested and died in prison in 1984.

44. On the role of language as a field for the miraculous, see Bamyeh 1999, 115–40.

45. On the subject of control for the story of Islam, Rushdie writes: "One day [Muslims] may agree that . . . the row over *The Satanic Verses* was at bottom an argument about who should have the power of the grand narrative, the Story of Islam, and that that power must belong equally to everyone" (Salman Rushdie, "One Thousand Days in a Balloon," reprinted in MacDonogh 1993, 17).

46. Pipes 1990, 116–17. See also Slaughter 1993, 164, n. 57.

47. Cave 1979. I am grateful to James Boon for pointing out the relevance of Cave's work to me. Jussawalla (1996, 67) argues that *The Satanic Verses* is an example of a Persian *dastan*, a "long-winded stream-of-consciousness tale that incorporates many related and sometimes loosely strung-together frame tales and assorted humorous anecdotes." But while the *dastan* form, or those shorter Arabic tales familiar from *The Arabian Nights*, may allow the author to portray some degree of role reversal, neither establishes the implicit claim to its own self-validation of moral and spiritual truths that informs both cornucopian novels and *The Satanic Verses*. On the Arab frame tradition generally, see Gittes 1983.

48. Cave 1979, 332. Sadik Al-Azm also notes this similarity to the work of the French writers: "Rushdie's sarcastic attacks on Islam's ossified spirituality, on the profound obsolescence of its piously reiterated narratives, on the backwardness of its current dogmatic formulations, on the rigid and perilous refusal of its establishments to look seriously into its current contradictions, anomalies, paradoxes and weaknesses, are very much in the spirit of Rabelais' debunking of the fundamental dogmas, sacraments and narratives of an outmoded medieval scholastic Christianity" (Al-Azm 1991, 5).

49. Cave 1979, 327. Cave also writes that such texts "give license to an interpretive approach which is itself self-conscious and which stresses the indeterminate character of its products" (idem).

50. Cave 1979, 328. See also his discussion at p. 22.

51. Cave 1979, 34.

52. Cave 1979, 182.

53. Cave 1979, 330.

54. Cave 1979, 332.

55. The relation of this self-creation to the position—indeed the needs—of one who crosses boundaries is stated quite clearly in the novel:

> A man who sets out to make himself up is taking on the Creator's role,
> according to one way of seeing things; he's unnatural, a blasphemer, an
> abomination of abominations. From another angle, you could see pathos
> in him, heroism in his struggle, in his willingness to risk: not all mutants
> survive. Or, consider him sociopolitically: most migrants learn, and can
> become disguises. Our own false descriptions to counter the falsehoods in-
> vented about us, concealing for reasons of security our secret selves.
>
> A man who invents himself needs someone to believe in him, to prove
> he's managed it. Playing God again, you could say. Or you could come

down a few notches, and think of Tinkerbell; fairies don't exist if children
don't clap their hands. Or you might say: it's just like being a man.

Not only the need to be believed in, but to believe in another. You've
got it: Love. (Rushdie 1988, 49)

On the almost God-like creation of such a text through a "magic realism" that reconstructs the
very bases of perception, see Kronagel 1991; and Seminck 1993, 65: "Writers act like Gods creating
their own universes, alternatives for the Only, True world described in the Quran. . . . Muhammad
did not like fiction, which he regarded as untrue. *The Satanic Verses* even widens this gap between
fiction and Islam by turning the novel into a pastiche of the Quran."

56. Rushdie has the character Baal give one poetic answer to this question at the time of the
Prophet's hegira, when he writes: "What kind of idea / does 'Submission' seem today? / One full of
fear. / An idea that runs away" (Rushdie 1988, 126). Elsewhere the questions are framed thus: "Any
new idea, Mahound, is asked two questions. The first is asked when it's weak: WHAT KIND OF
AN IDEA ARE YOU? Are you the kind that compromises, does deals, accommodates itself to society, aims to find a niche, to survive; or are you the cussed, bloody-minded, ramrod-backed type
of damnfool notion that would rather break than sway with the breeze?—The kind that will almost
certainly, ninety-nine times out of a hundred, be smashed to bits; but the hundredth time will
change the world" (Rushdie 1988, 335; original bold [i.e., all capitals]). Referring to the poet Baal,
Rushdie writes: "His verses, he thought, what had they been? *What kind of idea* damn it, he
couldn't even remember them properly *does Submission seem today* yes, something like that, after
all this time it was scarcely surprising *an idea that runs away* that was the end anyhow" (Rushdie
1988, 369; original italics), and, referring to an interlocutor's question to Ayesha, as she leads her
followers into the Arabian Sea: "His offer had contained an old question: *What kind of idea are you?
And she, in turn, had offered him an old answer. I was tempted, but am renewed; am uncompro-
mising; absolute; pure*" (Rushdie 1988, 500; original italics). See also at pp. 101 and 111 of the novel
where, the doubts about the idol-gods of the pre-Islamic cosmos and of the Prophet himself lead
Gibreel and another character beyond "What kind of idea is he" to "What kind of idea am I?"

57. "Facing the utter intransigence, the Philistine scorn of so much of Actually Existing Islam,
I reluctantly concluded that there was no way for me to help bring the Muslim culture I'd dreamed
of, the progressive, irreverent, skeptical, argumentative, playful and *unafraid* culture which is what
I've always understood as *freedom*. Actually Existing Islam, . . . which makes literalism a weapon
and redescriptions a crime, will never let the likes of me in" (in MacDonogh 1993, 22; original italics). It is such an "unafraid Islam" that Rushdie feels he has failed to help create. Rushdie re-
emphasized this point after the terrorist events of September 11, 2001, when he argued that the conflict was indeed about Islam (Rushdie 2001). Indeed, Rushdie even suggests that fear lies at the
heart of the way many Muslims approach their religion: "For a vast number of 'believing' Muslim
men, 'Islam' stands, in a jumbled, half-examined way . . . for the fear of God—the fear more than
the love, one suspects . . ." (Rushdie 2001). The whole question of the role that fear plays in the
Qur'anic vision remains to be given full critical attention.

On the two questions he poses, Rushdie told an interviewer: "Basically, there's two questions
that the book seeks to answer. When an idea comes into the world, it's faced with two big tests:
when you're weak, do you compromise; when you're strong, are you tolerant? . . . [T]he answer to
the first question is that, when weak, there seems [in the case of Mohammed] to have been a brief
flirtation with a possible compromise—about monotheism—which was very rapidly rejected. . . .
When Mohammed returned to Mecca in power, he was very, very tolerant" (interview of January 27, 1989, reprinted in Appignanesi and Maitland 1990, 22).

58. The Prophet is not represented as having himself experienced doubts about the content
of the precepts voiced through him by God, though he is sometimes portrayed as being uncertain
of his own role as a prophet. One unusual literary representation of doubt is contained in the
novelized life of the Prophet written by the well-known North African author Driss Chraibi.

The muted tone of doubt that runs through the whole of the book is indicated by the following passage:

> In a cave stands a man in a sleeveless seamless mantle of undyed wool.
> *All the questions have been asked, their answers furnished; and now, in this the aftermath of human history, may the days of the imagination begin— the days of ascendant dreams and restoring doubt turned on headlong certainties.* (Chraibi 1998, 13; original italics)

59. As Talal Asad has put it: "[W]hat is really interesting . . . is the way *representations* of questioning, doubt, and so on, *in* the text are read backward into an authorial intention (the 'spirit' of the writing) that *produced* the text" (Asad 1993, 275; original italics). Even former president Carter couched his criticism of Rushdie in terms of what the author intended: "The author, a well-versed analyst of Moslem beliefs, must have anticipated a horrified reaction throughout the Islamic world" (Carter 1989). Others have seen the issue in the light of the migrant's experience: "The literary theorist Homi Bhabha says that the immigrants have taken 'The Satanic Verses' outside the realm of fiction and 'into the realm of intention'—and that the important question is therefore not whether the book is insulting to Islam but who *sees* it as insulting to Islam, and what this means to what Professor Bhabha calls 'the project of modernity.'" (Kramer 1991, 65; original italics). See also Chakravorty 1995, 2241. By contrast, Pnina Werbner's structuralist analysis of *The Satanic Verses* and the role of authorial intent concludes that "from a modernist perspective *The Satanic Verses* did not intend to defame Islam and mock Muslims and their Prophet" (Werbner 1996, S69).

60. "In Good Faith," in Rushdie 1991, 410.

61. Goody 1996, 678. Goody continues (p. 679): "Questioning is in fact built into the human situation in which language-using animals create representations of entities to help deal with their intellectual, social and psychological needs. There are cognitive (and other) contradictions involved in the conceptualization of supernatural beings whose presence can only be deduced from their possible effects. Such dilemmas involve doubts as well as doctrines; this fact is part of the social universe that humanity creates for itself by the very use of language, a universe which represents experience in a totally transforming way and always contains a kernel of doubt." See also Goody 1997, esp. 238–70.

62. MacGregor 1987, 425.

63. Pouillon 1982, 5

64. The Arabic term employed here is *fitna,* which is usually translated as "chaos" or "disorder" (especially of a political nature). But as Bernard Lewis points out, it may better be thought of as "political disaffection," which in turn engenders such disorder. It does not, he argues, imply dissent in any acceptable sense of that term (Lewis 1988, 95). For some Muslim thinkers, fitna—which also translates as "temptation," "fascination," "commotion," and "disbelief"—may stem either from sensuality or from that doubt which is itself a weakness of knowledge intensified by ill-intent. See, generally, Williams 1995. Importantly, for understanding the reaction to the publication of *The Satanic Verses,* doubt is best countered by believers asserting the truth collectively. See Kamali 1993.

65. See Rosen 1995b. Others have put the issue in similar terms. "What does not contravene is permitted. Short of its arbitrary, religious and legal obligations Islam admits what the generality do" (Cragg 1965, 186). "Phenomenologically, Islam is whatever Muslims say it is; and prescriptively, Islam is whatever any Muslim believes it should be" (Mottahedeh 1993, 25). Pouillon's argument that Western scholars often assume that something is a matter of belief which is experienced by the people themselves as a form of direct knowing is expressed in his aphorism: "[I]t is the unbeliever who believes that the believer believes in the existence of God" (Pouillon 1982, 2).

66. Steiner 1995, 117.

67. Bardolph 1994, reprinted in Fletcher 1994, 217.

68. Paul Gray, "An Explosive Reception," *Time*, February 13, 1989, quoted in Bardolph 1989, 217, n. 17.

69. In this regard my disagreement is clear with other critics: See Enright 1989 and Engblom 1994, reprinted in Fletcher 1994, 302–3. As Seminck notes: "Surprisingly, however, *The Satanic Verses* is Rushdie's first novel *not* to end in total destruction. 'Some terrible doom . . . was in store' (541), but the disaster never takes place. True, Gibreel commits suicide (546), but Chamcha is saved, because Gibreel has broken the unending chain of betrayal and revenge by saving Chamcha's life (468): a 'small redeeming victory for love' (468). . . . After pages of squalidness, the text ends in a truly Dickensenian 'sentimental resolution'" (Seminck 1993, 21; internal page references are to *The Satanic Verses*).

Erickson, following the idea of "magical realism"—i.e., that Rushdie's text, by creating an alternative, fantastical world, challenges authority by leveling differences—argues that "the natural and the supernatural in Rushdie's narrative are never reconciled" (Erickson 1998, 156). But reconciliation is not the same as being conjoined in an orderly fashion: When, in his earlier works, Rushdie does not rely on the fantastic, eventual orderliness, as represented in his chosen style of closure, invariably remains elusive.

70. On these changes, see chapter seven in this volume.

71. Akbar Ahmed (personal communication).

72. The quoted phrase, as well as the overall idea, derives from a statement by Malise Ruthven quoted in Craige 1992, 133, n. 1.

73. Albert R. Jonsen and Stephen Toulmin raise these criteria in their assessment of Pascal's attack on casuistry when they write: "Was Pascal's critique of casuistry fair? That is a hard question. Fairness is not, of course, the prime virtue demanded of satire. Yet this particular satire has a serious purpose: namely, the intellectual demolition of an entire body of theological and moral doctrine. So its avowed appeal to the broad public did not absolve it from the demands of intellectual honesty—for as Pascal himself would have agreed, the ends do not justify the means" (Jonsen and Toulmin 1988, 243).

74. Suleri 1990, reprinted in Fletcher 1994, 223.

75. Remark by Salman Rushdie during the course of a 1988 radio interview, re-broadcast on BBC Radio 4 on September 25, 1998.

76. "Dr. Aadam Aziz, the patriarch in my novel *Midnight's Children,* loses his faith and is left with 'a hole inside him, a vacancy in a vital inner chamber.' I, too, possess the same God-shaped hole. Unable to accept the unarguable absolutes of religion, I have tried to fill up the hole with literature" (quoted from the *Observer* [London], January 22, 1989, in Webster 1990, 53–54).

Bibliography

Abdallah, Anouar, et al., eds. 1994. *For Rushdie: Essays by Arab and Muslim Writers in Defense of Free Speech*. New York: George Braziller.

Abou El Fadl, Khaled M. 2001. *And God Knows the Soldiers: The Authoritative and the Authoritarian in Islamic Discourses*. Lanham, MD: University Press of America.

Abu-Haidar, Farida. 1996. "The Moroccan Community in the Netherlands." *Maghreb Review* 21 (1–2): 62–69.

Ahmed, Akbar. 1991. "Salman Rushdie: A New Chapter." *Guardian* (London), January 17. Review 21–22.

Ahmed, Mohammed Shahab. 1999. "The Satanic Verses Incident in the Memory of the Early Muslim Community: An Analysis of the Early Riwayas and Their Isnads." Ph.D. diss., Princeton University.

Ahsan, M. M., and A. R. Kidwai, eds. 1991. *Sacrilege versus Civility: Muslim Perspectives on "The Satanic Verses" Affair*. Leicester, UK: Islamic Foundation.

Alami, Mohammed Hamdouni. 2001. "The Fiction of Architectural Identity in Contemporary Morocco." *ISIM Newsletter* (International Institute for the Study of Islam in the Modern World), 8 (September): 27.

Al-Azm, Sadik J. 1991. "The Importance of Being Earnest about Salman Rushdie." *Die Welt des Islams* 31: 1–49.

———. 1994. "Is the Fatwa a Fatwa?" In *For Rushdie: Essays by Arab and Muslim Writers in Defense of Free Speech*, edited by Anouar Abdallah, et. al., 21–23. New York: George Braziller.

Al-Azmeh, Aziz. 1997. *Muslim Kingship: Power and the Sacred in Muslim, Christian, and Pagan Polities*. London: I. B. Tauris.

al-Laheidan, Sheikh Saleh Ibn Mohammad. 1980. "Means of Evidence in Islamic Law." In *The Effects of Islamic Legislation on Crime Prevention in Saudi Arabia*, 149–92. Rome: Kingdom of Saudi Arabia and United Nations Social Defense Research Institute.

Allievi, Stefano. 1996. "The Muslim Community in Italy." In *Muslim Communities in the New Europe*, edited by Gerd Nonneman, Tim Niblock, and Bogdan Szajkowski, 315–29. Reading, UK: Ithaca Press.

Al-Madani, 'Izz Al-Din. 1995. "The Zanj Revolution." In *Modern Arabic Drama: An Anthology*, edited by Salma Khadra Jayyusi and Roger Allen, 159–85. Bloomington: Indiana University Press.

Ammons, A. R. 1990. *The Really Short Poems of A. R. Ammons.* New York: W. W. Norton.

Anderson, Lisa. 1995. "Democracy in the Arab World: A Critique of the Political Culture Approach." In *Political Liberalization and Democratization in the Arab World: Theoretical Perspectives,* vol. 1, edited by R. Brynen, B. Korany, and P. Noble, 77–92. London and Boulder: Lynne Rienner Publishers.

Anderson, Perry. 1974. *Lineages of the Absolutist State.* London: N.L.B.

An-Naim, Abdullahi Ahmed. 1986. "The Islamic Law of Apostasy and Its Modern Applicability: A Case from the Sudan." *Religion* 16: 197–224.

Appignanesi, Lisa, and Sara Maitland, eds. 1990. *The Rushdie File.* Syracuse: Syracuse University Press.

Arberry, Arthur J. 1964. *The Koran Interpreted.* Oxford: Oxford University Press.

Arkoun, Mohammed. 1989. "The Concept of Authority in Islamic Thought: La Hukma illa lillah." In *The Islamic World: From Classical to Modern Times,* edited by C. E. Bosworth, Charles Issawi, Roger Savory, and A. L. Udovich, 31–53. Princeton, NJ: Darwin Press.

Armstrong, Karen. 2000. *Islam: A Short History.* New York: Modern Library.

Asad, Talal. 1993. *Genealogies of Religion: Discipline and Reasons of Power in Christianity and Islam.* Baltimore: Johns Hopkins University Press.

Awret, Irene. 1984. *Days of Honey: The Tunisian Boyhood of Rafael Uzan.* New York: Schocken Books.

Ayubi, Nazih N. 1995. *Over-Stating the Arab State: Politics and Society in the Middle East.* London: I. B. Tauris.

Bahloul, Joëlle. 1996. *The Architecture of Memory: A Jewish-Muslim Household in Colonial Algeria, 1937–1962.* Cambridge: Cambridge University Press.

Baker, Keith Michael. 1985. "Memory and Practice: Politics and the Representation of the Past in Eighteenth-Century France." *Representations* 11: 134–64.

Balz, Kilian. 1997. "Submitting Faith to Judicial Scrutiny through the Family Trial: The 'Abu Zayd Case.'" *Die Welt des Islams* 37 (2): 135–55.

Bamyeh, Mohammed. 1999. *The Social Origins of Islam.* Minneapolis: University of Minnesota Press.

Banville, John. 1993. "An Interview with Salman Rushdie." *New York Review of Books,* March 4, 34–36.

Bardolph, Jacqueline. 1994. "Language Is Courage." In *Reading Rushdie: Perspectives on the Fiction of Salman Rushdie,* edited by M. D. Fletcher, 209–19. Amsterdam: Rodopi.

Barfield, Thomas, ed. 1997. *The Dictionary of Anthropology.* Oxford: Blackwell.

Bargach, Jamila. 2001. *Orphans of Islam: Family, Abandonment, and Secret Adoption in Morocco.* Blue Ridge Summit, PA: Rowman & Littlefield Publishing Group.

Barrada, Hamid. 1999. "Voyage au coeur de l'Islamisme marocain: Un entretien avec Mohamed Tozy." *Jeune Afrique,* February 9–15, 8–19.

Basdevant-Gaudemet, Brigitte. 2000. "The Legal Status of Islam in France." In *Islam and European Legal Systems,* edited by Silvio Ferrari and Anthony Bradney, 97–124. Aldershot: Ashgate/Dartmouth.

Bearak, Barry. 2001. "Pakistan: Death Sentence Upheld." *New York Times,* July 27, A6.

Bellah, Robert N., et al. 1985. *Habits of the Heart: Individualism and Commitment in American Life.* Berkeley: University of California Press.

Bennani-Chraibi, Mounia. 1994. *Soumis et rebelles: Les jeunes au Maroc.* Paris: C.N.R.S.

Bennison, Katherine N. 2002. *Jihad and Its Interpretations in 19th Century Morocco: State-Society Relations during the French Conquest of Algeria.* London: Routledge/Curzon, 2002.

Bergson, Henri. [1896] 1988. *Matter and Memory.* New York: Zone.

Berque, Jacques. 1958. *Al-Youssi: Problèmes de la culture marocaine au XVIIème siècle.* The Hague: Mouton.

————. 1978. *Cultural Expression in Arab Society Today.* Austin: University of Texas Press.

————, and Jean-Paul Charnay, eds. 1967. *L'ambivalence dans la culture arabe.* Paris: Editions Anthropos.

Bhabha, Homi. 1994. *The Location of Culture.* London: Routledge.

Black, Max. 1967. "Probability." In *The Encyclopedia of Philosophy,* vol. 6, edited by P. Edwards, 464–79. New York: Macmillan.

Boehm, Christopher. 1989. "Ambivalence and Compromise in Human Nature." *American Anthropologist* 91 (4): 921–39.

Bohannon, Laura. 1966. "Shakespeare in the Bush." *Natural History* 75 (August/September): 28–33.

Boon, James. 1982. *Other Tribes, Other Scribes.* Cambridge: Cambridge University Press.

Borges, Jorge Luis. 1993. *Ficciones.* London: Everyman.

Boullata, Issa. 1987. "I'jaz." In *Encyclopedia of Religion,* vol. 5, edited by Mircea Eliade, 87–88. New York: Macmillan.

————. 1988. "The Rhetorical Interpretation of the Qur'an: I'jaz and Related Topics." In *Approaches to the History of the Interpretation of the Qur'an,* edited by Andrew Rippin, 139–57. Oxford: Clarendon Press.

Boyarin, Jonathan, ed. 1994. *Remapping Memory: The Politics of Timespace.* Minneapolis: University of Minnesota Press.

Bradney, Anthony. 2000. "The Legal Status of Islam within the United Kingdom." In *Islam and European Legal Systems,* edited by Silvio Ferrari and Anthony Bradney, 181–97. Aldershot: Ashgate/Dartmouth.

Bravmann, M. M. 1972. *The Spiritual Background of Early Islam.* Leiden: E. J. Brill.

Brett, Michael, and Elizabeth Fentress. 1996. *The Berbers.* Oxford: Blackwell Publishers.

Brown, Kenneth L. 1976. *People of Salé: Tradition and Change in a Moroccan City, 1830–1930.* Cambridge: Harvard University Press.

Burgel, J. C. 1970–71. "Die beste Dichtung ist die Lugenreichste." *Oriens* 23–24: 7–102.

————. 1979. "Love, Lust, and Longing: Eroticism in Early Islam as Reflected in Literary Sources." In *Society and the Sexes in Medieval Islam,* edited by Afaf Lutfi al-Sayyid Marsot, 81–117. Malibu, CA: Undena Pub.

Burke, Edmund, III. 1976. *Prelude to Protectorate in Morocco: Precolonial Protest and Resistance, 1860–1912.* Chicago: University of Chicago Press.

————. 1993. "Mohand N'Hamoucha: Middle Atlas Berber." In *Struggle and Survival in the Modern Middle East,* edited by Edmund Burke III, 100–13. Berkeley: University of California Press.

Bushnaq, Inea, ed. 1986. *Arab Folktales.* New York: Pantheon Books.

Calder, Norman. 1989. "Doubt and Prerogative: The Emergence of an Imami Shi'i Theory of IJTIHAD." *Studia Islamica* 70: 57–78.

Campbell, Donald T. 1965. "Altruistic Motives." In *Nebraska Symposium on Motivation,* edited by D. Levine, 283–311. Lincoln: University of Nebraska Press.

Carter, Jimmy. 1989. "Rushdie's Book Is an Insult." *New York Times,* March 5, E23.

Caton, Steven C. 1987. "Power, Persuasion, and Language: A Critique of the Segmentary Model in the Middle East." *International Journal of Middle East Studies* 19: 77–102.

Cave, Terence C. 1979. *The Cornucopian Text: Problems of Writing in the French Renaissance.* Oxford: Oxford University Press.

Chakravorty, Pinaki. 1995. "The Rushdie Incident as Law-and-Literature Parable." *Yale Law Journal* 104: 2213–47.

Chraibi, Driss. 1998. *Muhammad: A Novel,* translated by Nadia Benabid. Boulder: Lynne Rienner Publishers.

Christian, Nichole M. 2000. "Challenging Islamic Myth on Organ Transplants as Ailments Rise." *New York Times,* May 20, A9.

Chtatou, Mohamed. 1996. "Saints and Spirits and Their Significance in Moroccan Cultural Beliefs and Practices: An Analysis of Westermarck's Work." *Morocco* 1 (n.s.): 62–84.

Clastres, Pierre. 1974. *Society against the State,* translated by Robert Hurley. Oxford: Basil Blackwell.

Clifford, James. 1988. *The Predicament of Culture.* Cambridge: Harvard University Press.

Cohen, Mark R. 1991. "The Neo-Lachrymose Conception of Jewish-Arab History." *Tikkun* 6 (3): 55–64.

Cohen, Roger. 2000. "Europe's Migrant Fears Rend a Spanish Town." *New York Times,* May 8, A1.

———. 2001a. "Germany Ponders Opening Door, Just a Crack, to Immigration." *New York Times,* July 5, A3.

———. 2001b. "How Open to Immigrants Should Germany Be? An Uneasy Country's Debate Deepens." *New York Times,* May 13, 11.

Cohn-Sherbok, Dan, ed. 1990. *The Salman Rushdie Controversy in Interreligious Perspective.* Lewiston, NY: Edwin Mellen Press.

Collingwood, R. G. 1940. *An Essay on Metaphysics.* Oxford: Oxford University Press.

Combs-Schilling, M. Elaine. 1989. *Sacred Performances: Islam, Sexuality, and Sacrifice.* New York: Columbia University Press.

———. 1991. "Etching Patriarchal Rule: Ritual Dye, Erotic Potency, and the Moroccan Monarchy." *Journal of the History of Sexuality* 1 (4): 658–81.

Commission for Racial Equality. 1990. *Free Speech: Report of a Seminar Organised by the Commission for Racial Equality and the Policy Studies Institute.* London: Commission for Racial Equality.

Connerton, Paul. 1989. *How Societies Remember.* Cambridge: Cambridge University Press.

Connolly, William E. 1987. "Modern Authority and Ambiguity." In *Authority Revisited,* Nomos 29, edited by J. R. Pennock and J. W. Chapman. New York: New York University Press.

Cotran, Eugene, and Adel Omar Sherif, eds. 1999. *Democracy, the Rule of Law and Islam.* The Hague: Kluwer Law International.

Cragg, Kenneth. 1965. *Counsels in Contemporary Islam.* Edinburgh: Edinburgh University Press.

———. 1994. *Troubled by Truth: Biographies in the Presence of Mystery.* Cleveland: Pilgrim Press.

Craige, Betty Jean. 1992. *Laying the Ladder Down: The Emergence of Cultural Holism.* Chicago: University of Chicago Press.

Crane, Susan A. 1997. "Writing the Individual Back into Collective Memory." *American Historical Review* 102 (5): 1372–85.

Croisette, Barbara. 1998. "Democracy's Desert: A Rising Tide of Freedom Bypasses the Arab World." *New York Times,* April 26, Section 4, 1.

———. 2001. "As Democracies Spread, Islamic World Hesitates." *New York Times,* December 23, A14.

Crone, Patricia, and Shmuel Moreh. 2000. *The Book of Strangers: Medieval Arabic Graffiti on the Theme of Nostalgia.* Princeton, NJ: Marcus Weiner Pub.

Dakhlia, Jocelyn. 1990. *L'oubli de la cité: La mémoire collective à l'épreuve du lineage dans le Jérid tunisien.* Paris: Editions la Découverte.

———. 1993. "Collective Memory and the Story of History: Lineage and Nation in a North African Oasis." *History and Theory* (Beiheft 32): 57–79.

Danforth, Sandra C. 1973. "Repaying Historical Debts: The Indian Claims Commission." *North Dakota Law Review* 49 (2): 359–403.

Danielson, Virginia. 1997. *"The Voice of Egypt": Umm Kulthum, Arabic Song, and Egyptian Society in the Twentieth Century.* Chicago: University of Chicago Press.

Dashti, Ali. 1985. *Twenty-three Years: A Study of the Prophetic Career,* translated by F. R. C. Bagley. London: Allen & Unwin.

Dassetto, Felice. 1996. *La construction de l'Islam européen: Approche socio-anthropologique*. Paris: L'Harmattan.

———. 2000. "The New European Islam." In *Islam and European Legal Systems*, edited by Silvio Ferrari and Anthony Bradney, 31–45. Aldershot: Ashgate/Dartmouth.

———, and Gerd Nonneman. 1996. "Islam in Belgium and the Netherlands: Towards a Typology of 'Transplanted' Islam." In *Muslim Communities in the New Europe*, edited by Gerd Nonneman, 187–217. Reading, UK: Ithaca Press.

Davidson, Donald. 1980. *Essays on Action and Events*. Oxford: Clarendon Press.

Dayan, Haviva. 1993. "The Patient Wife." In *Jewish Moroccan Folk Narratives from Israel*, edited by Haya Bar-Itzhak and Aliza Shenhar, 25–40. Detroit: Wayne State University Press.

Denoeux, Guilain, and Andeslam Maghraoui. 1998. "King Hassan's Strategy of Political Dualism." *Middle East Policy* 5 (4): 104–30.

Deprez, Jean. 1996. "Statut personnel et pratiques familiales des étrangers musulmans en France: Aspects de droit international privé." In *Familles-Islam-Europe: Le droit confronté au changement*, edited by Marie-Claire Foblets, 57–124. Paris: L'Harmattan.

Deshen, Shlomo. 1989. *The Mellah Society: Jewish Community Life in Sherifian Morocco*. Chicago: University of Chicago Press.

Diamond, Jared. 1997. *Guns, Germs, and Steel: The Fates of Human Societies*. New York: W. W. Norton.

Douglas, Allen, and Fedwa Malti-Douglas. 1994. *Arab Comic Strips: Politics of an Emerging Mass Culture*. Bloomington: Indiana University Press.

Douglas, Mary. 1986. *How Institutions Think*. London: Routledge & Kegan Paul.

———. 1995. "Forgotten Knowledge." In *Shifting Contexts: Transformations in Anthropological Knowledge*, edited by Marilyn Strathern, 13–29. London: Routledge.

Doutté, Edmond. 1914. *En tribu*. Paris: Paul Geuthner.

Dresch, Paul. 1988. "Segmentation: Its Roots in Arabia and Its Flowering Elsewhere." *Cultural Anthropology* 3 (1): 50–67.

———. 1990. "Imams and Tribes: The Writing and Acting of History in Upper Yemen." In *Tribes and State Formation in the Middle East*, edited by Philip S. Khoury and Josph Kostiner, 252–87. Berkeley: University of California Press.

Dugger, Celia W. 2000 "Rushdie Creates Sensation on His Return to India." *New York Times*, April 17, A4.

Dupree, Louis. 1984. "Tribal Warfare in Afghanistan and Pakistan: A Reflection of the Segmentary System." In *Islam in Tribal Societies: From the Atlas to the Indus*, edited by Akbar Ahmed and David M. Hart, 266–86. London: Routledge & Kegan Paul.

Dupret, Baudouin. 2000–2001. "Modern Law and Arab Societies in Recent French-Speaking Literature." *Journal of Law and Religion* 15 (1 and 2): 289–301.

Dworkin, Ronald. 1986. *Law's Empire*. London: Fontana.

Dwyer, Daisy Hilse. 1978. "Women, Sufism, and Decision-Making in Moroccan Islam." In *Women in the Muslim World*, edited by Lois Beck and Nikki Keddie, 585–98. Cambridge: Harvard University Press.

Earle, Timothy. 1997. *How Chiefs Come to Power*. Stanford: Stanford University Press.

Edelson, Edward. 1986. "The Ubiquity of Nonlinearity." *Mosaic* 17 (3): 10–17.

Eickelman, Dale F. 1977. "Time in a Complex Society: A Moroccan Example." *Ethnology* 16 (1): 39–55.

———. 1985. *Knowledge and Power in Morocco: The Education of a Twentieth-Century Notable*. Princeton: Princeton University Press.

Engblom, Philip. 1994. "A Multitude of Voices: Carnivalization and Dialogicality in the Novels of Salman Rushdie." In *Reading Rushdie: Perspectives on the Fiction of Salman Rushdie*, edited by M. D. Fletcher, 293–304. Amsterdam: Rodopi.

Enright, D. J. 1989. "So, and Not So." *New York Review of Books* 36 (3): 25–26.

Erickson, John. 1998. *Islam and Postcolonial Narrative.* Cambridge: Cambridge University Press.

Evans-Pritchard, E. E. 1940. *The Nuer.* Oxford: Oxford University Press.

———. 1949. *The Sanusi of Cyrenaica.* Oxford: Oxford University Press.

Evers-Rosander, Eva. 1993. "Some Wedding Customs in Qbila Anjra Now (1976–87) and Then (1900–1910): Comparisons and Reflections Based on Westermarck's 'Marriage Ceremonies in Morocco.'" In *Westermarck et la société marocaine,* edited by Rahma Bourqia and Mokhtar al-Harras, 111–24. Publications de la Faculté des Lettres et des Sciences Humaines–Université Mohammed V, in the series Colloques et Séminaires 27. Rabat: Imprimerie El Maarif Al-Jadida.

Ewing, Katherine Pratt. 2000. "Legislating Religious Freedom: Muslim Challenges to the Relationship between 'Church' and 'State' in Germany and France." *Daedalus* 129 (4): 31–54.

Fakhry, Majid. 1970. *A History of Islamic Philosophy.* New York: Columbia University Press.

Fentress, James, and Chris Wickham. 1992. *Social Memory.* Cambridge, MA: Blackwell.

Feynman, Richard P. 1998. *The Meaning of It All.* London: Allen Lane.

Fisher, Michael M. J. 1996. "Comments on Pnina Werbner's 'Allegories of Sacred Imperfection.'" *Current Anthropology* 37 (Supplement): S72.

———, and Mehdi Abedi. 1990. "Bombay Talkies, the Word, and the World: Salman Rushdie's Satanic Verses." *Cultural Anthropology* 5 (2): 107–59.

Fletcher, M. D., ed. 1994. *Reading Rushdie: Perspectives on the Fiction of Salman Rushdie.* Amsterdam: Rodopi.

Florescano, Enrique. 1994. *Memory, Myth, and Time in Mexico.* Austin: University of Texas Press.

Foblets, Marie-Claire. 1996. "Un droit pour ou par ses destinataires? Les complexités du rattachement juridique de l'alliance matrimoniale entre partenaires immigrés." In *Famille-Islam-Europe: Le droit confronté au changement,* edited by Marie-Claire Foblets, 125–51. Paris: L'Harmattan.

———. 1999. "Femmes immigrées et conflits conjugaux: Plaidoyer pour plus de protection juridique." *Droit et Cultures* 37 (1): 255–76.

———, and Jinske Verhellen. 2000. "Marokkaanse migrantenvrouwen in gezinsgeschillen: Wat zijn passende juridische oplossingen?" *RIMO: Vereniging tot bestudering van het Recht van de Islam en het Midden Oosten Recht van de Islam* 17: 90–115.

Foucault, Michel. 1970. *The Order of Things: An Archaeology of the Human Sciences.* New York: Pantheon.

———. 1980. *Power/Knowledge.* Brighton, UK: Harvester Press.

Freud, Sigmund. [1899] 1989. "Screen Memories." In *The Freud Reader,* edited by Peter Gay, 117–26. New York: Norton.

Fried, Morton H. 1966. "On the Concepts of 'Tribe' and 'Tribal Societies.'" *Transactions of the New York Academy of Sciences* 28 (4): 527–40.

Friedman, Thomas L. 1989. *From Beirut to Jerusalem.* New York: Doubleday.

———. 2002. "A Traveler to Saudi Arabia." *New York Times,* February 24, WK13.

Frisch, Hillel. 1997. "Modern Absolutist or Neopatriarchal State Building? Customary Law, Extended Families, and the Palestinian Authority." *International Journal of Middle East Studies* 29: 341–58.

Fuentes, Carlos. 1985–86. "Remember the Future." *Salmagundi* 68–69: 333–52.

Galbraith, John Kenneth. 1983. *The Anatomy of Power.* London: Hamish Hamilton.

Gandjieh, Ayatollah Djallal. 1994. "For Rushdie." In *For Rushdie: Essays by Arab and Muslim Writers in Defense of Free Speech,* edited by Anouar Abdellah, et al., 149–56. New York: George Braziller.

Gardet, Louis. 1976. "Moslem Views of Time and History: An Essay in Cultural Typology." In *Cultures and Time,* edited by Louis Gardet. Paris: Unesco Press.

————. 1977. "The Prophet." In *Time and the Philosophies,* edited by H. Aguessy, 197–209. Paris: Unesco Press.

Geary, Patrick J. 1994. *Phantoms of Remembrance: Memory and Oblivion at the End of the First Millennium.* Princeton: Princeton University Press.

Geertz, Clifford. 1968. *Islam Observed.* New Haven: Yale University Press.

————. 1973. *The Interpretation of Cultures.* New York: Basic Books.

————. 1979. "The Bazaar." In *Meaning and Order in Moroccan Society,* by Clifford Geertz, Hildred Geertz, and Lawrence Rosen, 123–313. New York: Cambridge University Press.

————. 1988. *Works and Lives: The Anthropologist as Author.* Stanford: Stanford University Press.

————. 1989. "Toutes Directions: Reading the Signs in a Urban Sprawl." *International Journal of Middle East Studies* 21: 291–306.

————. 2000. *Available Light: Anthropological Reflections on Philosophical Topics.* Princeton: Princeton University Press.

————, Hildred Geertz, and Lawrence Rosen. 1979. *Meaning and Order in Moroccan Society: Three Essays in Cultural Analysis.* New York: Cambridge University Press.

Gellner, Ernest. 1959. *Words and Things.* Harmondsworth, UK: Penguin Books.

————. 1974. *Legitimation of Belief.* Cambridge: Cambridge University Press.

————. 1981. *Muslim Society.* Cambridge: Cambridge University Press.

————. 1983. *Nations and Nationalism.* Ithaca: Cornell University Press.

————. 1988. "Trust, Cohesion, and Social Order." In *Trust: Making and Breaking Cooperative Relations,* edited by Diego Gambetta, 142–57. Oxford: Basil Blackwell.

————. 1997. *Nationalism.* New York: New York University Press.

Gerholm, Tomas, and Yngve Georg Lithman, eds. 1988. *The New Islamic Presence in Western Europe.* London: Mansell Publishing Limited.

"Germany Bans Radical Organization." 2001. *USA Today,* December 13, 9A.

Getches, David H., Charles F. Wilkinson, and Robert A. Williams. 1998. *Cases and Materials on Federal Indian Law.* 4th ed. St. Paul, MN: West Publishing Co.

Gibb, H. A. R. 1949. *Mohammedanism.* Oxford: Oxford University Press.

"Gibraltar in Reverse?" 2002. *Economist,* February 23, 52.

Gilsenan, Michael. 1976. "Lying, Honor, and Contradiction." In *Transaction and Meaning: Directions in the Anthropology of Exchange and Symbolic Behavior,* edited by Bruce Kapferer, 191–219. Philadelphia: Institute for the Study of Human Issues.

————. 2000. "Signs of Truth: Enchantment, Modernity, and the Dreams of Peasant Women." *Journal of the Royal Anthropological Institute* (n.s.) 6 (4): 597–615.

Gittes, Katherine Slater. 1983. "The *Canterbury Tales* and the Arabic Frame Tradition." *PMLA (Publications of the Modern Language Association)* 98: 237–51.

Glain, Stephen J. 2000. "Sword Play: The Secret Weapon in Saddam's Arsenal May Drive an SUV and It May Backfire: Tribes of Iraq Are a Key Source of Loyalty and Rebellion." *Wall Street Journal,* May 23, 1ff.

Glass, Charles. 1990. *Tribes with Flags: A Dangerous Passage through the Chaos of the Middle East.* New York: Atlantic Monthly Press.

Gleve, Robert. 2000. *Inevitable Doubt: Two Theories of Shi'i Jurisprudence.* Leiden: E. J. Brill.

Glieck, James. 1987. *Chaos: Making a New Science.* New York: Viking.

Goitein, S. D. 1977. "Individualism and Conformity in Classical Islam." In *Individualism and Conformity in Classical Islam,* edited by Speros Vryonis, 3–18. Weisbaden: Otto Harrasowitz.

Goldberg, Ellis. 1991. "Smashing Idols and the State: The Protestant Ethic and Egyptian Sunni Radicalization." *Comparative Studies in Society and History* 33 (1): 3–35.

Goldberg, Harvey. 1988. *The Book of Mordechai.* Philadelphia: Institute for the Study of Human Issues.

Goldman, Shalom. 1995. *The Wiles of Women / The Wiles of Men: Joseph and Potiphar's Wife in Ancient Near Eastern, Jewish, and Islamic Folklore.* Albany: State University of New York Press.

Gonzalez-Quijano, Yves. 1987. "Les 'nouvelles' generations: Issues de l'immigration maghrébine et la question de l'Islam." *Révue Française de Science Politique* 37 (6): 820–31.

Goodstein, Laurie. 2001. "Stereotyping Rankles Silent, Secular Majority of American Muslims." *New York Times,* December 23, A20.

Goody, Jack. 1987. *The Interface between the Written and the Oral.* Cambridge: Cambridge University Press.

———. 1996. "A Kernel of Doubt." *Journal of the Royal Anthropological Institute* 2 (4): 667–81.

———. 1997. *Representations and Contradictions: Ambivalence Towards Images, Theatre, Fiction, Relics, and Sexuality.* Oxford: Blackwell Publishers.

Grove, Valerie. 1998. "Back in the Light after a Decade of Darkness." *Times* (London), September 26, 7.

Grunebaum, Gustave E. von. 1974. *A Tenth-Century Document of Arabic Literary Theory and Criticism: The Sections on Poetry of al-Bâqillâni's I'jâz al-Qur'ân.* Chicago: University of Chicago Press.

———. 1986. "I'djaz." In *Encyclopedia of Islam,* vol. 3, edited by H. A. R. Gibb, et. al., 1018–20. Leiden: E. J. Brill.

Hacking, Ian. 1975. *The Emergence of Probability.* Cambridge: Cambridge University Press.

———. 1995. *Rewriting the Soul: Multiple Personality and the Sciences of Memory.* Princeton: Princeton University Press.

Haddad, Mohammed. 1998. "Pour comprendre Hasan Hanafi." *IBLA: Révue de l'Institut des Belles Lettres Arabes* 61 (1): 49–69.

Haddad, Yvonne Yazbeck, and Jane Idleman Smith, eds. 1994. *Muslim Communities in North America.* Albany: State University of New York Press.

Haenni, Patrick. 2000. "Divergent Trajectories: Islam and Ethnicity in Switzerland." *ISIM Newsletter* (International Institute for the Study of Islam in the Modern World), 6: 31.

Halbwachs, Maurice. 1925. *Les cadres sociaux de la mémoire.* New York: Harper & Row.

Hall, John A., and Ian Jarvie, eds. 1996. *The Social Philosophy of Ernest Gellner.* Amsterdam: Rodopi.

Hallaq, Wael B. 1990. "On Inductive Corroboration, Probability, and Certainty in Sunni Legal Thought." In *Islamic Law and Jurisprudence: Studies in Honor of Farhat J. Ziadeh,* edited by Nicholas L. Heer, 3–31. Seattle: University of Washington Press.

Hammoudi, Abdellah. 1993. *The Victim and Its Masks: An Essay on Sacrifice and Masquerade in the Maghreb.* Chicago: University of Chicago Press.

———. 1994. "The Path of Sainthood: Structure and Danger." *Princeton Papers in Near Eastern Studies* 3: 71–88.

———. 1997. *Master and Disciple: The Cultural Foundations of Moroccan Authoritarianism.* Chicago: University of Chicago Press.

———. 2001. "From Recognition to Political Nationalization: The Tribal, the Ethnic and Their Relation to the Moroccan State." In *State Formation and Ethnic Relations in the Middle East,* edited by Usuki Akira, 143–62. Japan Center for Area Studies Symposium Series. Osaka, Japan: Japan Center for Area Studies.

Harris, Marvin. 1968. *The Rise of Anthropological Theory: A History of Theories of Culture.* New York: Thomas Y. Crowell.

Hart, David M. 1993. "Faulty Models of North African and Middle Eastern Tribal Structures." *Révue des Mondes Musulmans et de la Méditerranée* 68–69 (2–3): 225–38.

Hasnaoui, Ahmed. 1977. "Certain Notions of Time in Arab-Muslim Philosophy." In *Time and the Philosophies,* edited by H. Aguessy, 49–79. Paris: Unesco Press.

Hefner, Robert W. 2000. *Civil Islam: Muslims and Democratization in Indonesia*. Princeton: Princeton University Press.

Henderson, J. B. 1998. *The Construction of Orthodoxy and Heresy: Neo-Confucian, Islamic, Jewish, and Early Christian Patterns*. Albany: State University of New York Press.

Herzfeld, Michael. 1992. *The Social Production of Indifference: Exploring the Symbolic Roots of Western Bureaucracy*. New York: Berg.

Heydeman, Steven. 1999. *Authoritarianism in Syria: Institutions and Social Conflict, 1946–1970*. Ithaca: Cornell University Press.

Hoebel, E. Adamson. 1978. *The Cheyennes: Indians of the Great Plains*. 2nd ed. New York: Holt, Rinehart and Winston.

Holmes, Oliver Wendell. 1915. "Ideals and Doubts." *Illinois Law Review* 10: 1–4.

Homola, Victor. 2002. "Germany: Muslim Animal Slaughter Approved." *New York Times*, January 16, A9.

Hourani, Albert. 1991. *A History of the Arab Peoples*. Cambridge: Harvard University Press.

Hutton, Patrick H. 1993. *History as an Art of Memory*. Hanover, NH: University Press of New England.

Ibrahim, Abdullahi Ali. 1994. *Assaulting with Words: Popular Discourse and the Bridle of Shariah*. Evanston: Northwestern University Press.

Irwin-Zarecka, Iwona. 1994. *Frames of Reference: The Dynamics of Collective Memory*. New Brunswick, NJ: Transaction Publishers.

Izutsu, Toshihiko. 1966. *Ethico-Religious Concepts in the Qur'ān*. Montreal: McGill University Press.

Johnson, Allen W., and Timothy Earle. 2000. *The Evolution of Human Societies*. 2nd ed. Stanford: Stanford University Press.

Johnson, George. 1991. *In the Palaces of Memory: How We Build the Worlds Inside Our Heads*. New York: Knopf.

Jonsen, Albert R., and Stephen Toulmin. 1988. *The Abuse of Casuistry: A History of Moral Reasoning*. Berkeley: University of California Press.

Jussawalla, Feroza. 1996. "Rushdie's Dastan-e-Dilruba: The Satanic Verses as Rushdie's Love Letter to Islam." *Diacritics* 26 (1): 50–73.

Kamali, Mohammad H. 1993. "Freedom of Expression in Islam: An Analysis of *Fitnah*." *American Journal of Islamic Social Science* 10 (2): 178–200.

Kammen, Michael. 1995. "Review of Iwona Irwin-Zarecka, Frames of Reference: The Dynamics of Collective Memory." *History and Theory* 34 (3): 245–61.

Kapchan, Deborah. 1996. *Gender on the Market: Moroccan Women and the Revoicing of Tradition*. Philadelphia: University of Pennsylvania Press.

Katz, Jonathan. 1992. "Visionary Experience, Autobiography, and Sainthood in North African Islam." *Princeton Papers in Near Eastern Studies* 1: 85–118.

Kerr, Malcolm. 1963. *Arab Radical Notions of Democracy*. St. Anthony's Papers. No. 16: 9–40. London: Chatto and Windus.

Khaldun, Ibn. 1967. *The Muqaddimah: An Introduction to History*. Abridged edition, translated by Franz Rosenthal. Princeton: Princeton University Press.

———. 1987. *An Arab Philosophy of History: Selections from the Prolegomena of Ibn Khaldun of Tunis (1332–1406)*, translated by Charles Issawi. Princeton: Darwin Press.

Khuri, Fuad I. 1990. *Tents and Pyramids: Games and Ideology in Arab Culture from Backgammon to Autocratic Rule*. London: Saqi Books.

Kierkegaard, Søren. 1971. *Philosophical Fragments*, translated by D. F. Swenson. Princeton: Princeton University Press.

King, Bruce. 1989. "Who Wrote 'The Satanic Verses'?" *World Literature Today* 63 (3): 433–35.

King, Michael. 1993. *Muslims in Europe: A New Identity for Islam,* EUI Working Paper ECS no. 93/1, EUI Working Papers in European Cultural Studies. Florence: European University Institute.

Knapp, Steven. 1989. "Collective Memory and the Actual Past." *Representations* 26: 123–49.

Knibiehler, Yvonne, Geneviève Emmery, and Françoise Leguay, eds. 1992. *Des Français au Maroc: La présence et la mémoire (1912–1956).* Paris: Editions Denoël.

Kramer, Jane. 1991. "Letter from London." *New Yorker,* January 14, 60–75.

Kraus, Wolfgang. 1998. "Contestable Identities: Tribal Structures in the Moroccan High Atlas." *Journal of the Royal Anthropological Institute* (n.s.) 4 (1): 1–22.

Kronagel, Alex. 1991. "*The Satanic Verses:* Narrative Structure and Islamic Doctrine." *International Fiction Review* 18 (2): 69–75.

Kruger, Hilmar. 2000–2001. "The Study of Islamic Law in Germany: A Review of Recent Books on Islamic Law." *Journal of Law and Religion* 15 (1 and 2): 303–30.

Krüger, Lorenz, Lorraine J. Daston, and Michael Heidelberger, eds. 1987. *The Probabilistic Revolution,* 2 vols. Cambridge: MIT Press.

Kubler, Clark George. 1944. *The Argument from Probability in Early Attic Oratory.* Chicago: University of Chicago Press.

Kuchler, Susanne, and Walter Melion, eds. 1991. *Images of Memory: On Remembering and Representation.* Washington: Smithsonian Institution Press.

Kuper, Adam. 1996. "Ernest Gellner: The Last of the Central Europeans." *Anthropology Today* 12: 19–20.

Lahbabi, Mohamed Aziz. 1964. *Le personnalisme musulman.* Paris: Presses Universitaires de France.

Landau, Misia. 1991. *Narratives of Human Evolution.* New Haven: Yale University Press.

Landau-Tasseron, Ella. 2000. "From Tribal Society to Centralized Polity: An Interpretation of Events and Anecdotes of the Formative Period of Islam." *Jerusalem Studies in Arabic and Islam* 24: 180–216.

Landman, Nico. 1999. "Imams in the Netherlands: Home-Made Better Than Import?" *ISIM Newsletter* (International Institute for the Study of Islam in the Modern World), 2: 5.

Layish, Aharon, and A. Shmueli. 1979. "Custom and *Shari'a* in the Bedouin Family According to Legal Documents from the Judean Desert." *Bulletin of the School of Oriental and African Studies* 42: 29–45.

Le Goff, Jacques. 1992. *History and Memory.* New York: Columbia University Press.

Leaman, Oliver. 1985. *An Introduction to Medieval Islamic Philosophy.* Cambridge: Cambridge University Press.

Lequin, Yves, and Jean Métal. 1980. "À la récherche d'une mémoire collective: Les métallurgistes retraités de Givors." *Annales: Économies, Sociétés, Civilisations* 35 (1): 149–63.

Leveau, Remy. 1997. "The Political Culture of the 'Beurs.'" In *Islam in Europe: The Politics of Religion and Community,* edited by Steven Vertovic and Ceri Peach, 147–55. London: Macmillan Press Ltd.

Levine, Donald N. 1985. *The Flight from Ambiguity: Essays in Social and Cultural Theory.* Chicago: University of Chicago Press.

Levy, André. 1997. "To Morocco and Back: Tourism and Pilgrimage among Moroccan-Born Israelis." In *Grasping Land: Space and Place in Contemporary Israeli Discourse and Experience,* edited by E. Ben-Ari and Y. Bilu, 25–46. Albany: State University of New York Press.

———. 2000. "Playing for Control: Card Games between Jews and Muslims on a Casablancan Beach." *American Ethnologist* 26 (3): 632–53.

Levy, Leonard W. 1993. *Blasphemy: Verbal Offense against the Sacred, from Moses to Salman Rushdie.* New York: Knopf.

Lewis, Bernard. 1975. *History: Remembered, Recovered, Invented.* Princeton: Princeton University Press.

———. 1982. *The Muslim Discovery of Europe.* New York: W. W. Norton.

———. 1988. *The Political Language of Islam.* Chicago: University of Chicago Press.

———. 1990. *Race and Slavery in the Middle East.* New York: Oxford University Press.

———. 1991. "Behind the Rushdie Affair." *American Scholar* 60: 185–96.

———. 2000. *A Middle East Mosaic: Fragments of Life, Letters, and History.* New York: Random House.

———, and Dominique Schnapper, eds. 1994. *Muslims in Europe.* London: Pinter Publishers.

Lewis, I. M. 1968. "Tribal Society." In *International Encyclopedia of the Social Sciences,* vol. 16, edited by David L. Sills, 146–51. New York: Macmillan.

Lewis, Philip. 1997. "The Bradford Council for Mosques and the Search for Muslim Unity." In *Islam in Europe: The Politics of Religion and Community,* edited by Steven Vertovic and Ceri Peach, 103–28. London: Macmillan Press Ltd.

Lifton, Robert Jay. 1993. *The Protean Self: Human Resilience in an Age of Fragmentation.* New York: Basic Books.

Lightman, Alan. 1994. *Good Benito.* New York: Pantheon Books.

Lindholm, Charles. 1995. "The New Middle Eastern Ethnography." *Journal of the Royal Anthropological Institute* (n.s.) 1: 805–20.

Lloyd-Bostock, Sally. 1983. "Attributions of Cause and Responsibility as Social Phenomena." In *Attribution Theory and Research: Conceptual, Developmental, and Social Dimensions,* edited by J. Jaspers, F. D. Fincham, and M. Hewstone, 261–89. New York: Academic Press.

López-García, B., ed. 1993. *Inmigración magrebí en España.* Madrid: Mapfre.

Luciani, Giacomo, ed. 1990. *The Arab State.* London: Routledge.

Lukes, Steven. 1974. *Power: A Radical View.* London: Macmillan.

———, ed. 1986. *Power.* Readings in Social and Political Theory. Oxford: Basil Blackwell.

MacDonogh, Steve, ed. 1993. *The Rushdie Letters: Freedom to Speak, Freedom to Write.* Kerry, Ireland: Brandon Book Publishers Ltd.

Macfarlane, Alan. 1978. *The Origins of English Individualism.* Oxford: Oxford University Press.

MacGregor, Geddes. 1987. "Doubt and Belief." In *The Encyclopedia of Religion,* vol. 4, edited by Mircea Eliade, 424–30. New York: Macmillan.

Maher, Vanessa. 1984. "Possession and Dispossession: Maternity and Mortality in Morocco." In *Interest and Emotion: Essays on the Study of Family and Kinship,* edited by Hans Medick and David Warren Sabean, 103–28. Cambridge: Cambridge University Press.

Mahfouz, Naguib. [1983] 1992. *The Journey of Ibn Fattouma,* translated by Denys Johnson-Davies. New York: Doubleday.

Malka, Victor. 1978. *La mémoire brisée des Juifs du Maroc.* Paris: Editions Entente.

Mamdani, Mahmood. 1999. "Historicizing Power and Responses to Power: Indirect Rule and Reform." *Social Research* 66 (3): 859–86.

Manna, Hyatham. 1997. *Islam et hérésies: L'obsession blasphématoire.* Paris: L'Harmattan.

Marcus, Michael E. 1985. "'The Saint Has Been Stolen': Sanctity and Social Change in a Tribe of Eastern Morocco," *American Ethnologist* 12 (3): 455–67.

Marmura, Michael E. 1968. "Causation in Islamic Thought." In *Dictionary of the History of Ideas,* vol. 1, edited by P. P. Weiner, 286–89. New York: Charles Scribner's Sons.

Marsh, Joss. 1998. *Word Crimes: Blasphemy, Culture, and Literature in Nineteenth-Century England.* Chicago: University of Chicago Press.

Martinez-Torron, Javier. 2000. "The Legal Status of Islam in Spain." In *Islam and European Legal Systems,* edited by Silvio Ferrari and Anthony Bradney, 47–71. Aldershot: Ashgate/Dartmouth.

Matar, Nabil. 1998. *Islam in Britain, 1558–1685.* Cambridge: Cambridge University Press.

McMurray, David. 1993. "Haddou: A Moroccan Migrant Worker." In *Struggle and Survival in the Modern Middle East*, edited by Edmund Burke III. Berkeley: University of California Press.

Meeker, Michael E. 1979. *Literature and Violence in North Arabia*. Cambridge: Cambridge University Press.

Mehta, Ved. 1962. *Fly and the Fly Bottle*. Boston: Little, Brown.

Meital, Yoram. 1997. "Revolutionizing the Past: Historical Representation during Egypt's Revolutionary Experience, 1952–62." *Mediterranean Historical Review* 12 (2): 60–77.

Melotti, Umberto. 1997. "International Migration in Europe: Social Projects and Political Cultures." In *The Politics of Multiculturalism in the New Europe: Racism, Identity, and Community*, edited by Tariq Modood and Pnina Werbner, 73–92. London: Zed Books Ltd.

Memmi, Albert. 1971. *The Scorpion: Or the Imaginary Confession*. New York: Grossman Publishers.

Mernissi, Fatima. 2002. *Islam and Democracy: Fear of the Modern World*. Boulder, CO: Perseus Publishing.

Merton, Robert. 1976. *Sociological Ambivalence and Other Essays*. New York: Free Press.

Milicia, Joe. 2001. "At the Workplace, Worship: Companies Accommodate Religious Practices of Muslim Employees." *New York Times*, May 20, D1–D2.

Miller, Arthur G. 1991. "Transformations of Time and Space: Oaxaca, Mexico, circa 1500–1700." In *Images of Memory: On Remembering and Representation*, edited by Susanne Kuchler and Walter Melion, 141–75. Washington: Smithsonian Institution Press.

Miller, Judith. 1996. "New Tack for Egypt's Islamic Militants: Imposing Divorce." *New York Times*, December 28, 22.

Mills, Edgar W., Jr. 1983. "Sociological Ambivalence and Social Order: The Constructive Uses of Normative Dissonance." *Sociology and Social Research* 67 (3): 279–287.

Mir-Hosseini, Ziba. 1993. *Marriage on Trial: A Study of Islamic Family Law*. London: I. B. Tauris.

———. 1996. "Powers and Limits of Negotiations: Women's Strategies in Marriage and Divorce." In *Femmes en Iran*, edited by N. Yavari. Paris: L'Harmattan.

Modood, Tariq, and Pnina Werbner, eds. 1997. *The Politics of Multiculturalism in the New Europe*. London: Zed Books Ltd.

Montagne, Robert. 1930. *Les Berbères et le Makhzen dans le Sud du Maroc: Essai sur la transformation politique des Berbères sedentaires (Groupe Chleuh)*. Paris: Félix Alcan.

———. 1973. *The Berbers: Their Social and Political Organisation*, translated by David Seddon. London: Frank Cass.

Moore, Kathleen M. 1995. *Al-Mughtaribun: American Law and the Transformation of Muslim Life in the United States*. Albany: State University of New York Press.

"Morocco: Breaching the Ramparts." 1999. *Economist*, January 2, 48–49.

Morris, Colin. 1972. *The Discovery of the Individual: 1050–1200*. New York: Harper and Row.

Morris, Pam, ed. 1994. *The Bakhtin Reader*. London: Edward Arnold.

Mottahedeh, Roy P. 1993. "Toward an Islamic Theology of Toleration." In *Islamic Law Reform and Human Rights*, edited by Tore Lindholm and Kari Vogt, 25–36. Oslo: Nordic Human Rights Publications.

Mozaffari, Mehdi. 1995. "Rushdie Affair." In *Oxford Encyclopedia of the Modern Islamic World*, vol. 3, edited by John Esposito, 443–45. Oxford: Oxford University Press.

Muñoz, Gema Martín, ed. 1999. *Islam, Modernism and the West*. London: I. B. Tauris.

Munson, Henry. 1984. *The House of Si Abd Allah: The Oral History of a Moroccan Family*. New Haven: Yale University Press.

———. 1989. "On the Irrelevance of the Segmentary Lineage Model in the Moroccan Rif." *American Anthropologist* 91: 386–400.

———. 1991. "Morocco's Fundamentalists." *Government and Opposition*, 26 (Summer): 331–44.

Muslehuddin, Mohammad. 1975. *Islamic Jurisprudence and the Rule of Necessity and Need*. Islamabad: Islamic Research Institute.

Neisser, Ulric, ed. 1982. *Memory Observed: Remembering in Natural Contexts.* San Francisco: W. H. Freeman and Co.

———, and Robyn Fivush, eds. 1994. *The Remembering Self: Construction and Accuracy in the Self-Narrative.* New York: Cambridge University Press.

Niebuhr, Gustav. 2001. "Study Finds Number of Mosques Up 25% in 6 Years." *New York Times,* April 27, A21.

Nonneman, Gerd, Tim Niblock, and Bogdan Szajkowski, eds. 1996. *Muslim Communities in the New Europe.* Reading, UK: Ithaca Press.

Noonan, John. 1984. *Bribes.* New York: Macmillan.

Nora, Pierre. 1989. "Between Memory and History: Les lieux de mémoire." *Representations* 26 (Spring): 7–25.

O'Brien, Jay, and William Roseberry, eds. 1991. *Golden Ages, Dark Ages: Imagining the Past in Anthropology and History.* Berkeley: University of California Press.

Ong, Walter J. 1982. *Orality and Literacy: The Technologizing of the Word.* New York: Routledge.

Ormsby, Eric L. 1991. "The Taste of Truth: The Structure of Experience in al-Ghāzalī's *al-Munqidh min al-dalāl.*" In *Islamic Studies Presented to Charles J. Adams,* edited by Wael B. Hallaq and Donald P. Little, 133–52. Leiden: E. J. Brill.

Osiel, Mark J. 1995. "Ever Again: Legal Remembrance of Administrative Massacre." *University of Pennsylvania Law Review* 144 (2): 463–704.

Pandolfo, Stefania. 2000. "The Thin Line of Modernity: Some Moroccan Debates on Subjectivity." In *Questions of Modernity,* edited by Timothy Mitchell, 115–47. Minneapolis: University of Minnesota Press.

Parsons, Talcott. 1986. "Power and the Social System." In *Power,* edited by Steven Lukes. Oxford: Basil Blackwell.

Patai, Raphael. 1981. "Violence, the Islamic Curse." *Chicago Tribune,* December 6, Section 2, 1.

Patey, Douglas Lane. 1984. *Probability and Literary Form: Philosophic Theory and Literary Practice in the Augustan Age.* Cambridge: Cambridge University Press.

Pearl, David. 1986. *Family Law and the Immigrant Communities.* Bristol: Family Law Publications.

Peters, Emyrs L. 1990. *The Bedouin of Cyrenaica: Studies in Personal and Corporate Power.* Cambridge: Cambridge University Press.

Pfaff, William. 1993. *The Wrath of Nations: Civilization and the Furies of Nationalism.* New York: Simon & Schuster.

Pipes, Daniel. 1983. *In the Path of God: Islam and Political Power.* New York: Basic Books.

———. 1990. *The Rushdie Affair: The Novel, the Ayatollah, and the West.* New York: Carol Publishing Group.

Popham, Peter. 1998. "Bangladeshi Feminist Goes into Hiding." *Independent* (London), September 19, 16.

Popular Memory Group. 1982. "Popular Memory: Theory, Politics, Method." In *Making Histories,* edited by Richard Johnson, et. al., 205–52. Minneapolis: University of Minnesota Press.

Potter, David, et al., eds. 1999. *Democratization.* New York: Columbia University Press.

Pouillon, Jean. 1982. "Remarks on the Verb 'To Believe.'" In *Between Belief and Transgression: Structuralist Essays in Religion, History, and Myth,* edited by Michael Izard and Pierre Smith, 1–8. Chicago: University of Chicago Press.

Poulter, Sebastien. 1986. *English Law and Ethnic Minority Customs.* London: Butterworths.

———. 1989. "Cultural Pluralism and Its Limits: A Legal Perspective." In *Britain: A Plural Society,* edited by the Commission for Racial Equality and the Runnymede Trust, 3–28. London: Commission for Racial Equality and the Runnymede Trust.

———. 1998. *Ethnicity, Law, and Human Rights: The English Experience.* Oxford: Clarendon Press.

Pratt, David. 2001. "Taliban Surrender to Hugs and Kisses." *Sunday Herald* (Scotland). November 25, 1.

Pryce-Jones, David. 1989. *The Closed Circle: An Interpretation of the Arabs.* New York: Harper-Collins.

Queens Bench. 1978. "Ahmad v. Inner London Education Authority." *Queens Bench* 1978: 36.

Rappaport, Joanne. 1990. *The Politics of Memory: Native Historical Interpretation in the Colombian Andes.* New York: Cambridge University Press.

R'chid, A. Moulay. 1991. *La femme et la loi au Maroc.* Casablanca: Le Fennec.

Read, Kenneth. 1986. *Return to the High Valley: Coming Full Circle.* Berkeley: University of California Press.

Renteln, Alison Dundes. 2002. *The Cultural Defense.* New York: Oxford University Press.

Richards, Audrey I. 1956. *Chisungu: A Girl's Initiation Ceremony among the Bemba of Northern Rhodesia.* London: Faber and Faber.

Roberts, Hugh. 2002. "Perspectives on Berber Politics: On Gellner and Masqueray, or Durkheim's Mistake." *Journal of the Royal Anthropological Institute* 8 (1): 107–26.

Rodinson, Maxime. 1987. *Europe and the Mystique of Islam,* translated by Roger Veinus. Seattle: University of Washington Press.

Rorty, Amelie Oksenberg. 1992. "Power and Powers: A Dialogue between Buff and Rebuff." In *Rethinking Power,* edited by Thomas E. Wartenberg, 1–13. Albany: State University of New York Press.

Rorty, Richard. 1986. "The Contingency of Language." *London Review of Books,* April 17: 3–6.

Rosaldo, Renato. 1980. *Ilongot Headhunting, 1883–1974.* Stanford: Stanford University Press.

Rose-Ackerman, Susan. 1999. *Corruption and Government: Causes, Consequences, and Reform.* Cambridge: Cambridge University Press.

Rosen, Lawrence. 1968. "A Moroccan Jewish Community during the Middle East Crisis." *American Scholar* 37 (3): 435–51.

———. 1970. "'I Divorce Thee': Moroccan Marriage and the Law." *Transaction* 7 (8): 34–37.

———. 1972a. "Muslim-Jewish Relations in a Moroccan City." *International Journal of Middle East Studies* 3 (4): 435–49.

———. 1972b. "Rural Political Process and National Political Structure in Morocco." In *Rural Politics and Social Change in the Middle East,* edited by Richard T. Antoun and Iliya Harik, 214–36. Bloomington: Indiana University Press.

———. 1977. "The Anthropologist as Expert Witness." *American Anthropologist* 79 (3): 555–78.

———. 1984. *Bargaining for Reality: The Structure of Social Relations in a Moroccan City.* Chicago: University of Chicago Press.

———. 1989a. *The Anthropology of Justice: Law as Culture in Islamic Society.* New York: Cambridge University Press.

———. 1989b. "Responsibility and Compensatory Justice in Arab Culture and Law." In *Semiotics, Self, and Society,* edited by Benjamin Lee and Greg Urban, 101–20. Berlin and New York: Mouton de Gruyter.

———. 1991. "The Integrity of Cultures." *American Behavioral Scientist* 34 (4): 594–617.

———. 1995a. "Have the Arabs Changed Their Mind? Intentions and the Discernment of Cultural Change." In *Other Intentions: Cultural Contexts and the Attribution of Inner States,* edited by Lawrence Rosen, 178–200. Santa Fe, NM: School of American Research Press.

———. 1995b. "Law and Custom in the Popular Legal Culture of North Africa." *Islamic Law and Society* 2 (2): 194–208.

———. 2000. *The Justice of Islam: Comparative Perspectives of Islamic Law and Society.* Oxford: Oxford University Press.

Rosenthal, A. M. 1999. "Daring to Speak the Truth about Democracy in the Arab World." *International Herald Tribune,* May 8–9, 6.

Rosenthal, Franz. 1970. *Knowledge Triumphant: The Concept of Knowledge in Medieval Islam.* Leiden: E. J. Brill.

———. 1974. "Plotinus in Islam: The Power of Anonymity." In *Plotino e il Neoplatonismo*, 371: 439–46. Rome: Accademia Nazionale dei Lincei.

———. 1975. *Gambling in Islam*. Leiden: E. J. Brill.

———. 1983. *"Sweeter Than Hope": Complaint and Hope in Medieval Islam*. Leiden: E. J. Brill.

———. 1995. "The 'Time' of Muslim Historians and Muslim Mystics." *Jerusalem Studies in Arabic and Islam* (no. 19): 5–35.

———. 1997. "The Stranger in Medieval Islam." *Arabica* 44 (1): 35–75.

Roth, Michael S. 1995. *The Ironist's Cage: Memory, Trauma, and the Construction of History*. New York: Columbia University Press.

Roy, Olivier. 1990. "Afghanistan: Modèles anthropologiques et pacification." *Cahiers du Monde Russe et Sovietique* 31 (2–3): 405–12.

———. 1999. *Vers un Islam européen*. Paris: Editions Esprit.

———. 2000a. "Muslims in Europe: From Ethnic Identity to Religious Recasting." *ISIM Newsletter* (International Institute for the Study of Islam in the Modern World), 5: 1 ff.

———. 2000b. *The New Central Asia: The Creation of Nations*. London: I. B. Tauris.

Royal Anthropological Institute. 1951. *Notes and Queries on Anthropology*. 6th ed. London: Routledge & Kegan Paul.

Ruolt, Adolf. 1996. *Code Pénal Annoté*. Rabat: Royaume du Maroc, Ministère de la Justice.

Rushdie, Salman. 1988. *The Satanic Verses*. Dover, DE: Consortium, Inc.

———. 1991. *Imaginary Homelands: Essays and Criticism*. London: Granta Books/Penguin.

———. 1999. "Sneakers and Burgers Aren't the Real Enemies." *International Herald Tribune*, March 6–7, 6.

———. 2000. "Letter From India: A Dream of Glorious Return." *New Yorker*, June 19 and 26, 94–112.

———. 2001. "Yes, This Is About Islam." *New York Times*, November 2, A25.

"Rushdie's Nightmare Is Over." 1998. *Guardian* (London), September 25.

Saaf, Abdallah. 1989. "Vers la décrepitude de l'état neo-patrimonial." In *Annuaire de l'Afrique du Nord*, vol. 28, 73–106. Paris: Editions du CNRS.

Sachs, Susan. 2001. "Muslims in U.S. Seek Financing: Pursuing an American Dream While Following the Koran." *New York Times*, July 5, C1–7.

Said, Edward W. 1978. *Orientalism*. New York: Pantheon Books.

Said, Zkik. 1994. *La répression de l'abandon de famille en droit marocain*. Rabat: Arabian Al Hilal.

Sambursky, S. 1956. "On the Possible and the Probable in Ancient Greece." *Osiris* 12: 35–48.

Sander, Ake. 1996. "The Status of Muslim Communities in Sweden." In *Muslim Communities in the New Europe*, edited by Gerd Nonneman, Tim Niblock, and Bogdan Szajkowski, 269–89. Reading, UK: Ithaca Press.

Sandler, R. 1976. "The Changing Concept of the Individual." In *Introduction to Islamic Civilisation*, edited by R. M. Savory, 137–45. Cambridge: Cambridge University Press.

Sartorius, Rolf, ed. 1983. *Paternalism*. Minneapolis: University of Minnesota Press.

Scelles-Millie, J., and Boukhari Khelifa. 1966. *Les quatrains de Medjdoub le Sarcastique: Poète maghrébine du XVIe siècle*. Paris: G.-P. Maisonneuve et Larose.

Schachter, Daniel L. 1996. *Searching for Memory: The Brain, the Mind, and the Past*. New York: Basic Books.

Schieffelin, Edward L., and Robert Crittenden. 1991. *Like People You See in a Dream: First Contact in Six Papuan Societies*. Stanford: Stanford University Press.

Schiffauer, Werner. 1997. "Islam as a Civil Religion: Political Culture and the Organisation of Diversity in Germany." In *The Politics of Multiculturalism in the New Europe: Racism, Identity, and Community*, edited by Tariq Modood and Pnina Werbner, 147–66. London: Zed Books Ltd.

Schmidt di Friedberg, Ottavia. 1998. "Stratégies des migrants et positionnement de l'Islam en

Italie." In *Islam(s) en Europe, approaches d'un nouveau pluralisme culturel européen,* edited by Remy Leveau, 83–103. Berlin: Centre Marc Bloch.

Seligman, Adam B. 1997. *The Problem of Trust.* Princeton: Princeton University Press.

Seminck, Hans. 1993. *A Novel Visible But Unseen: A Thematic Analysis of Salman Rushdie's "The Satanic Verses."* Gent: Studia Germanica Gandensia.

Sennett, Richard. 1980. *Authority.* New York: Vintage Books.

Sertel, Ayse Kudat. 1972. "Images of Power." *American Anthropologist* 74 (3): 639–657.

"Le seuil de tolérance et une notion aussi hideuse qu'incontournable." 1999. *Le Monde* (Paris), electronic edition.

Shahid, Irfan. 1983. "Another Contribution to Koranic Exegesis: The Sura of the Poets (XXVI)." *Journal of Arabic Literature* 14: 1–21.

Shah-Kazemi, Sonia Nurin. 2001. "Untying the Knot: Divorce and Muslim Law in the UK." *ISIM Newsletter* (International Institute for the Study of Islam in the Modern World), 7: 31.

Shapiro, Barbara. 1983. *Probability and Certainty in the Seventeenth Century.* Princeton: Princeton University Press.

Sharabi, Hisham. 1988. *Neopatriarchy: A Theory of Distorted Change in Arab Society.* Oxford: Oxford University Press.

Shelley, Percy Bysshe. 1904. *A Defense of Poetry.* Indianapolis: Bobbs-Merrill.

Sherley, Sir Anthony. 1609. *A true historicall discourse of Muley Hamets rising to the three kingdomes of Moruecos, Fes, and Sus. . . . The Adventures of Sir Anthony Sherley and diuers other English gentlemen, in those countries.* London: Thomas Purfoot.

Shotter, John. 1990. "The Social Construction of Remembering and Forgetting." In *Collective Remembering,* edited by David Middleton and Derek Edwards, 120–38. London: Sage Publications.

Shourie, Arun. 1995. *The World of Fatwas, or Shariah in Action.* New Delhi: ASA Publications.

Simons, Marlise. 2000a. "Between Migrants and Spain: The Sea That Kills." *New York Times,* March 30, A3.

———. 2000b. "Resenting African Workers, Spaniards Attack." *New York Times,* February 12, A3.

Slaughter, M. M. 1993. "The Salman Rushdie Affair: Apostasy, Honor, and Freedom of Speech." *Virginia Law Review* 79: 153–204.

Smoller, Laura A. 1998. "Miracle, Memory, and Meaning in the Canonization of Vincent Ferrer, 1453–1454." *Speculum* 73 (2): 429–54.

Sonn, Tamara. 1990. *Between Qur'an and Crown: The Challenge of Political Legitimacy in the Arab World.* Boulder, CO: Westview Press.

Spruyt, Hendrik. 1994. *The Sovereign State and Its Competitors.* Princeton: Princeton University Press.

Steiner, Wendy. 1995. *The Scandal of Pleasure: Art in an Age of Fundamentalism.* Chicago: University of Chicago Press.

Stillman, Norman A. 1977. "Muslims and Jews in Morocco." *Jerusalem Quarterly* 5: 74–83.

———. 1982. "Saddiq and Marabout in Morocco." In *The Sephardi and Oriental Jewish Heritage,* edited by Issachar Ben-Ami, 489–500. Jerusalem: Magnes Press, Hebrew University.

———. 1991. "Myth, Countermyth, and Distortion." *Tikkun* 6 (3): 60–64.

Stoll, Georg. 1998. "Immigrant Muslim Writers in Germany." In *The Postcolonial Crescent: Islam's Impact on Contemporary Literature,* edited by John C. Hawley, 266–83. New York: Peter Lang Publishing, Inc.

Strathern, Andrew J. 1975. "Why Is Shame on the Skin?" *Ethnology* 14: 347–56.

Stroumsa, Sarah. 1999. *Freethinkers of Medieval Islam: Ibn al-Rawāndī, Abū Bakr al-Rāzī and Their Impact on Islamic Thought.* Leiden: E. J. Brill.

Sturzenhofecker, Gabriele. 1998. *Times Enmeshed: Gender, Space, and History among the Duna of Papua New Guinea.* Cambridge: Cambridge University Press.

Suleri, Sara. 1990. "Contraband Histories: Salman Rushdie and the Embodiment of Blasphemy." In *Reading Rushdie: Perspectives on the Fiction of Salman Rushdie,* edited by M. D. Fletcher, 221–36. Amsterdam: Rodopi.

Sullivan, Anita. 1985. *The Seventh Dragon: The Riddle of Equal Temperament.* Portland, OR: Metamorphous Press.

Taheri, Amir. 1987. *Holy Terror: The Inside Story of Islamic Terrorism.* London: Hutchinson.

Tayler, Jeffrey. 2000. "Another French Revolution: In Marseilles, Europe Confronts Its North African Future." *Harper's* 301: 58–66.

Teski, Marea C., and Jacob J. Climo, eds. 1995. *The Labyrinth of Memory: Ethnographic Journeys.* Westport, CT: Bergin & Garvey.

Thelan, David. 1989. "Memory and American History." *Journal of American History* 75 (4): 1117–29.

Toledano, Henry. 1981. *Judicial Practice and Family Law in Morocco.* Boulder: Social Science Monographs.

Torfs, Rik. 2000. "The Legal Status of Islam in Belgium." In *Islam and European Legal Systems,* edited by Silvio Ferrari and Anthony Bradney, 73–95. Aldershot: Ashgate/Dartmouth.

Toulmin, Stephen. 1958. *The Uses of Argument.* Cambridge: Cambridge University Press.

Tozy, Mohamed. 1998. *Monarchie et Islam politique au Maroc.* Paris: Presses de Sciences Po.

United Nations Development Program. 1998. *Human Development Report 1998.* New York: Oxford University Press.

Unsworth, Clive. 1995. "Blasphemy, Cultural Divergence, and Legal Relativism." *Modern Law Review* 58 (5): 658–77.

Valensi, Lucette. 1986. "From Sacred History to Historical Memory and Back: The Jewish Past." *History and Anthropology* 2 (2): 283–305.

———. 1992. *Fables de la mémoire: La glorieuse bataille des trois rois.* Paris: Editions de Seuil.

———, and Nathan Wachtel. 1991. *Jewish Memories.* Berkeley: University of California Press.

Van Bijsterveld, Sophie C. 2000. "The Legal Status of Islam in the Kingdom of the Netherlands." In *Islam and European Legal Systems,* edited by Silvio Ferrari and Anthony Bradney, 125–45. Aldershot: Ashgate/Dartmouth.

Vatikiotis, P. J. 1987. *Islam and the State.* London: Croom Helm.

Vertovec, Steven. 1996. "Muslims, the State, and the Public Sphere in Britain." In *Muslim Communities in the New Europe,* edited by Gerd Nonneman, Tim Niblock, and Bogdan Szajkowski, 169–86. Reading, UK: Ithaca Press.

Vertovec, Steven, and Ceri Peach, eds. 1997. *Islam in Europe: The Politics of Religion and Community.* London: Macmillan Press Ltd.

Vicén, Nuria del Olmo. 1996. "The Muslim Community in Spain." In *Muslim Communities in the New Europe,* edited by Gerd Nonneman, Tim Niblock, and Bogdan Szajkowski, 303–14. Reading, UK: Ithaca Press.

Viorst, Milton. 1996. "The Muslims of France." *Foreign Affairs* 75 (5): 78–96.

Voinot, L. 1948. *Pèlerinages judéo-musulmans du Maroc.* Paris: Editions Larose.

Wachtel, Nathan. 1986. "Introduction: Memory and History." *History and Anthropology* 2 (2): 207–24.

Walzer, Michael. 1974. "Political Action: The Problem of Dirty Hands." In *War and Moral Responsibility,* edited by M. Cohen, 62–82. Princeton: Princeton University Press.

Ward, Mrs. Humphrey [Mary Augusta]. [1888] 1987. *Robert Elsmere.* Oxford: Oxford University Press.

Warraq, Ibn. 1995. *Why I am Not a Muslim.* Amherst, NY: Prometheus Books.

Waterbury, John. 1970. "Legitimacy Without Coercion: or How to Live Without Weber." Review of Ernest Gellner, *Saints of the Atlas. Government and Opposition* 5 (2): 253–60.

———. 1972. *North for the Trade: The Life and Times of a Berber Merchant.* Berkeley: University of California Press.

———. 1976. "Corruption, Political Stability, and Development: Comparative Evidence from Egypt and Morocco." *Government and Opposition* 11 (4): 426–45.

Watt, W. Montgomery. 1972. *The Influence of Islam on Medieval Europe.* Edinburgh: Edinburgh University Press.

Weaver, Mary Anne. 1994. "A Fugitive from Injustice." *New Yorker,* September 12, 48–60.

———. 1998. "Revolution by Stealth." *New Yorker,* June 8, 38–48.

Weber, Max. 1964. *The Theory of Social and Economic Organization.* New York: Free Press.

Webster, Richard. 1990. *A Brief History of Blasphemy: Liberalism, Censorship, and "The Satanic Verses."* Southwold, UK: Orwell Press.

Wehr, Hans. 1994. *A Dictionary of Modern Written Arabic.* Ithaca: Spoken Language Services.

Weingrod, Alex. 1990. *The Saint of Beersheba.* Chicago: University of Chicago Press.

Weiss, Bernard. 1985. "Knowledge of the Past: The Theory of Tawattur According to Ghazzali." *Studia Islamica* 61: 81–105.

Wells, Peter S. 1999. *The Barbarians Speak.* Princeton: Princeton University Press.

Werbner, Pnina. 1996. "Allegories of Sacred Imperfection: Magic, Hermeneutics, and Passion in 'The Satanic Verses.'" *Current Anthropology* 37 (Supplement): S55–86.

Westermarck, Edward. 1914. *Marriage Ceremonies in Morocco.* London: Macmillan and Co.

———. 1926. *Ritual and Belief in Morocco,* vol. 1. London: Macmillan.

White, Jefferson. 1996. "Analogical Reasoning." In *A Companion to Philosophy of Law and Legal Theory,* edited by Dennis Patterson, 583–90. Oxford: Blackwell Publishers.

Wikan, Unni. 2000. "Citizenship on Trial: Nadia's Case." *Daedalus* 129 (4): 55–76.

Williams, John Alden. 1995. "Fitnah." In *The Oxford Encyclopedia of the Modern Islamic World,* vol. 2, edited by John Esposito, 26–28. Oxford: Oxford University Press.

Williams, Tennessee. 1970. *The Glass Menagerie.* New York: New Directions Publishing Corp.

Wilson, Peter Lamborn. 1988. *Scandal: Essays in Islamic Heresy.* Brooklyn, New York: Autonomedia, Inc.

Wittgenstein, Ludwig. 1972. *On Certainty,* translated by Denis Paul and G. E. M. Anscombe. New York: Harper & Row.

Wolf, Eric R. 1951. "The Social Organization of Mecca and the Origins of Islam." *Southwestern Journal of Anthropology* 7 (4): 329–56.

Wright, Robert. 1988. "Did the Universe Just Happen?" *Atlantic Monthly* 261 (4): 29ff.

Yapp, Malcolm. 1990. "The Hubris of the Hidden Imam." In *The Rushdie File,* edited by Lisa Appignanesi and Sara Maitland, 91–94. Syracuse: Syracuse University Press.

Yerushalmi, Yosef H. 1988. *Usage de l'oubli.* Paris: Editions du Seuil.

Zafrani, Haim. 1998. *Deux mille ans de vie juive au Maroc.* Paris: Maisonneuve et Larose.

Zonabend, Françoise. 1984. *The Enduring Memory: Time and History in a French Village,* translated by Anthony Forster. Manchester: Manchester University Press.

Index

The boldface number following each foreign term refers to the place where the most complete definition of that term will be found in the text.